Night
in the *Middle Ages*

Night

in the

Middle Ages

Jean Verdon

translated by
George Holoch

University of Notre Dame Press • *Notre Dame, Indiana*

English Language Edition Copyright © 2002 by
University of Notre Dame
Notre Dame, Indiana 46556
http://www.undpress.nd.edu
All Rights Reserved

Manufactured in the United States of America

Translated by George Holoch from *La Nuit au Moyen Age* by Jean Verdon, published by Perrin.

The publisher is grateful to
THE FRENCH MINISTRY OF CULTURE—CENTRE NATIONAL DU LIVRE
for support of the costs of translation.

© Librarie Académique Perrin, 1994 et 1998.

Library of Congress Cataloging-in-Publication Data
Verdon, Jean.
[Nuit au Moyen Age. English]
Night in the Middle Ages / Jean Verdon ; translated by George Holoch.
p. cm.
Includes bibliographical references (p.   ) and index.
ISBN 0-268-03655-1 (cloth : alk. paper)
ISBN 0-268-03656-X (pbk. : alk. paper)
1. Night—Social aspects. 2. Night—History. 3. Sleeping customs—History.
4. Compline—History. 5. Civilization, Medieval.
I. Title.

HM1033 .V4713   2002
304.2'3'0902—dc21
2002013377

∞ *This book is printed on acid-free paper.*

FOREWORD

A power failure plunged New York into darkness on Wednesday July 13. . . . Trains and subways were stopped, imprisoning their passengers. Mayor Abraham Beame asked citizens to keep calm while off-duty police and firefighters were urgently mobilized. Governor Hugh Carey declared that he was putting the National Guard on a state of alert to assist the local police. The police department announced that it had arrested nearly fourteen hundred looters who had taken advantage of the darkness to loot stores (*Le Monde*, July 15, 1977, p. 16).

The contemporary world is uncomfortable with night, more precisely with night it has not domesticated with electricity. What was it like in the Middle Ages when darkness was nearly unbroken from the setting to the rising of the sun?

CONTENTS

ACKNOWLEDGMENT

I am very grateful to Dominique Malezieux-Pastol, who was kind enough to read my manuscript before publication and who made many helpful suggestions.

Introduction

"God said, 'Let there be light,' and there was light; and God saw that the light was good, and he separated the light from the darkness. He called the light 'day', and the darkness 'night'. So evening came, and morning came, the first day."

So says the author of the Book of Genesis, relating the creation of the world. Night appears above all as the length of time that passes from the setting of the sun to its rising. As Isidore, bishop of Seville and author of a veritable encyclopedia called the *Etymologies*, wrote in the early seventh century, during the day the sun is above the land, at night it is underneath. The day is thus divided in two periods, daytime and nighttime.

Let us consider night, along with Isidore, who distinguishes seven periods in the course of the night. There is evening, so called because of the star which follows the setting sun and precedes the darkness; twilight, marked by an uncertain light; and the first period, when silence reigns. The middle period is free from activity, for a deep sleep has brought about a flawless tranquility—we become aware of time only through human activity; the middle of the night is free of all movement and as a result corresponds in some sense to an absence of time. Then there is the moment when the cock crows, heralding the first light; morning, between the departure of the first light and the arrival of dawn, and daybreak, when a bit of sunlight begins to shine through.

I

Night—darkness. But in addition to this night, which is nothing specifically medieval, there emerges more and more clearly in the thought of the time a legal night, the limits of which seem to some extent independent of the notion of darkness.

That night is not defined by the rising and the setting of the sun, but by the ringing of bells that in the evening announce the putting out of hearth fires, and in the morning the resumption of work. When darkness falls, a whole ceremony unfolds. In the thick wall surrounding the city, the gates that allow an escape into the countryside or conversely an entrance for provisions are closed, making the city an enclosed space deprived for a few hours of all relation to the external world. In the streets, chains are stretched out to block an attack or to slow the flight of malefactors after a robbery.

This is not a cosmic night but one characterized, in principle at least, by the absence of urban activities. Urban, because the countryside lives according to the rhythm of nature, and even today peasants know nothing of the bustle of large cities.

The distinction between these two types of night does not appear to be rigorous. The evening bell that marks the end of the artisan's day (working by candlelight was prohibited) and the morning bell that calls the workers to their task shortly after the break of day do not sound at the same time in every season; they take account of the very precious light given off by the sun.

When one moves from night to its constituent parts, one notices an evolution: the "time of the Church" is followed by the "time of the merchant." Of course, an entire day includes, in the Middle Ages as in our time, twenty-four hours, divided either into minutes and seconds, or into points (an hour contains four points), moments (a point is equivalent to ten moments), ounces (a moment represents twelve ounces), and atoms (there are forty-five atoms in an ounce). To these theoretical divisions, medieval writers prefer the quarter-hour or the half-hour. But hours do not have the same duration in the course of the year, for they always count twelve hours from the rising to the setting of the sun and twelve hours from the setting of the sun to its rising, so that the hours of the night are much longer in December than in June, shifting from thirty to ninety minutes.

Offices, the canonical hours recited by monks, permit distinctions among the different moments of the day—compline at sunset, matins or lauds at sunrise. Bells ring then as well as, in certain regions, for the evening Angelus.

Mechanical clocks make possible the movement from unequal to equal hours. At night, as during the day, hours now have the same duration. There were public clocks—one is noted in Paris in 1370—but also domestic clocks. In 1369, Froissart writes in *The Clock in Love:*

> For night and day it teaches us the time,
> With the subtlety it has in mind
> Even in the absence of the sun.

These clocks do not prevent the bells from continuing to ring, like the one named Marie, installed in the chapel of the Sorbonne, which announces curfew in the University. Villon remembers it well one cold night in December while writing his *Lais,* when he hears

> . . . in the Sorbonne the bell
> Which always at nine will tell
> Salvation the Angel foretells.

Stopping work, he then begins to pray.

Medieval man has to integrate into his existence this inevitable night, to which are connected Eros, Hypnos, and Thanatos: love, which it conceals from indiscreet glances; sleep at night; and in the end eternal sleep, death. From the very beginning, this night is identified with evil; if God is light, the darkness can only be the realm of the Evil One. But there is a way that is specific to the Middle Ages of subduing night and the fears that it provokes. More than technology or human action in general, this is sublimation through unconscious or conscious turning toward God.

PART ONE

Satan or
Horrific Night

The Medieval Nocturnal Landscape

The Countryside

The land was covered with many forests, a refuge for hermits or outcasts, a source of essential products, but forests where it was not wise to wander at night, as revealed by an adventure that happened to Philip the Good, duke of Burgundy, as told by the chronicler Georges Chastellain.

Seeking to avoid pleas for assistance from the dauphin Louis—the future Louis XI—who had taken refuge at his court, Philip decided to leave his house surreptitiously one night to meet a few lords who were his friends. The days were short and it was already "basse vesprée" when the duke mounted his horse. A thaw following a long and bitter freeze and a dense mist that had held on all day before changing into light rain soaked the ground. Nevertheless, the duke rode off, thinking that he would easily find his way.

Daylight disappeared and night was upon him. This great prince who ruled over thousands of people rode thus, alone and lost, but he did not wish to return to Brussels; "he liked to endure the adventure of the perilous night." The further he went, the more lost he became, but he held to his intent to reach Halsenberg, the appointed meeting place. And yet, "night, so hideous and so full of peril as it was, would terrify the heart of any man and lead him to despair."

The dauphin went off to look for him. But as time passed, considering "the night and the weather full of danger," he returned home.

The duke wandered aimlessly, for the world at that hour was nothing but darkness. He found himself in a dense and vast forest with no sense of a way out of it. But he kept up his courage, paying no heed to either cold or the darkness of night, awaiting the break of day and telling himself that a night, even a hard one, is soon over. His shouts produced no reply. His horse stumbled three or four times.

He finally saw a distant light, but it was a lump of earth with flame coming out of all sides. It could have been midnight. He took up his road again, famished. Long he wandered. Finally, he heard a dog barking and reached a cottage where a poor man was sleeping along with his wife. In spite of his shouts and violent blows on the door, the man was in no hurry to answer, "for he thought it was brigands of the woods or wicked people since, at that hour and in such weather and so far from any road, they were out and about. 'Go on your way, it is now after midnight, let us sleep and go away.'"

The duke managed to persuade the fellow to let him into his little house to sit by the fire and to bring him a frugal meal and then, in return for good hard currency, to go with him to show him the right way. The duke continued on to Halsenberg; it was about four hours after midnight. He reached the home of his huntsman, Loykin, and spent the rest of the night there.

Meanwhile, the lords whom he had planned to meet were troubled. They remained in place, vigilant, "while daylight began to deeply fade and night came on, black and hideous, full of mist and ice, that seemed to them very hard and full of perils, and they began to have fantasies and various thoughts about how and why he could be taking so much time to come, since it was already dark night and the weather was harsh and foul." They sought him in vain. The lord of Croy was deeply troubled; "considering the peril of the weather and the dark night, he could not help but think that an unfortunate accident had brought him to an evil, hard, and shameful death in open country."

Night and the forest thus came together to block light, multiply perils, and increase dread.

Fear of night, fear in the night. Fear of darkness amounts to a dread justified by nothing but the absence of visual perception. Man cannot live unharmed in darkness; he needs to see to act. There is also a fear in darkness, the one that the duke of Burgundy must have felt, unable as he was to discern the dangers surrounding him.

The City

The city—the castle had similar characteristics on a smaller scale— protected itself against the perils that threatened it, particularly at night. First of all, it was surrounded by a solid wall. In the Gallo-Roman era, walls enclosed the towns. More or less destroyed thereafter, by warfare or from lack of upkeep, these fortifications, or what remained of them, could not contain the demographic growth of the eleventh century, and suburbs spread beyond the walls that were literally embedded within houses. Toward the middle of the fourteenth century, armed conflict required the construction of new enclosures.

Toward the end of the Middle Ages, a traveler would thus try to reach the city where he hoped to find rest and safety before nightfall. Latecomers were at risk, for every night the gates were closed and the watch took up its post.

Within the city, there were narrow and irregular streets, a veritable labyrinth of alleys and gardens, a cutthroat place for anyone who walked at night alone or without a weapon to discourage purse snatchers. Take as an example the good city of Tours, well known thanks to the work of Bernard Chevalier.

As protection against the English, toward the middle of the fourteenth century it was decided to enclose the city, although two populated neighborhoods were left outside the fortifications that were less solidly constructed than originally planned. The walls with earthen facings often had to be shored up; the walk at the top of the parapet was generally only an overhanging platform; in place of watchtowers, there were simple shelters. To reach the top of the walls there were about twenty ladders.

Altogether the wall was 4.5 kilometers long, enclosing nearly 60 hectares, fronted by ditches and contrescarps. Entry was by way of ten gates, very different from one another. Some were simple openings in the wall, easily closed. Others, in contrast, were cut through thick stone fortifications between two round towers. All of them were equipped with drawbridges.

Crossing the gate just before the bells rang at La Riche and the Feu-Hugon tower and the heavy panels were closed, a traveler could now dawdle, wander at whim from street to street, unless he prudently decided to find beforehand a hospitable place to spend the night. In the neighborhood of Châteauneuf, the residents have just stopped working; the taverns are filling up, for the city is densely populated. The streets are a labyrinth in which a stranger can easily lose his way. The houses are lined up along the alleys, with interior courtyards but no room for gardens. From time to time there is a square. The largest, fifty meters long, contains large and small butcher shops; the market takes place there on Saturday.

Continuing, the traveler would reach the center of the city, which has a very different appearance, with two longitudinal streets, the rue de la Scellerie and the main street, a residential area of the bourgeois and well-to-do artisans. There is room here for large houses and their gardens, monasteries and their vast parks. There are a few modest houses scattered about, enclosed within the outbuildings of aristocratic establishments. The great square Foire-le-Roi, where mystery plays are performed and the pillory is set up, is 150 meters long and 100 meters wide. The neighborhood also has gardens belonging to prominent people, but not near their houses, that are sometimes neglected and look like waste ground. Also, at the end of the day, prostitutes are strolling in search of clients, while thieves watch out for the bourgeois hurrying home in hope of stealing a purse.

Facing it, the neighborhood of la Cité seems more tranquil—a few men at arms in the château, canons in the cloister that shelters their houses, little movement on the vast terrain covered by the still unfinished buildings of the cathedral. In the center, the carroi des Arcis, there are no large houses, but many narrow dead ends running off the main street, festooned with houses constructed haphazardly, according to each builder's whim and the space available. These streets offer little temptation to stroll at night.

But let us leave Touraine on a witch's broom and fly over the regions between the joyous Loire and Paris, where Master François Villon, unrepentant night-owl, will be happy to guide us.

Darkness begins to cover the city. Vespers has just been rung in the churches and convents, work has come to a stop. In the street, before the evening meal, children go to get freshly ground mustard; they go in groups, striking up cheerful or indeed bawdy songs like "Open your door, Guillemette."

The workers have something to eat, generally a modest meal made up of bread, peas and beans, bacon, and cabbage. Curfew is rung: at seven for Notre-Dame, at eight in the other churches of Paris, at nine for the Sorbonne bell.

Night has now fallen—several hours ago in winter, just now in the long days of summer. Some candles are still burning in the workshops of a few artisans who have gotten special permission to carry on urgent work. In the city, darkness is complete. Next to the entry of the porte du Châtelet a lantern glows before the image of the Virgin Mary. The drinkers have left the taverns and are staggering toward home.

The wicked, the poor who have found no place to sleep and settle in under tables used to display goods for sale, and lovers going to meet their beloved whose father is asleep or whose husband is away have taken over the capital. Villon depicts them without apology:

> And to those who lie beneath the merchants' stalls,
> I leave to each a punch in the eye;
> They shiver, faces contracted by cold,
> Thin, hairy, and sniffling,
> I leave them then short pants, shortened dress,
> They are freezing, battered, and dripping wet.

The thieving Villon really has no pity for the shameful poor!

As for this foot patrol, he describes them very amusingly, "feeling among the stalls," that is, pilfering the shops. Many texts mention lovers who injure themselves by colliding with carts or house doors. Marot writes:

> I fear the watch; he's far from nice.
> And then at night you find a cart;
> You break your nose like so much ice,
> For the pleasure of a little tart.

Night is coming to a close. Daybreak sounds from atop the keep of the Louvre, from the towers of the Grand and the Petit Châtelet. Troublemakers have returned to bed and sleep without remorse. The bells ring prime. The city resumes its activities.

CHAPTER I

Violence

Night, the realm of fear, was apparently the realm of the devil, of sin. The sin was "venial" if it were only a matter of the nighttime uproar of young men leaving taverns after copious drinking or schoolboys taking down the signs of honest sleeping merchants. But it was "mortal sin" when such escapades ended in homicide, when robbers took advantage of the sleep of honest folk to loot their houses, when fearsome mercenaries silently going through the walls of a city threw themselves on the harmless residents, or when in the absence of her husband a spouse indulged in extramarital pleasures.

Trials frequently mention the time of offenses. The detail refers especially to those committed at a "suspect hour," an "hour that favors misdeeds," a "forbidden hour," that is, after curfew. If we are to believe the documents, most bad actions took place in darkness.

The civil regulations of Lyon prohibited "any tavern keeper from being so bold as to keep a tavern open publicly after the great curfew bell, with a penalty of sixty sous." But many taverns did not respect the rules, and late at night young bachelors left them to wander the streets looking for mischief or for a girl to attack.

Private Violence

Disorders

In Dijon, on Thursday June 22, 1464, four or five companions in disguise ran through the city several times—each time in different clothes, and once dressed as devils—from midnight to two o'clock in the morning, and threw stones at doors and windows. They tried to get into one house and shouted at the master of the house, named Jacot: "In the voice of a devil, hoarse and unclear: Jacot, Jacot, la, la, la, sus, sus; get up, by the devil." Then they emitted truly diabolical cries to the great terror of the neighbors.

In December 1452, the "subalterns" of the school rector, who were unhappy with him, organized an uproar. Around nine o'clock at night, while the rector was in a room conversing with some of his pupils, he heard a loud noise. Stones were thrown at the house. The rector, very frightened, tried to find out what was happening. From the window he could see sixteen to eighteen people and hear shouts, without distinguishing anything but "oaf, oaf" or "bru, bra." Before leaving, the young men broke three doors, "still shouting, making noise, and singing."

Here is an even more serious incident. On Assumption Sunday in 1473, Jean Aigneaul, bourgeois and magistrate, was on watch with several servants and neighbors to see whether anyone in the city was causing a disturbance or whether there were strangers about, for it was said that "in the city, there had been various noises, brawls, and other great disturbances at night."

The little troop passed by a butcher shop at around eleven-thirty at night. One of Aigneaul's young servants bringing up the rear had a waxen torch ripped from his hands by a butcher named Jean Fèvre. His master came to his help and asked the butcher why he was out at this unseemly hour. As Jean Fèvre refused to give up the torch, Aigneaul arrested him. Fèvre's wife protested, the neighbors came running. One of them, Étienne Dacier, said to Aigneaul, "By God, you will not put him in prison, Jean Aigneaul, Jean sheep, Jean ewe. [Aigneaul is a near homonym of *agneau*, lamb.] What a misfortune that we are ruled by a dyer."

Jean Aigneaul agreed to release Fèvre, but Fèvre immediately grabbed him by the throat and tried to throw him to the ground and to seize the weapon that he was carrying. He was restrained. Jean Fèvre and Étienne Dacier were imprisoned, the former fined a hundred livres tournois, the latter fifty livres tournois, and both required to make formal apologies.

In university towns with their hundreds of students the situation was most troubling for the sleepy bourgeois. For example, there was the episode of the stone called the *Pet-au-Diable* [devil's fart].

This was a raised stone of unknown origin, perhaps a former milestone, in the shape of a bladder or a bag, its name apparently derived from a scabrous fabliau, *Dou pet au vilain*. Located in front of the house of an old and pious lady, Mademoiselle de Bruyères, it had become an object of many student pranks. One fine day in 1451, Parisian students carried the stone to the top of the montagne Sainte-Geneviève. The Parlement decided to open an investigation, and the stone was carried to the courtyard of the Palais de Justice.

The students later returned to Mademoiselle de Bruyères's house and removed the stone with which she had replaced the *Pet-au-Diable*. Having baptized it as the Silent Fart, they carried it off to the montagne Sainte-Geneviève where they set it firmly in the ground. Every night, they came and danced to the sound of flutes and drums.

Moreover, according to police lieutenant Jean Bezon, the students had been guilty of many excesses for several years. At night, they noisily removed signs firmly attached to houses with iron clamps and shouted "Kill! Kill!" to terrify the bourgeois who, hearing noise in the street, would cautiously open their windows to find out what was happening. They removed the signs from the butcher shops of Sainte-Geneviève and performed wedding ceremonies with them, boasting for instance that they had the Serf to celebrate the union of the Sow and the Bear. But this nighttime— and sometimes daytime—uproar finally seriously angered the authorities. Toward the end of 1452, the stone and the signs were removed from the montagne Sainte-Geneviève.

The students were a turbulent community, many of whose members could proclaim, "I set my heart on other things than study." And indeed, waking the bourgeois at night by creating an uproar, tossing off insults, courting chambermaids, and frequenting taverns were the favorite activities of a good number of them. Unfortunately, many pranks ended with a wound or a mortal blow.

Homicides

In December 1471, Toussaint Bouton "a poor young child of twenty," was eating supper with four companions named Philippot Noblet, Barthélemy Bonhomme, Jean Davant, and Jean Hamelin in a Parisian tavern on rue de la Juiverie. After supper, around nine o'clock—by this time, curfew had sounded long before—they left the establishment and went to the house of la grosse Margot, near the cloister of Notre-Dame, where prostitutes were allowed. They stayed there for a while without making a scene and then decided to go home. On the way, Toussaint, Noblet, and Bonhomme saw Noël Mercier talking to a prostitute named Thomassine. The three companions approached, exchanged a few words with Noël, and then went on. But soon Noblet cried out, "Death! Murder!" And he called to Toussaint, saying, "Kill, kill." His friends came running and saw that he was wounded. Wanting to revenge his comrade, Toussaint went looking for Noël, whom he found outside a handball court called *la Plastrière*. Noël hit Toussaint with a stick and Toussaint drew his sword. Noël died three weeks later from a head wound.

From disturbing the peace, we have moved to homicide. How did people get to such extremes? We should first note the extent of the consumption of wine. In fifteenth-century Tours, the average annual consumption for an adult was between 148 and 178 liters, although a number of people, for reasons of age or health, drank only water. In Touraine, a third of violent incidents resulted from drinking. It was thus not uncommon for brawls to take place outside taverns at nightfall. Other contributing causes were poverty, a masculine sexuality frustrated by the late age of marriage, and the habit of carrying weapons.

The first stage of this violence was located at the level of language, where the barrier between the tolerable and the intolerable was soon crossed. From everyday insults, like "bastard" or "oaf," one would move on to doubts about the opponent's virility, the worst insult being to question his wife's behavior. Insults were followed by obscene gestures and then a slap or a punch and finally a stabbing. Some examples will shed light on this movement toward homicide, even though the protagonists would at first meet in a harmless way.

On November 15, 1425, at around nine in the evening, Guillaume Bouyn, about sixty years old, was finishing supper with his wife Macé in their dwelling near the Pont Neuf in Paris. They were talking and, among other things, Guillaume told Macé that he had rented a little room with a window on the street near the hôtel des Tourelles to sell clothes, as he had always done to earn his living. She immediately retorted that she wouldn't be able to go to the shop because her bad leg made the distance from home too great. He told her to stay home then. Macé kept up her criticism, and Guillaume, who was tipsy like his wife, slapped her twice. Then, since she refused to keep quiet and kept on complaining, he went to get a stick to teach her a lesson. Instead of a piece of wood, next to his bed he found the sword that he used when he was on watch at the porte Saint-Jacques. He hit his wife on the shoulders a few times with the flat of the blade. She tried but failed to take the weapon from him and angrily left the room shouting "Assassin!" Thinking that she was heading toward the outside door to run away, she found herself in a little kitchen with a low window, then open, through which she fell. A little later, some passersby—there were some at that hour!—found her, and several neighbors came out to pick her up and bring her to one of their homes. A sergeant arrived, went to find Guillaume, and took him off to the *conciergerie* of the Palais de Justice where he was imprisoned.

Also in Paris, in November 1431, there was a violent dispute between Raoulin Petit, a forty-eight-year-old worker in the wine trade, and Velizon, a young disreputable woman whom he had taken up with a few months earlier and whom, he said, he had unsuccessfully been attempting to wean away from her former dissolute life. About six weeks before the letter of remission dated December 26, "around eight or nine o'clock at night," Raoulin returned home. He found Velizon drunk and criticized her for her behavior, telling her that he would kick her out if she didn't change her ways. The young woman answered that she wouldn't leave under any circumstances, called him "a wicked traitor," and, with those words, suddenly came up to him and grabbed him by the genitals so that he fell to the floor with her on top of him. Raoulin, feeling himself grasped by "his lower parts," began to shout "Murder!" Despite his howls, Velizon continued to hold him, and she squeezed so hard that he was now in the hands of the doctors because of a swelling of those "lower parts." Fearing that the woman would kill him, Raoulin partly freed himself with great effort and, with the pommel of the sword he carried at his side, struck Velizon on the forehead, and she let him go. Then they made up—according to the petitioner. The next day, ignoring her wound, she left him to continue her dissolute life.

A final example, in which death was apparently caused by an accident, happened at Charzais in Poitou in the year 1335. Jean Moreau, father of four young children, having been drinking in the tavern and gotten drunk, came home "at night" where his wife, seeing him in that state, started to give him a tongue lashing. Jean Moreau got angry, took the child that she was holding out of her arms, and hit her several times. She struggled to hit him back and scratched him on the face while shouting insults, and then took refuge in the attic, which collapsed under her weight. She died during the night. Moreau had fallen asleep and, finding her dead when he woke up, ran away.

These three domestic scenes confirm the pattern set forth above. But these documents provoke some observations. Women were at the receiving end of the blows, mortal on two occasions. To be sure, Velizon died some time after the dispute, "as much from her bad living as from a stomach disease," but this is according to the petitioner. Forget for the moment that the fatal outcome was the result of anger provoked by the woman's insults—no one can verify the truth of these statements. It is important to note that drunkenness played a role in every case. Guillaume and Macé Bouyn must have drunk copiously during their meal. Raoulin Petit found Velizon drunk, and he himself, a wine merchant, had no doubt indulged before coming home. Jean Moreau got drunk in a tavern—we should note that to secure his remission it was pointed out as an attenuating circumstance "that at the time he was full of wine." Finally, the first scene began at nine o'clock at night, the second around eight or nine—and in November—and the third probably around the same time in the month of January. Before going to bed, when night has fallen, after too much drinking at home or in a tavern, these are the elements that unleash domestic violence.

Punitive expeditions tended to take place at night, when people's guard was down. Around 1350, the farmer-monk of a priory located near L'Isle-Jourdain gathered a number of men and led them to a village where they found a man named Brigant, whom they beat to death with sticks.

It appears that the forces of order were not always asleep at night, and this gave rise to occasional battles. Jacques de Belleville, a twenty-five-year-old squire, came to Poitiers in October 1462 to press a claim against the bishop of Luçon. The royal prosecutor of Poitou had him arrested on the grounds that he had thrown a sword at a certain Fortin and that he had taken grain and hay that he claimed belonged to him. Released, he remained in town to settle his affairs. On Saint Luke's Day, at around "eleven o'clock at night," there secretly came into his room in the Hotel du Mouton where he was staying (there was a lighted candle on the table) a certain Hilleret Tondeur, an officer of the city provost, armed with a large dagger and accompanied by two servants in cloaks, each one carrying a large knife or short sword. Terrified, Jacques stated to Hilleret that he had not sent for him and that this was no time to carry out police action. He got up and sat on the bed, dressed only in a nightshirt. Hilleret placed his right hand on his dagger and his left on the petitioner, who tried to flee, but fell on the chimney corner injuring his arm and shoulder. The candle had almost burned down, and since it was rather dark in the room, he managed to escape. While looking for the ladder that went up to the room, he found a lantern. While going down the rungs, and because he was bleeding, he shouted, "Murder! Help in the name of the king!"

All was dark at the foot of the ladder, but he found the open door of the unlit room of the hotel keeper. He went in protesting the outrage to which he had been subjected. As he heard Hilleret and his servants approaching, he tried to close the door, but in vain because a badly placed roasting spit prevented him. He then seized the spit and, thinking that the others would try to come into the room, shouted, "Don't come in and take care. I can't see a thing!" And he stuck the spit through the open doorway. He then heard Hilleret say, "Jesus, vile traitor, you've killed me!" He had not seen him, because there was no candle or any other light, and if he had struck him with the spit, it was by chance and not deliberately, and in defending himself—at least he so asserted in the letter of remission that relates the anecdote. The servants finally managed to get in and seize Jacques de Belleville.

Hotels were not safe, and at night, as other documents attest, some very strange things occurred. Of course, their principal function was to provide a place to sleep for travelers, and they were often therefore more populated at night than during the day, and darkness favored many crimes.

Violence seemed to be everywhere, particularly at night, fostered by drunkenness or by the explosion of resentful passions. Indeed, it sometimes broke out over trifles. Let us return to the streets of Paris along with Master François Villon.

One evening, François Villon went to see a certain Robin Daugis who lived on the rue de la Parcheminerie, at the sign of the Wagon, to be given supper, for he didn't have a red cent. Daugis generously granted his request and they ate with two other companions, Rogier Pichart and Hutin du Moustier. Then they decided to go to Villon's room, and with this in mind they went down the rue Saint-Jacques. It was about seven or eight o'clock at night.

On their left, next to the Mule Tavern, was the office of the pontifical notary, Master François Ferrebouc. His duties allowed him to work after the curfew, and young men were there copying documents by candlelight.

Seeing the light, Rogier Pichart stopped in front of the notary's window, engaged in some banter with the hard-working scribes, and spat into their room. They immediately came out cursing the thugs that would do such a thing. Pichart asked them if they wanted to "buy some flutes." With this question he no doubt wanted to show them what kind of wood these flutes were made of, since he intended to beat them with it. Master Ferrebouc's employees obviously didn't see things the same way and a brawl broke out. Hutin du Moustier was captured and carried into the notary's house, shouting, "Murder! They're killing me! I'm a dead man!" Master Ferrebouc rushed outside and shoved Robin Daugis who fell to the ground but immediately got up, drew his dagger and stabbed him. Robin then met up with Rogier Pichart in front of the church of Saint-Benoît-le-Bétourné and vehemently reproached him for his behavior. He then went home to bed, very worried about the consequences of this nocturnal brawl.

The author of the *Testament* was used to these fights. On June 5, 1455, Corpus Christi, at around nine o'clock at night, François was sitting on a stone bench on the rue Saint-Jacques with a priest and a woman going by the name of Isabeau. They were happily chatting when a priest, Philippe Sermoise, and Jean le Mardi suddenly appeared. Seeing Villon, Philippe shouted, "I deny God! Master François, I've found you; you can be sure that I'll make you angry." Villon replied, "Have I done you wrong? What do you want of me? I believe I have done you no harm. Dear brother, what are you angry about?"

He got up to offer him his seat, but Philippe refused. Villon sat down again. Then Sermoise drew his dagger and struck him in the face, cutting his lip. Villon's two companions had discreetly gone off, leaving only Philippe and François. Villon backed off, a stone in his right hand, a dagger in his left. As the priest pursued him, Villon stabbed him in the groin.

Then he went to a barber-surgeon to have his wound treated. To follow police rules, the barber asked his name. Villon said he was Michel Mouton and named Philippe Sermoise as the man who had wounded him. Meanwhile, neighbors had picked up Sermoise and put him to bed in a house near the gate opening onto the rue Saint-Jacques. He was treated and an official from the Châtelet questioned him. The next day, he was transported to the Hôtel-Dieu where he died the following Saturday.

It was more convenient to slay an enemy when the streets were almost deserted after curfew, when darkness allowed one to hide and made it easier to keep from being seen; thus, nocturnal and political violence sometimes coincided. For example, on the evening of November 23, 1407, the duke of Orléans was assassinated on orders of his cousin, the duke of Burgundy, Jean sans Peur. The story is told in many chronicles, here by Enguerran de Monstrelet. "In Paris, one Wednesday, the day of Saint Clement, pope and martyr, the duke was put to death around seven o'clock at night. And this homicide was perpetrated by about eighteen men who were staying at the hotel at the sign of *The Image of Our Lady* near the porte Barbette." A servant of Charles VI had been sent to the duke at around seven to tell him that the king was asking for him. "The duke, wishing to obey the king, although the latter was not in on the plot, immediately mounted his mule, and he was escorted by two squires on a horse and four or six servants in front and behind, carrying torches. When he approached the porte Barbette, the aforementioned eighteen men, who were carrying weapons under their cloaks, were waiting for him near a house. *It was dark enough for that night.* They threw themselves all together on the duke, and one of them shouted, 'Death! Death,' and striking him with an ax, cut off his hand."

Two other kinds of nocturnal violence can be noted, but they have peculiar characteristics. The first is self-inflicted violence that in some cases resulted in death. Suicides must have taken place in daylight, but in those instances the time is not mentioned. On the other hand, when poor unfortunates took their own lives at night, the time was always mentioned. For one suicide taking place during the day, there were eight at night: one at night without further precision, one in the evening, three toward midnight, three at dawn. Doctors observed further that those who were ill often carried out their plans during the second half of the night, for, sleeping little, they awoke in anguish faced with another miserable day to live through, while their tired caregivers relaxed their attention; they then carried out their mortal act. For example, near daybreak on July 3, 1423, Michelet le Cavelier, mentally ill, taking advantage of the sleep of his wife and his keeper who had watched over him all night, got up completely naked, opened a window looking out on the coppersmiths' market, threw himself out the window, and died immediately. In 1447, a mentally ill woman was lying next to her husband. As she got up, he asked her where she was going; she replied that she was answering a call of nature. She left the house completely naked and threw herself down a deep well.

Fortunately, such attempts sometimes failed. Jeannette Voidié, depressed because she could not nurse her last child and thinking herself a bad mother, lamented one night lying in bed next to her husband, "Ah, treacherous enemy, you really tricked me, I was going to succeed, and you took away the rope." In fact, she had several times tried to hang herself and twice had gotten up at night to throw herself into the river from a window of their house located on the pont Notre-Dame in Paris, but she had failed because of her husband's intervention. The unfortunate mother, still depressed, nevertheless ended up drowning her three-month-old son.

Children died at night, smothered by their parents with whom they shared a bed. "Have you found your child smothered in your bed, when you and your husband were lying together, without knowing who smothered it, you or its father, or whether the child died naturally?" asked Burchard de Worms at the beginning of the eleventh century, echoing Saint Colomban from the late sixth century, who dealt in his penitential with the case of a father or mother smothering a young child. These references can be compared with the sad story of Colette, a young wet-nurse of seventeen, the wife of a secondhand clothes dealer named Jean Mingois. Colette, who lived in Paris, had for seven months been nursing Jean, the son of Jean Cordier, a bourgeois of the city. On Monday, December 2, 1420, "at the hour of eight at night," after having fed the child, Colette put him in his cradle, breast-fed him at nine, and after he had gone to sleep, put him as usual next to her bed. She covered his head with a warm hat because of the cold and an hour later went to bed alone, since her husband was out. She slept until about four o'clock in the morning. When she woke up, delighted that the child had let her sleep, which he did not usually do, she went to get him, saw the hat covering his face, and realized that he was dead.

Thefts

Violence against people, violence against property. Note a reversal of values compared to our day: while brawling and physical violence in general did not necessarily give rise to social disapproval, the same thing was not true of theft, which provoked fear and havoc. In the criminal records of the Châtelet in Paris for the years 1389–1391, 67 percent of the accused were cited for theft. To what extent did this percentage correspond to reality? In fact, letters of remission give much more space to fights ending in homicide. Was royal pardon easier to obtain in those cases?

Theft and night seem to be linked, but this first impression needs to be nuanced and certain distinctions need to be made. A thief, who committed an inexcusable crime, had to remain unrecognized. It was therefore appropriate that the theft be carried out in an uninhabited place or at night, or sometimes both.

Gregory of Tours, in the Merovingian era, reports many illicit borrowings carried out in darkness. For instance, in the little town of Yzeure, on the border of the territory of Tours, there stood a church with windows of glass with wooden frames, which allowed light to come in more easily. One night, a bold thief came in the darkness; seeing that he could carry off none of the furnishings that had been carefully put away by the guardians, he decided to snatch the windows.

Another individual, during the vigils of Saint Julian, stole the horse of a man who had come to the ceremony and quickly rode off, hoping the theft would not be discovered before daybreak and "that night would conceal the criminal fraud of a thief whose conscience was clouded by the darkness of cupidity. It was of such men that the Lord said in the Gospels: 'Whoever does evil hates the light.'"

While people were leaving the church of Saint Julian after evening prayers, a thief hid in a corner of the basilica and, when the silence of the night had filled the entire building, left his hiding place and, as though urged on by Satan, ran toward the gate of the saint's tomb and ripped from the top of it a cross covered in dazzling stones. Then he returned to the place where he had been lying and went to sleep. The guardians making their rounds saw him and kept him under guard for the rest of the night; in the morning he confessed his crime.

All the same, it was the absence of worshipers at night in the basilica of Saint Julian and not night itself that encouraged this thief to commit his crime. Indeed, toward the end of the Middle Ages, judging by the letters of remission, many thefts were committed in daylight after thieves had spied out the owners' departure. Sometimes, however, darkness was actively sought out. This was particularly true in hotels. Common rooms, occupied by people who did not know one another, offered opportunities for theft at the expense of companions of a single night. For instance, in June 1460, in the hotel de l'Amour de Dieu on rue de la Barillerie in Paris, there were in the same room a man from Normandy, one from Nantes, and two companions whose origin was unknown. Alain Robert, the Breton, was caught while stealing the money from his bed-mate's bag.

In 1476, Étienne Maubec, from the parish of Maillé in Poitou, carried off the church bells, then "waited for nightfall" and, "when night had come," opened the door of the building and stole nine écus. One night in 1483 or 1484, Pierre Prévost, from Airvault, got into the house of Daniel Musset and stole two bushels of wheat from the attic. Another night, he went into Jean Saquet's garden and went through a window into the room where Saquet and his son-in-law were sleeping, but he was caught in the act. A little later, around nine at night, he got into Pierre Mercier's hayloft, remained hidden there until midnight, and then went into Mercier's bedroom where he stole the money kept in a purse. One night, along with his uncle Colin Prévost, he went to the house of Georges le Feure, got into the room where le Feure and his wife were sleeping, and took a certain sum of money. In an abbey, while the monks were saying matins, he stole a pair of black hose and a doublet.

Let us conclude by recalling the "career" of Christophe Micheau, a native of Secondigny-en-Gâtine, that clearly demonstrates that thieves did not systematically seek out darkness.

A letter of remission of May 1457 recounts that our hero, about twenty-seven years old and a prisoner in La Mothe-Saint-Héraye, had been passing through a nearby village the preceding October 24, "entered by force" into a house where he stealthily took a piece of cloth and two hats. Arrested for this theft, he then confessed many others. The preceding Thursday, traveling from Pamprou to Saint-Maixent, he had gone into a dwelling "at around ten in the morning" through an improperly closed window. On Sunday, October 23, in a neighboring town, "at an hour when people were at high mass," he went through a house where no one was home. He did the same thing on September 22 when he saw a house with an open door. Before that, at noon one day in Saintes, he stole various items from a chaplain. Three years earlier, in the town of Parthenay, he got into a gentleman's house around midnight. Then, afraid of being caught, he left the town by going over the walls with the help of a rope. In Thouars, while selling something he had stolen, he watched where the buyer took out the money to pay him. He then waited for the man to go out to dinner, and when no one was at home he stole many things. He also confessed that he had gone into the fortress of Pamprou around eleven at night and had forced the locks of several houses. In Vienne, in Dauphiné, having observed a money-changer, he got into his house one night. This list of misdeeds is not complete, but even so it makes it possible to specify the times at which thefts were committed.

Pillage cannot be assimilated to simple theft. Particularly intense in time of war, pillage did not necessarily require the absence of the owners, since it involved destruction carried out by people of superior force in addition to the seizure of particular goods.

Challenges to Authority

Beyond private violence, night harbored another more frightening danger, subversion of public order. It has been written that in Venice, night meant the "rejection of civic order." Gangs of young men caused disorder and committed acts of vandalism that came close to political crimes to the extent that they appeared to challenge the municipal or indeed the royal authorities.

A document edited and analyzed by Robert-Henri Bautier provides an excellent illustration. The scene took place in Orléans on February 27 and 28 of the year 1284. On the night of the Sunday of Torches, the population was in the habit of celebrating, and in particular of lighting bonfires to mark the beginning of Lent. That night after curfew, four royal sergeants from the Châtelet of Orléans were making the rounds to verify that nothing out of the ordinary was going on. According to three of them, on the rue du Retour-Saint-Benoît, they met a servant who, in spite of the ban, was carrying a dagger at his waist. There was a discussion. One of the sergeants seized the dagger, to the great displeasure of the servant, who began to yell. Thereupon, eight students, his masters, came out of a nearby house and demanded that the sergeants return the weapon. When the sergeants replied that they did not have the right to give it up, the students, who were armed, attacked them, wounded two, and took the sword from a third.

Jean de Boulonville, the provost of Orléans, decided to restore order and himself to lead the watch the following night to find the guilty men. Eleven sergeants and auxiliaries went along with him. Near the hotel des Tournemines, in the street where the episode had taken place, they heard a noise. Since a tavern was located at the spot, the sound could only be coming from there! The provost banged on the door and demanded that it be opened. The tavern-keeper and his wife—who were asleep—were harshly criticized for keeping their house open so late. This was a mistake, because the noise was coming from a nearby house where the students were living. During the discussion movements were heard; it was the young men gathering stones, as they had in fact been doing throughout the day.

The provost left the tavern. According to his testimony, he was wounded before he had identified himself. It seems, however, to judge from other testimony, that voices from a window one flight up asked, "Who's there?" and that the provost answered, "It's the king's provost." Now knowing with whom they were dealing, the students shouted "Shit on the king!" and "Hurry off to a bad end! May God send it to you!" and "Run off to Spain with your king!" These were not thoughtless words, for a few days earlier the king had decided to undertake the crusade to Aragon. Even worse, matching actions to words, the royal officer's antagonists bared their bottoms and slapped their buttocks.

The provost replied and a brawl ensued. Stones rained down on him and his sergeants. He ordered that the door be opened, but was met with more shouts and projectiles. The provost received only a slight wound in the cheek, but his pelvis was shattered by a well-aimed paving stone. Stones were followed by iron-tipped crossbow arrows, clearly revealing premeditation. Three sergeants were wounded, one of whom lost an eye.

The provost then decided to launch an attack. But first he ordered all the bourgeois to help him, and in order to enforce the king's command, he appeared in person at each house. All joined him except for a man who did not want to leave his sick wife alone. Noticing that the insurgents were continuing to receive supplies, a neighbor tried to reason with them. The provost once again called on the students to surrender, but received only louder shouts in reply. The bourgeois who had come to the aid of the watch were called "dogs of Orléans"; arrows and stones flew through the air. This went on through a good part of the night. Several bourgeois did not escape unscathed, one was wounded in the back, another in the knee. Finally, the provost ordered an attack, which lasted until daybreak. Shielding themselves with doors that had been taken off their hinges from neighboring houses or with tables, his troops reached the troublemakers' house and broke down the door. But the besieged had left by the windows giving on an orchard, taking their swords and shields with them, so that when the provost and seven men entered the house, they found it empty. He called for a torch, since it was still dark. They discovered a monk, who broke the torch with his sword and was then made prisoner. There were three clerics hiding in the school, four students in the cellar of a nearby house, and another fleeing in the street.

Aside from a prank that degenerated into a brawl, this incident displays a challenge to royal authority. The references to the Aragon crusade and the persistence in a battle whose outcome was not in doubt are evidence of a particular state of mind.

Let us go beyond this brawl with political connotations to consider the deeper problem of opposition to authority, premeditated or not. When political opinions were subject to repression, there was always the night in which they could be expressed secretly or indeed given concrete illustration. Hence, night gave birth to conspiracies, a movement from licentiousness to liberty.

In the course of difficult periods, like the fourteenth and fifteenth centuries, it was not uncommon for opposition forces to meet at night, or indeed to attempt to seize power by force. Attempts to overthrow the authorities were particularly evident during the quarrel between the Armagnacs and the Burgundians. Nicolas de Baye, clerk of the Parlement de Paris, noted that rumors of sedition were rife in the city. On Tuesday night, December 10, 1415, a pastry cook who lived across from the central butchers' market in Paris was arrested because he had written letters and used a ten- or twelve-year-old boy to get them to the duke of Burgundy to encourage him to come to Paris at once. According to Juvénal des Ursins, this pastry cook was decapitated on the 11th and his body hung on the gallows, at night, no doubt in order to avoid a disturbance. Also on that Wednesday night, and for the same reason, the authorities incarcerated in the name of the king "a large number of people in Paris, only to prevent them from making any commotion in the city." One night in 1416, while Charles VI was "absent," and the duke of Guyenne was governing in the name of his father, some rebels hung placards on the churches: "Dear fellow citizens, know that the chains will soon be removed from your streets and your defensive arms taken from you. So prepare to resist with energy and courage; you will soon receive powerful reinforcements." The royal authorities had to take action, all the more because civil war and foreign war were coming together. It was thus prohibited, on pain of imprisonment, to hold gatherings or secret meetings or to ring church bells from curfew until daybreak, in order to allow the night watch to be able better to hear both internal and external noises. And, "in order to forestall the plots of certain people inspired by the spirit of treason, who, by viciously and at an ungodly hour throwing fire through basement windows, might foment popular uprisings while people were hurrying to put out the fire, it was also ordered by the voice of the herald that those windows be closed, and everyone had to have a barrel full of water at the door of his house."

In 1417, the community of Rouen rose up and put to death the bailiff, Messire Raoul de Gaucourt. At the urging of supporters of the duke of Burgundy, some people of no great standing went to the king's bailiff. Armed with weapons and sticks, they loudly knocked at the door and asked to speak to him in order to turn over a traitor that they had just arrested. It was about ten at night. The bailiff's servants told them to secure their prisoner until the following day. Nevertheless, these individuals were so persistent that the servants opened the door. The bailiff got up and, draped in a large coat, came to talk to them. At that point, some of them killed him. In the course of the night, the conspirators went to other houses and killed a dozen people.

On August 20, 1418, at around ten at night, the people of Paris started to murmur that the Châtelet and other establishments of the same kind held several prisoners said to be favorable to the Armagnac side. Some prisoners accused of the same crime had been freed, but these had not. The police authorities were accused of negligence or corruption, ignorance or concealment. That night the Parisians in great numbers went to the Grand and the Petit Châtelet, broke down the doors, and seized everyone who had been imprisoned for supporting the cause of the count of Armagnac. The rumors and the troubles lasted throughout the night and the following day.

Fifteen years later, on Ascension night, the inhabitants of Ghent tried to come together to revolt against the prince's officials and the governors of the town. The reply given to these people who wanted to meet with their prince leaves no doubt about the political implications of the night: "[They] could gather by night, and at a time when he and all of us his servants were asleep, could come and attack and try to kill everyone, the master and his family."

WAR

Conspiracy is in essence linked to night, but on the strictly military plane, darkness is unquestionably ambivalent. Night attracts or repels armed actions depending on the prominence of one aspect or another, ruse or force.

Flight

Night turns out to have been favorable to war, first in a negative manner, to the extent that it allowed escape from a difficult situation by flight. In 1383, during the siege of Bergues by French troops, the commander of the garrison, who, if we are to believe the monk of Saint-Denis, was considered by the English a model of valor, lacking confidence in his forces, declared to his soldiers, "'My friends, I have come to tell you of my plans. Our position has become such that I have rather to show you what necessity demands than to give you advice. Our sole hope of safety is to leave this place and to escape; and this sortie has to take place during the night. Thus, since we have no hope of saving the city, let us take advantage of the time of night when men are sunk in deepest sleep, and let us go and join our compatriots in Gravelines.' All agreed and, carrying their baggage, they withdrew with a great booty after setting fire to the town. In the morning, at daybreak, the French found nothing to repay them for their efforts."

In 1414, a rebel, Enguerrand de Bournonville, seeing that the king's forces were winning, spoke as follows to those who were still with him in Soissons: "Listen, my friends, to the resolution I have made; the state of our affairs is such that it remains for me less to give you advice than to show you what we have been reduced to by necessity. We have no more hope of defending the city; our only hope of safety is to abandon it and to withdraw. We can only do that during the night. Let us leave then during the second watch, at a time when the besiegers are sunk in the deepest sleep; let us march silently and hold ourselves ready to open a way with our swords in hand if we happen to run into the sentinels on watch." Messire de Craon, suspecting Enguerrand's treachery, refused to let him leave at the appointed time.

The officers of the king of France used the same procedure. In 1385, Admiral Jean de Vienne called together his companions in arms and declared, "We have to trick the enemy; in my view, our only hope of safety is to leave the city [Edinburgh] and to escape.

This sortie has to be made during the night; I believe the most propitious time is the hour when mortals are sunk in the deepest sleep. The enemy will not be on the alert or prepared to defend themselves; we will meet neither guards nor sentinels and we will be able to go past their camp while keeping total silence." All agreed to this plan; and from then on, no one thought of sleeping or resting, but the time was taken up by selecting the objects they would carry off with them. Then the signal for departure was given. In the darkness of night, the French passed silently by the enemy and in two days crossed the wilderness to the border of Scotland.

The similarity of these speeches casts some doubt on the accuracy of the words reported by the monk of Saint-Denis. The fact remains that in all these cases the leaders decided to flee at night, as the most propitious moment to leave an indefensible position without attracting the attention of the besiegers.

Surprise

Darkness played a more positive role by facilitating the movement of troops. Surveillance could not detect maneuvers and in the morning the enemies that had come close were able to launch an unexpected attack. Chastellain recounts how, in 1421, the duke of Burgundy, Philip the Good, surprised his opponents. Having learned that the French were preparing to cross the Somme to attack his army, which was engaged in a siege, the duke decided to take the initiative in order to prevent them from coming into Picardy.

The siege was therefore lifted: "At least it was decided to lift it during the following night, so that their enemies would not be aware of their enterprise." At "basses vêpres," the duke summoned two knights and ordered them to leave with six hundred soldiers to scout the enemy position. He would follow them at night to help them if they ran into difficulty. The two knights set out when it was already "black night." They arrived at a gate to Abbeville, had it opened, crossed through the city, went out through a gate on the other side of the river, and went on their way with their ears on the alert for any noises of people or horses. At the same time, the duke of Burgundy left with his army and arrived before Abbeville at daybreak. He thereby took advantage of the night to attempt to reverse the situation in his favor.

Monstrelet recounts that, in 1435, the French crossed the Somme at night at la Blanquetaque, and from there reached the town of Rue, held by the English. Using ladders, they secretly entered the town, and before their opponents noticed anything, seized it without encountering any resistance.

Obviously, antagonists used the same ruses, which sometimes produced unexpected results. In that same year of 1435, the duke of Bedford, who was in Rouen, learned of the capture of the town of Rue. Realizing the danger to the region under English influence created by this loss, he wrote to the count of Arundel, then in Nantes, telling him to set siege to Rue. Informed on the way that the French were restoring an old fortress called Gerberoy, the count decided to capture it. He took on supplies, artillery, and other war engines at Gournay, set out "shortly after midnight," and arrived before the château of Gerberoy toward eight in the morning. But the fortress contained many more soldiers than expected. While his army was settling in, La Hire, Pothon, and other valiant French warriors deliberated. They too had "come the night before," which explains the English lack of knowledge. They immediately decided to fight. "And thus were those English as it were half surprised and defeated, and the greater part put to death and turned to great misfortune."

It even happened that armies in a sense sought each other in darkness—or rather tried to avoid each other. In 1436, Messire Jean de Croy, bailiff of Hainaut, assembled fifteen hundred combatants to lay siege to Calais and other fortresses on the English side. The assembly took place in a village named Le Waast, which the soldiers left at night to approach their opponents. The latter, that very night, abandoned their garrison to move to the Boulonnais. Since the two forces were unaware of their respective positions and did not wish to meet up, Jean de Croy, near the border between Picardy and the Boulonnais, sent out expert scouts who knew the country well to gather information. The scouts caught sight of the English at daybreak.

Let us leave the conclusion to *Le Jouvencel,* a work written by Jean de Bueil between 1461 and 1468, which recounts the exploits of this hero. "Night is the time when all animals take their rest and believe they are in safety, in which they are often deceived; it thus appears from the bustard and other birds; similarly also with several reptiles of the earth which are taken in and deceived by their confidence in the night, just as men surprise one another and carry out betrayals and perilous deeds."

And indeed, night not only permitted the clandestine approach to enemy fortresses or cities but especially their capture with the help of various stratagems.

Betrayal

The flight of enemies could be put to good use if it was known in time. In 1383, the French who had captured Bergues after the nocturnal departure of the English went off to lay siege to Gravelines. They set up camp not far from the town, which contained a warlike population. The besieged refused to surrender and very carefully arranged soldiers to guard their town day and night and to take turns keeping watch. The leaders oversaw all positions, made the rounds of the walls, and spent most of the night without sleeping. But when the English saw the French preparing siege machines, they decided to flee. The inhabitants vainly tried to dissuade them. The English killed the guards at the gate, left in total silence on the side that was not blocked, and reached Bourbourg.

News of this furtive retreat soon came to the ears of the French. While confusion reigned in the town, three Picard prisoners managed to escape and brought news of the events to the admiral of France, Messire Jean de Vienne, who was keeping watch at night. They told him that the opportunity was favorable, that he could easily capture the city, but that he had to act at once. Suspicious, the admiral put the three men under heavy guard; then he called the knights together to hear their views. They advised him to attack. They soon crossed the river and reached the top of the walls, silently, so that the guards heard nothing and even the dogs did not bark. They thus reached the center of town and put to death every armed man they encountered. The others fled and tried to hide. After setting some of his soldiers to guard the gates, the admiral left the town to be pillaged. At daybreak, he sent word of this nocturnal victory to the king.

It seems that the mentality of the time considered nighttime attacks more akin to betrayal than to shrewdness. In 1412, the Parisians were indignant when they learned of the capture of the Saint-Cloud bridge by the duke of Orléans. A messenger gave them a few details. "Colin de Puiseux, who had recently been assigned to guard the bridge, could only be discontent when, in the name of the king, this post was assigned to Guillaume de Beaumont; consequently, he deliberately neglected the duty he had been given. I do not know whether he allowed himself to be corrupted with gold and if that was the reason that he did not even want a child to keep watch at night." Taking advantage of the situation, a knight, Jean de Gaucourt, crossed the Seine with the help of ropes, along with three hundred men, in complete silence. A Gascon soldier scaled the wooden bridge, broke the lock, and thus allowed his companions to get in. It was not possible to have done so without noise, but Colin pretended not to hear. He even restrained the fervor of his men and several times ordered them to go back to bed. The invaders were thus able to open the doors to his chambers with skeleton keys. They surprised him in bed with his wife and allowed him to take refuge with his brother-in-law, who belonged to the Orleanist party. With some of them left behind to guard the bridge, the soldiers then went on to attack men at arms and bourgeois, who were completely unprepared, and so could not resist. The victors seized huge spoils.

In May 1418, civil war between Armagnacs and Burgundians was still prevalent. A goodly number of Parisians wanted to see the duke of Burgundy seize power, but they did not know how to help him. There was no question of entering into contact with him, because they were under the eye of many soldiers of the Armagnac party, who were ready to repress harshly any attempt at rebellion. Nevertheless, a few young men "of middling estate and of slight will" managed to reach the lord of l'Isle-Adam, who was garrisoned in Pontoise. Among them was Perrenet Le Clerc. They talked with the lord of l'Isle-Adam, who agreed to assemble a number of soldiers and to lead them on May 29 to the gate of Saint-Germain-des-Prés. For their part, they promised him that they would open the gate. The lord of l'Isle-Adam then gathered about eight hundred combatants and led them to the designated place on the day that had been set. There they found Perrenet Le Clerc, who had taken the keys for the gate of Saint-Germain from under the pillow of his father, who was the guardian of the gate. Perrenet and his companions opened the gate as promised, and approached the lord of l'Isle-Adam to tell him to enter boldly; they would lead him through the city. The soldiers of the Burgundian party thus entered Paris on horseback. It was about two in the morning. Perrenet Le Clerc then relocked the gate with the keys, and threw them over the wall. And they made their way in the night to the Châtelet, where they found twelve hundred Parisians ready to join them. This capture of the city was thus tied to a conspiracy, since external forces were joined by inhabitants of the place. All agreed to take several mansions by storm. Then some of them went through the streets, encouraging those who wanted peace to take up their weapons and join them. Thus it was that a large multitude marched to the hôtel Saint-Pol where the insurgents broke down the doors, and did so much that they secured a meeting with the king. And "all that night and the next day and the day following," they rifled the great houses and made many high officials prisoner.

Such occurrences were not restricted to the capital. Flanders, an economically developed region, was also the scene of nocturnal conspiracies. Men of Ghent led by a certain François Ackermann reached the gate of Damme "with the perfidious aim" of aiding the English army. They discreetly inquired among the inhabitants to learn whether it was possible, under cover of darkness, surreptitiously to get to the king's ships in order to set them on fire. In the neighboring port of l'Écluse, they found accomplices who were to indicate the opportune moment to put their plan into operation. At twilight, the men of l'Écluse discreetly removed the locks and the bars from the great gate. Silence reigned, almost all the inhabitants were asleep. But the conspirators could not fulfill their plans and succeed in "their execrable plot," because the captain had learned of it. His soldiers seized the principal leaders. The next day, he hastily went to the king to tell him of "this odious conspiracy." The chronicler's indignation here seems to derive less from the nocturnal aspect of the enterprise than from the fact that the people of Ghent were helping the English.

Such attempts thus did not always meet with success. The lord of Offemont also had this experience around 1421. The inhabitants of Meaux, under siege by royal troops, went through terrible suffering, in particular not being able to sleep by day or night. The lord of Offemont decided to come to their aid. To this end, he gathered together about forty hand-picked men to get into the town at night. Inhabitants of the town had informed him that they would throw down a ladder to allow him to get in. At what he considered an auspicious moment, the lord of Offemont noiselessly approached the English army, but in his progress toward the walls he encountered sentries. He managed to kill them without a sound and went on his way. The first soldiers even managed to climb the ladder provided by the besieged, but the expedition ended in failure.

Night was also feared because it made arson easy. On Wednesday, September 5, 1414, "at night, at around twelve o'clock," a man, "impelled by ill will," set fire to the dwelling of the lord of Alençon, writes Monstrelet. Fire broke out on Tuesday, September 11, "at around three hours after midnight," according to the *Journal d'un bourgeois de Paris*, which says nothing of a criminal act. In any event, the two narrators agree about subsequent events. The Gascons, who had been forbidden to make fires for fear of the rapid spread of fire through wooden sheds, did not obey, either because they wanted to celebrate the recently signed peace or because they wanted to show their disapproval. The fire, moving from tent to tent, finally reached the rear of the royal pavilion. The king was moved to a safe place, but many of the ill were unable to flee and perished in the flames.

The success of a small group could be the result of chance. On the tenth day of December 1419, a few knights and five hundred combatants, supporters of the dauphin, left Compiègne and rode to the town of Roye in Vermandois where, in the absence of a watch, they entered without striking a blow, gathered in the marketplace, and began to shout, "Conquered town! Long live the king and the dauphin!" These shouts awakened some inhabitants, who realized that they could not resist and fled by climbing over the walls. The gate was opened, and all the soldiers and their horses entered the town. The Burgundian captain also ran off, abandoning his wife, his children, and a good part of his wealth.

Thus, night did not put a stop to war but even favored it at times. A nocturnal scaling of the walls, usually connected to a betrayal, carried out by a few men permitted the conquest of a badly guarded town. But an assault could consist of a full-scale attack, carried out both day and night. Instead of scaling the walls, the combatants would enter the town through a breach opened by artillery or undermining. In those cases, obviously, nocturnal surprise played no role. To reinforce the troops of the duke of Burgundy before Compiègne, two English counts brought two thousand combatants to him. The duke continued his unrelenting attack because he was determined to take the town. He used war machines night and day and left those inside no rest. One night, after two months of this kind of siege—after the besieged had been sorely pressed during the day—the attacking army launched a new assault at a point where resistance turned out to be weakest, and some defenders, trying to retreat quickly into the town, fell into the Oise and drowned. The others were killed, except for a few made prisoner.

When one makes war, writes the author of Le Jouvencel, it is important to use time for one's best interests, to act sometimes in daylight, sometimes at night. The troops of the Jouvencel waited until morning to enter a town. They hadn't acted at night, "for war is such that you must labor according to the time you have, and take it sometimes coldly and sometimes at full heat. And because one of the great points of warfare is to know the situation of your enemies, and they knew it quite well; and this is why they waited for daylight and captured the city without striking a blow. Otherwise they would have played for double or nothing."

For all that, for the men of the Middle Ages, night was not the best time for fighting. At night, it was hardly possible to accomplish notable exploits, and armies moved with difficulty. They thus preferred to wait for daylight. The duke of Burgundy, Philip the Good, wanting to avenge his father, ardently wished for "daylight to advance to be closer to the revenge he desired to take," and as soon as day dawned his army set forth.

In 1430, after engaging in a large skirmish, when the French had returned for the night to Compiègne and evening was coming on, the English count of Huntington and Messire Jean de Luxembourg, realizing that the battle had ended for that day, assembled their captains for consultations. The result of their discussion was that for that night they would return to their tents and would go to bed fully armed, and that the next day they would present themselves before the town ready for battle to see whether their opponents wanted to fight.

In 1404, deciding to take revenge on the English, the Bretons embarked on ships, went toward the place where the presence of their opponents had been noted, and came upon them toward sunset. The young men wanted to attack instantly, but the leaders advised against it, telling them, "You see that the sun is about to set; night will increase the dangers for us. So do not think of waging battle at the approach of night. For the coming battle you need more daylight than still remains. Tomorrow, at sunrise, you will begin the attack, and you will see the enemy close up, you can be sure of that. But now that it is hardly light, it would be neither wise nor prudent to fight."

Thus day and night corresponded to two very different kinds of warfare. In daylight, in a pitched battle, you could demonstrate your courage. At night, you could hope to win with the help of stratagems. Valor was a greater virtue than craftiness, but for some the end justified the means.

SEXUALITY

Night was a propitious time for sexual relations, which could take place far from prying eyes. Literature, like reality, provides clear evidence of this. We will consider sexuality here solely as a transgression of the norms propounded by the Church in the moral realm.

Adultery and Prostitution

Lustful women took advantage of the absence of their husbands to deceive them. It was tempting when a husband had left the conjugal dwelling at night to fulfill his military obligations—to shiver in a sentry box in order to be able to warn the inhabitants of the town of the possible approach of the enemy—to send for a young lover. For example, on October 20, 1415, to fulfill his official obligations, the mayor of Chauny went out at night to visit the watchmen and recommend that they guard the town well and keep a close eye on the environs, for the English were only six or seven leagues away. Toward four or five in the morning, as it began to rain, he returned home and found the door of his bedroom locked. He had it opened by his wife who was lying in bed. And between the bed and the wall, he saw a young man without trousers, dressed only in a shirt. Furious, he dealt him a mortal blow with his *badelaire* (a short sword with a curved blade).

A letter of remission of 1392 mentions the guilty relations of Jean de Bègues with the mother of Lancelot Rouault. Even though Lancelot had forbidden it, Jean de Bègues deliberately went at night into Lancelot's house.

The woman's consent in each of these cases is not open to doubt. It sometimes seems less obvious. Colette la Buquette recounts, in 1391, that one evening the Sire de Nouvion went to the hotel de l'Épée, where she was in the habit of amusing herself with the chambermaids, for she lived in a nearby house. She went into this gentleman's room, and he had sex with her. According to her statement, she was then a virgin. She then spent the rest of the night with Jean de Boisance with whom she also went to bed. After a virgin (?), a "common woman."

Toward the hour of curfew, on the Monday after Saint Martin's Day in the winter of 1380, three young men went to amuse themselves in a prostitute's house. In the course of their lovemaking, she told them that a neighbor in the same building was also a willing partner, despite her marriage to a carter. Hearing this, one of the companions named Jean du Poiz went into the neighbor's room and asked her to make love. Refusing at first, she finally accepted and, "without great refusal and violence"—

according to the petitioner—had carnal knowledge of him. Thereupon, the two others appeared and "knew" her without her consent, for one of them made as if to strike her. However, bearing them no grudge, she invited them to eat and drink. The two women and three men then agreed: the said petitioner and Jean du Poiz would sleep that night with the neighbor and the other one would sleep with Mahaut. But three or four days later, because Mahaut reproached her for her misbehavior, the neighbor filed a complaint.

It goes without saying that the oldest profession in the world was often practiced at night. A letter of 1382 indicates that two companions went to Guillette la Demoiselle, who kept loving little girls in her house in Rouen. They asked for two of her lodgers for the night and gave her five sous. A regulation of 1420 indicates that prostitutes had invaded several good streets on the île de la Cité, where some of them had bought houses to set up taverns. Others ran shops and, under cover of a profession, received clients, who were frequently foreigners, day and night.

Rapes

Love for pay, love by force. According to a letter of February 1389, at midnight on the first Sunday of the preceding Lent, the lord of Pauléon and his servants forcibly entered a house where they found Simone, wife of Pierre Millot; the lord raped her.

We know nothing about countless instances of nocturnal violence of the kind in which a master would not hesitate to abuse a young servant girl. We know of some of them by chance. In 1449, Marguerite Guillaume had to suffer the abuse of her master Humbert de Ravet. "And when night had come, she withdrew to a *couchote* in Ravet's bedroom where it was her custom to sleep. Ravet, who was already lying down, got up and went to her, picked her up entirely naked, and carried her to his bed, and as soon as she was there slept with her. . . . She also declares that, after Ravet had done that, she wanted to get up, but he held her arms behind her back and kept her that way until it was nearly daylight when he remounted her and did again what he had already done before. He then got up and went into town, leaving her in bed, and he forbade her to say a word about it, or else he would beat her." However, a few weeks later, it was at noon that Ravet "did what he had done the two other times."

Collective rapes by young men were almost always committed at night. At least twenty public rapes were committed every year in Dijon in the fifteenth century. Eighty percent of them were attacks carried out by two to fifteen individuals whose preferred targets were available women. These hooligans often got into the houses of single women, having no hesitation in using trickery or, more often, force. For example, in the years around 1447 in Dijon, a certain Sancenot Bauchet, along with other hooligans like himself, had the habit at night of breaking the locks of houses and perpetrating outrages on the women and girls in them. At around midnight on July 19, 1445, he got into the home of Gillot du Balay, a weaver, and did no more than frighten his wife Jaquotte by threatening to "cut off her nose" and "rip out her guts," but things went a lot further on Wednesday, August 30, 1447. At nightfall, Sancenot Bauchet, his brother, and two other companions broke into the house of a carpenter who was then away. Despite the protests of his wife Catherine, one of the companions punched her several times in the head and face, so that "her head is all swollen and battered"; the other companion "also joined in" and, drawing their daggers, they swore they would kill her if she said a word.

As Catherine called for help, the one who was hitting her said, "Shut up, shut up," and kept on hitting her. Finally, the two hooligans raped the young woman, "stopping up her mouth" to prevent her from crying out. In the meantime, Sancenot Bauchet and his brother were keeping a lookout and threw so many stones into the street, according to a neighbor woman, that all the devils seemed to be there. Then the scoundrels left the house, and no one dared to intervene. And yet, Catherine's screams and her aggressors' threats had been heard throughout the neighborhood. Several women were spinning yarn not far from there, but knowing that Sancenot was "a wicked scoundrel, outrageous, and a man who had several times done many things at night in the city," they did not dare leave the basement where they were working.

When Sancenot and his companions left, they thought of throwing stones at the women, but they didn't because one of them said that the women had left them alone.

The satisfaction of sexual desire sometimes even led to murder. Two weeks before All Saints' Day in 1390, "at the hour of sunset," a certain Thévenin asked Belon, wife of Drion Anceau, to become his mistress, telling her that her husband was no good to her and that he would not live until All Saints' Day. He begged her not to close her door; she would see what he would do. Once her husband was dead, he would marry her. She accepted. That night, Belon left the door to her bedroom open; she was in bed with her husband and, after her first sleep, she felt someone touching her knee. She woke up and recognized Thévenin, who said to her, "Keep quiet, it's me; I've done it." When she turned toward her husband, from whom she had been facing away, she found him dead. Thévenin had strangled him according to his promise. She helped him carry the body to the river, the Essonne, near her house, after putting clothes and shoes on it. Then they went back to bed.

Nocturnal Emissions

Doctors and theologians agreed to the extent that they considered an individual responsible when the emission was due to his imagination. Albertus Magnus points out that a natural purgation does not imply bodily corruption, but that virginity is lost when the emission flows from thoughts about coition or genital organs.

As early as the fifth century, Caelius Aurelius, a Roman doctor and author of a treatise *On the Illnesses of Women*, wrote: "During their sleep, under the influence of images without reality, patients experience the emission of sperm. Now the name comes from the symptom, since the dream is the origin of the venereal effect and provokes it. But, in general, it is neither an illness nor even the attribute of an illness—which the Greeks call a symptom—but it is the consequence of images, to which the Greeks give the name *phantasia*, affecting patients during their sleep because of the desire for sexual pleasure, that is, either from a constant and uninterrupted desire, or, in contrast, by reason of a long interruption in sexual activity and from continence." Thus, even during sleep, the individual remains responsible, since "the perceptions one receives in a state of wakefulness change into the form of images in a dream."

The problem lay in the fact that it was sometimes difficult to establish a distinction between voluntary thought and the fortuitous sight of an attractive daughter of Eve. To what extent was spermatorrhea a matter of sensation or of will? The responsibility of the individual was therefore sometimes subject to debate.

Given the importance attributed to the male seed in the mechanism of generation, while female "seed" played only a secondary role, it is easy to understand why a man's loss of seed could constitute a deadly sin, not only in the individual realm but in relation to the whole species.

Literary Evidence

In works of fiction as well, night provides love the means to succeed, particularly outside the bounds of conjugal ties. In *Cligès*, a romance by Chrétien de Troyes (c. 1135–c. 1183), the hero and Fenice confess their mutual passion. Since Fenice is married, she suggests that she feign death so that she can be carried off in the darkness and live with Cligès. When the watchers of her body are asleep, the abduction is carried out.

When lovers cannot satisfy their passion, night becomes the moment in which their pain is felt the most intensely. Insomnia is only the prelude to more exquisite torments, nocturnal visions in which the lover believes that he is holding the naked body of his beloved in his arms. "It is painful to be in bed when you are not asleep and not resting . . . and night does not go by quickly, for if it were light, I would get up. Oh, sun, in the name of God, hurry up then, do not stay still! Banish dark night and its torments that seem too long to me!" wrote Guillaume de Lorris in *Le Roman de la Rose* in the thirteenth century. In this case, the lover does not achieve his recompense. For Jean de Meung, the continuator of the work, dreams are no longer a torment, but a trick used to gain the lady's favors.

And physical love does find its place. Lancelot and Guenivere have "much joy and pleasure" all night, Chrétien de Troyes writes modestly, and he adds that not everything can be told in a tale. This love is thus more often than not a transgression, and darkness is above all the domain of the violation of law. Iseut in the French verse *Tristan*, a lover by night, in daylight again becomes the queen who belongs to the world of light and respect for the law. Even more serious than violation of law is deceit. The expected husband or wife is replaced by a stranger. In *Ami et Amile*, Charlemagne's daughter Belissant replaces her companion in Amile's bed, while he is completely unaware of the substitution. On the contrary, in *Athis et Prophilias*, Athis suggests to his friend Prophilias, madly in love with Athis's future wife, that he take his place in the nuptial bed on the wedding night, of course without the bride's knowledge. Night thus appears at the source of lying and of pleasure. The beloved object is changed from dream to reality; the barriers imposed by light can then be transgressed.

In a Latin comedy entitled *The Three Virgins*, the heroine, after the preliminaries to love, tells her suitor, "Do what you will with me quickly, for night is flying and day returns." The gap between eroticism and bawdiness is easily crossed, and this is true in all nations, both north and south.

In Italy, with Boccaccio's *Decameron* in the middle of the fourteenth century: in the plain of Mugnone, there lives a good man who is accustomed to receive acquaintances as paying guests. His wife, a still young and pleasing woman, has given him a daughter who is fifteen or sixteen and a baby a few months old. A man in love with the daughter, accompanied by a friend, asks the man for hospitality so he can meet his beloved.

The house contains only one bedroom furnished with three rather narrow beds that barely fit, two against one wall and the third opposite them. The innkeeper assigns the best bed to the two companions, who pretend to go to sleep. His daughter takes the second and he and his wife the third; the child's cradle is nearby. When everyone is asleep, Pinuccio, the lover, joins his beloved, and in her arms tastes the pleasures they have long desired. During this pleasant activity, a cat knocks something over in the next room and awakens the wife, who gets up. Awakened as well, Adriano, Pinuccio's friend, wants to go out to answer a call of nature; the cradle is in his way, so he moves it next to his bed. On his return, he forgets to replace it and goes back to bed. Meanwhile, the hostess comes back, feeling her way in the darkness, moves toward the conjugal bed and, not finding the cradle, thinks she has made a mistake. She finally finds it and slips into the bed occupied by Adriano, not her husband. Without saying a word, "he took her on a journey that she did not hope for at that hour of the night and which gave her great satisfaction."

For his part, for fear of being caught, Pinuccio tries to get back to his bed, but finding the cradle next to what he thinks is the innkeeper's bed, gets into the other one with the master of the house whom he takes for Adriano. He whispers, "That Nicolette is fit for a king! Never has a woman given me so much pleasure as what I have just tasted with her! And I partook no less than five times!"

Very shocked by these words, the host explodes. His cries awaken his wife who becomes aware that Adriano is beside her. Since she is intelligent, saying nothing, she gets up, takes the cradle, carries it over to her daughter's bed, and lies down next to her. Then, pretending to awake, she asks her husband what is going on.

"Didn't you hear," he answers, "what he said he did to Nicolette?"

"He hasn't touched our daughter. I have been next to her all night, and you are an imbecile to believe his story. You men drink so much at night that you take your dreams for reality. And sometimes you even sleepwalk. But what is Pinuccio doing next to you?"

At this moment, Adriano intervenes to support his hostess. "Pinuccio! I've told you more than a hundred times not to sleepwalk! Come back to your bed."

After sunrise, the two friends have a good laugh over the night's adventures and delightedly return to Florence.

In England, with Chaucer's *Canterbury Tales c.* 1390, early in the work, "The Miller's Tale" and "The Reeve's Tale" recount the nighttime dalliance of lustful men and women. These disorders involve a certain order in the sense that the daughter cannot sleep with a stranger unless the mother does the same thing with another. In "The Reeve's Tale," which recounts the story of a miller cuckolded by two Cambridge students, there unfolds in a single room a ballet in which the students leave their bed for that of the daughter, following a cradle-signpost moved by the miller's wife next to their bed—a scenario quite similar to that of the *Decameron*.

At the court of Burgundy, with the *Cent nouvelles nouvelles* toward the middle of the fifteenth century: a carter who has brought willow charcoal to a Parisian goldsmith finds the gates of the city closed before he has finished his delivery. The goldsmith welcomes him with open arms, and they eat a meal together, washed down with plenty of wine. Midnight comes on to their great surprise, for the time has passed very quickly. Because of the hour, the goldsmith invites the carter to sleep in his house, wanting to spare his having to go out and meet the soldiers of the watch. But, since he does not have a spare bed, he is obliged to have the carter share the conjugal bed. With not the slightest suspicion, he has his wife lie between his guest and himself. The wife, feeling the carter move closer to her because of the cold and the narrowness of the bed, turns toward her husband and places her head on his chest, so that her large backside ends up at the level of the carter's groin. Husband and wife fall asleep. But, despite his fatigue, the carter cannot imitate them, "his stallion raising its head high on feeling itself so close to the goldsmith's wife. Thereupon, it was no longer in his power to prevent it from joining her and from grasping her very tightly." Things remain that way for a long time, with the wife apparently not waking up. As for the husband, he would have continued to sleep "if there were not lying on his chest his wife's head which, from the repeated thrusts of the stallion, began to shake him so much that he soon woke up." Getting angry, he quickly "chases off the stallion." When daylight comes, the carter thanks his hosts and returns to his cart.

All these stories show the dangers of nocturnal promiscuity associated with feminine infidelity. Woman and night are linked together.

•   •   •

Is there a necessary opposition between night and day, sin and virtuous life, as for Duke Louis of Orléans, the brother of Charles VI? "And notwithstanding the fact that the duke of Orléans showed himself to be so pious during the day, nevertheless he led a very dissolute life at night. For almost every night he got drunk, played at dice, and slept with dissolute women." It is true that, "finally, he so increased the disorderly life that he had secretly led for a certain time at night and continued it for so long day and night, that it became quite open and notorious."

To what extent did acts of violence take place at night? It is logical that domestic scenes would tend to take place at night, when the husband returned home, sometimes affected by drink, before the couple went to bed. But did a brawl ending in murder in an alley or a dispute concluding with a knife blow on a country road happen more frequently at night than during the day? It is important on this point to conduct a quantitative study. In fact, we have chosen documents that attest to nocturnal violence, but there are many others that reveal violence in daylight. It is therefore appropriate to take into account all available sources. On the basis of letters of remission, Claude Gauvard has attempted to do this for the late Middle Ages in France. She concludes that 44 percent of crimes took place during the day, 25 percent at night, and 31 percent at twilight. More important than nightfall was the weariness of the day—young workers after ten to sixteen hours in a cramped workshop or on a construction site were on edge; taverns were numerous and opportunities for distraction infrequent, and in taverns you could drink, or gamble, or find a woman who would help you forget the weariness of your work. Men would fight when they left taverns, when it was time to pay the bill, or on the way home.

The fears inspired by night also explain the relatively small number of crimes committed then. People hesitated to go out at night. Darkness was dreaded, but that does not mean that it fostered crime. Indeed, it sometimes had the opposite effect, because of fear of making a mistake in the darkness. The deep shadows that prevented you from recognizing those you encountered could bring about various effects. Returning from the fair of Bernezay near Loudun on Saint Laurent's Day in 1398, "when it was more night than day," Jean de la Rajace thought he was striking one of the men who had just attacked his companions, but he killed his friend Gillet Bargnet with a sword blow. In 1476, Marsault Guyot, a participant in the abduction of a married woman, was assigned to keep watch at the door of her house. "His face turned toward the street and unable to see anything because of the very dark night," he heard someone come up behind him and say to him, "What's there? What's there?" Frightened, he turned around, and in doing so, involuntarily struck the man who had spoken to him with the blade of his spear, mortally wounding him in the throat. In the darkness, the tone of a voice could produce relief or worry. In Dohem, in 1527, two individuals saw someone at "an hour in the night, when it was dark, and not knowing him." They asked, "Who goes there?" The man replied, "Friend," and they had a quiet conversation.

Homicide in France did not reach explosive proportions in the course of the night, since it made up 57 percent of the crimes committed then, compared with 63 percent of those during the day and 73 percent of those at twilight. Nor did thieves seek out the night, although this was not the opinion of certain writers, who believed that crimes, especially robberies, often took place in darkness. Thieves apparently preferred to carry out their crimes in daylight, when the victims were absent, particularly when they were attending mass. Only looters showed a predilection for darkness, for unlike burglars who were dealing with people they knew, they attacked strangers whom they wanted to surprise in a state of lowered defenses.

Adultery and rape occurred as frequently during the day as at night, except for collective rapes carried out by gangs of idle young men who wandered around at night and pursued the women they encountered, or even broke into houses, similar in that way to the looters. Of course, darkness could allow the concealment of a crime, the disposal of a body after an infanticide. For example, Jeannette, wife of Nicolas Rollant, had been seduced and made pregnant by a priest named Jean Jouaye when she was about eighteen. When she gave birth to the child, the priest was disturbed and claimed he was dishonored. She told him then to do as he would. He took the child, wrapped it in a cloth, and placed it in the lap of Jeannette's dress, advising her to squeeze hard so that no cries could be heard. At night, they left the house, Jouaye with a shovel, and they carried the child near to the cemetery of Bouin in unconsecrated ground. The man dug a hole and asked the young woman to throw the child into it. They then returned home.

The same phenomenon can be observed outside France. Although violence seemed to be omnipresent in Venice, it did not appear to increase at night.

Moreover, the influence of the imaginary on criminals seems to have been slight. A certain number of petitioners invoked as an excuse the temptation that the devil led them into to incite them to commit their crime. But 24 percent said they had been urged by the devil during the day, compared to 17 percent at night and 6 percent at twilight. And yet, the imaginary held an important place in the Middle Ages.

CHAPTER 2

Fantasies

On a dark night in the year 1300, Dante, astray in a dark wood, begins his voyage to the other world, at first guided by the Latin poet Virgil. He moves through Hell filled with sighs, sobs, and piercing cries echoing in a night bereft of stars, through Purgatory where the moon as red as a glittering copper cauldron seems to have banished the stars, to the radiant Paradise revealed to him by Beatrice.

This vast canvas contains the entire imaginary world of the men of the Middle Ages, assimilating Satan and Hell to lugubrious night, bereft of stellar or lunar light, propitious for the demonic manifestations that their imaginations seemed unable to avoid.

THE DEVIL AND HIS MINIONS

The Evil One frequently appears in literary or narrative works of the Middle Ages. He was the supreme tempter and, in a society in which imagination played such a predominant role, it is not surprising that he took on various forms, terrifying for those who feared him and who, precisely because of this fear, had him so much in mind that they envisioned him in even the most harmless circumstances.

The demon manifested himself in various ways:

- *Through violence.* In the *Life of Saint Anthony,* we read that one night, entering with his minions the sepulcher where the saint has taken refuge, the devil rains blows down on him to the point that the poor man collapses in pain on the ground, unable to speak. This violence is found in narratives of saints' lives to the extent that it became a commonplace.
- *Through fear.* The same narrative contains scenes of nocturnal aggression by calling up horrible beasts. After making a dreadful noise and shattering the walls of the hermit's cell, the animals surround him in a threatening manner. Bishop Gregory of Tours, author of the celebrated late sixth-century *Gesta Francorum,* but also of eight books on miracles, reports that Saint Venant, getting up "one night" to say the office, saw at his door two great rams that threw themselves at him with fury. Another night, returning from the chapel, he found his cell filled with demons. But the saint easily mastered the minions of Satan by invoking Christ.
- *By possession.* Writers provide few details about the moment at which it occurs; they merely describe those possessed.
- *By temptation.* The devil frequently assumed an attractive appearance or called on honorable feelings to encourage sin. "The tempter appeared during the night, in the form of our Lord, to deacon Secondellus [companion of Saint Friard], and said to him, 'I am the Christ to whom you pray every day. You are already a saint, and your name is written in the book of life with the names of the other saints; leave this island, then, and go to do cures among the people.'" Taken in by this lie, the deacon left the island without telling his companion.

These documents show that appearances of the demon occurred particularly at night. The testimony of the monk Raoul Glaber, author of *Histoires* relating the events of the first half of the eleventh century, corroborates this assertion. As for Guibert de Nogent, who wrote an autobiography in the early twelfth century, he noted that three times out of four the demon acted in darkness. It does not follow that his remaining activity occurred in broad daylight, for no such details are presented.

At twilight, the devil manifested himself especially in fields and forests. The disquiet prevailing over uninhabited areas gradually penetrated into human habitations. Those who could not sleep, the ill, and the dying found themselves alone, without help, in the dark.

The link between darkness and demon is clearly highlighted by a childhood adventure of Guibert. "So, one night (in winter, it seems to me), awakened by a great and appalling fear, I was lying in bed; a nearby lamp cast an intense brightness that reassured me. And suddenly the noise of many nearby voices, seeming to come from above, burst out from the deep night. They were only cries without words. All at once, the violence of this horror, striking my temples, was enough to make me lose consciousness, as though I were falling into sleep. Then I thought I saw a dead man, who some had said had died in his bath. Terrified by this phantom, I threw myself at the foot of the bed, crying out in my turn, and then, turning around during these first movements, I saw that the lamp had gone out. Then, quite near, in the midst of the darkness of that enormous shadow, I contemplated the demon in his own shape." Further on, Guibert describes swarms of demons who come to torture a priest in Reims, throw him on the floor, and violently attempt to remove his habit. "It was especially at night that he was tortured in this way by these horrible afflictions, accompanied by frightful howling."

Although Raoul Glaber does not describe Satan himself, he does provide a precise representation of his familiar devil. He saw him as short, with a slender neck, a thin face, dark eyes, a furrowed brow, a flat nose, a pointed chin, a goat's beard, hair coming out of his ears, thick hair, a stooped back, and dressed in rags. Holding on to the edge of the monk's bed, he shakes it violently. The scene takes place when Glaber wakes up. The monk is being punished for his laziness; he has not joined his companions for matins—a frequent sin, as he says. Glaber leaves the monastery of Saint-Léger in Champeaux to go to Saint-Bénigne in Dijon, but his devil does not abandon him. He reappears in the monastery's sleeping quarters. As dawn begins to break, he comes out of the latrine asking for "his scholar." The next day at the same time, a friar breaks his vows and rejoins the world—for a time, before repenting. A third visit takes place in the abbey of Moutiers in the Yonne. There, too, the monks are less than fervent in their attendance at matins, and Glaber is among those who prefer to remain in bed. It is then that the demon shows himself, proclaiming that he stands by those who remain in bed. Awakened by the voice, Raoul recognizes him.

These narratives reveal a propensity to transform the imaginary into reality. But the diabolical does not leave material traces. One night, while Guibert de Nogent was in a reverie in the church of Saint-Germer, it seemed to him that two demons carried him to the top of the building and then dropped him into the chancel unhurt.

Despite the narrators' claims of being awake, it can thus be seen that demonic appearances take place when they are falling asleep or waking up. Likewise with those who claim not to have slept all night, while they have drowsed a part of the time, unaware. Guibert, for example, on the night he saw the devil, noted that he was taken out of his senses "as though the hour of falling into sleep had rung." Night troubled minds to the point that a watcher set in a room above the entry gate of a castle would sing to keep up his courage.

Noteworthy among the minions of Satan were the incubi, lubricious demons who were supposed to rape women during their sleep. Female devils copulating at night with men bore the name of succubi.

Guibert de Nogent recounts how his mother suffered the attacks of an incubus. "One particularly dark night, full of this atrocious anxiety [her husband had been imprisoned], when she was huddled deep in her bed, the devil, who usually prefers to attack souls afflicted with sadness, the Enemy in person suddenly appeared, he came and lay upon her while she was awake, and his great weight crushed her so much that she almost died. While her breath was taken away by this pressure and she was totally deprived of the free use of her limbs, while her voice was literally incapable of emitting the slightest sound, as free in her mind as she was mute, she could only implore divine help. And then at her bedside a spirit [a beneficent spirit, undoubtedly] began to pronounce, in a tone that was as warm as it was clear, this invocation: 'Holy Mary, help!' When he had spoken thus for a few moments—and she understood perfectly the meaning of his words—violently tortured as she was, she realized that he had thrown himself on the evil one with great hostility."

Much further on, Guibert de Nogent goes on to say that "on all sides we hear of demons avidly seeking out the love of women, and even trying to possess them." The notion of the incubus is thus linked to the realm of sexuality against which the clergy were so intent on warning their contemporaries, a realm that was both terrifying and alluring. This is how it is seen in the late fifteenth century in the celebrated work of demonology entitled *Le Marteau des Sorcières*. The authors, two inquisitors, who see woman as the source of evil, distinguish those who willingly submit to incubi, like witches, those whom the witches bring to meet incubi against their will, and finally those innocents who suffer the attacks of the demons.

It was thus possible—and the phenomenon was not restricted to the Middle Ages—to explain erotic dreams. Guibert de Nogent's mother was young, beautiful, separated from her captive husband—and her marriage, consummated several years after the wedding ceremony, turned out to be sexually a failure.

GHOSTS

Not only demons appeared in the course of the night, the souls of the dead also showed themselves in physical form. Ghosts were rare in the high Middle Ages and belonged to the elite, that is, the saints. Sometimes they appeared to the saints to urge them to demonstrate their supernatural gifts, as, for example, in the *Vie de saint Germain d'Auxerre*, by Constance de Lyon. "At one time, as he was traveling in winter and after he had spent the day in fasting and weariness, at sunset, his companions earnestly asked him to seek shelter for the night. Nearby was a half-ruined dwelling that had long been uninhabited. It had been so neglected that it was overgrown with brambles, so that it was almost better to spend the night in the cold, in the open air, than in this dangerous and horrible place. This was even more true because two old men in the neighborhood had warned Germain that the house was uninhabitable because it was infested with spirits. When he heard that, the holy man walked toward the frightful ruins as though toward a charming and idyllic spot. Amid what had once been many rooms, there was scarcely one fit for a resting place. He settled in with his modest belongings and his few companions. All save he took a little food. Finally, when night was at its darkest, overcome with fasting and weariness, Germain fell asleep while one of his clerics was reading.

"There suddenly appeared a frightful specter, who rose up before the face of the reader, while a hail of stones battered the walls of the house. The terrified reader implored the bishop's help. Germain woke up with a start and saw the outline of the fearsome phantom. After invoking the name of Christ, he ordered it to name itself and to say what brought it to this place.

"Immediately abandoning its horrible appearance, the phantom spoke in a humble and supplicating voice; he and his companion had committed many crimes, they lay unburied, and they tormented the living only because they themselves could find no rest. They begged him to pray to the Lord for them so that He might give them eternal peace. Moved by these words, the holy man was grieved and ordered him to indicate the place where they lay. Then, going before them with a candle and guiding them with great difficulty through the ruins in the dark of night, the shade pointed to the spot where their bodies had been thrown." As soon as day had dawned, Germain gave the dead a decent burial.

A sharp change took place in the eleventh and twelfth centuries. Sometimes alone, sometimes in countless troops, ghosts appeared, particularly in dreams. But a development could be discerned. Raoul Glaber reports that, on the night of Trinity Sunday in his monastery's church, the monk Vulferius of Moutiers-Saint-Jean, in the diocese of Langres, saw men dressed in white and purple led by a bishop. They had come, they said, to participate in the office. They were Christians who had been killed in battles against the Saracens. On the way to Paradise, they had stopped for a moment to gather some more companions.

A few decades later, Guibert de Nogent's mother saw her dead husband in a dream: "It thus happened, one Sunday night after matins, in midsummer, as she had stretched out on a narrow bench to rest, that she soon sank into sleep; it then seemed to her that her soul left her body in a palpable way. Then, after being led as though down a gallery, she came out of it and approached the opening of a well. When she got quite close, human phantoms rose up from the depths of this opening, phantoms whose scalps seemed to her pitted with ringworm, and sought to grasp her with their hands to draw her into the well. . . . When she was thus freed from the inhabitants of the well and had come to lean on the rim, nearby she saw my father, as he had been in his youth."

The diabolical quality of ghosts became more and more apparent, as exemplified by the appearance of the army of the dead to a Norman priest, reported by Orderic Vital in his *Ecclesiastical History*, written around 1140. On the night of New Year's Day in 1091, the priest saw a procession of a terrifying army led by a threatening giant followed by associates among whom he recognized recently deceased people. On a beam, a demon inflicted torments on a criminal. There followed cruelly tortured women. Finally there were the clergy, black monks, and knights bearing black standards. The priest then understood that he was witnessing the army of the dead, the *maisnie Hellequin*. He tried to stop one of the knights, who moved to strike him, but another knight came to his aid; this was his brother, who asked him to pray for a remission of his ordeal.

The clergy attempted to co-opt popular culture—derived from orally transmitted traditions—which experienced particular development in the twelfth century, and to make it fit into the framework of edifying literature. For example, around 1250, Vincent de Beauvais maintained that the participants in the *maisnie Hellequin* expiated their sins in the course of nocturnal processions. On the other hand, Guillaume d'Auvergne saw these stories as old wives' tales.

The places and dates of appearance of the *maisnie Hellequin* became more precise. The savage hunt appeared in particular on May 1, Walpurgisnacht, and was thus a manifestation of witchcraft. This was the time of the great witches' sabbath, and Martin Lefranc (1410–1461), secretary of the anti-pope Felix V, dedicated a poem to Philip the Good, duke of Burgundy, in which he spoke of an

> Old woman who on Walpurgisnacht
> On a stick would go off
> To see the whorish synagogue . . .

As early as the time of Étienne de Bourbon, who died in 1261, although the army of the dead, which had become essentially diabolical, might move from place to place, it had become attached to a particular place where sexual and satanic debaucheries were practiced. There thus took shape, between the middle of the thirteenth century and the fifteenth, the concept of the witches' sabbath.

WITCHES AND THE WITCHES' SABBATH

The nocturnal witch was not a medieval invention. Roman writings of the first two centuries of our era often mention a creature who flies at night, emits howls, and turns out to be fond of the flesh and blood of unfortunate humans. Named *stryge*, it resembled an owl but was in reality a being derived from the transformation of certain women. In *The Golden Ass*, Apuleius recounts that Pamphilia, a lady of Thessaly, is accustomed on certain nights to take on the form of a bird. To do this, she drinks a mixture of laurel and fennel dissolved in water and rubs her entire body with the mixture; her skin then grows feathers, her nose and nails become beak and talons, she hoots like an owl, and goes in search of a lover, for she turns out to be very sensual and severely punishes anyone who rejects her.

Intellectuals knew very well that this witch, a woman by day, a lustful and cannibalistic bird by night, existed only in their imaginations. However, things seemed to be different for the Germanic peoples, and the law of the Salian Franks referred to the *stryge* as though it really existed. Under the influence of Christianity, later barbarian laws—those of the Alemanni and the Lombards—no longer accepted the reality of this vampire, but evidence the belief in its existence.

In the early eleventh century, in Book XIX of his *Decretal* entitled *Healer or Doctor,* a penitential, Burchard, bishop of Worms, writes: "Have you shared the belief of many women who are followers of Satan? That in the silence of the night, after stretching out on your bed and while your husband is resting on your breast, you have the power, even though you are a corporal being, to go through a closed door, to move through space with other women like yourself? That you have the power to kill, with invisible weapons, Christians who have been baptized and redeemed by the Blood of Christ, to cook and eat their flesh, and to replace their hearts with straw or some other object? That you have the power, after eating them, to resurrect them and to grant them more time to live? If so: forty days of fasting and a penance of seven years."

The following was reported by Étienne de Bourbon: "I have heard on this subject that it happened in little Brittany, that is, in Armorica, that a woman lost two children before either one had reached the age of one. Some women told the mother that *stryges* were the cause and that they had sucked the children's blood. The mother believed them and told them that when her third child reached its first birthday, she would stay awake throughout the night before, putting on the child the iron cover she used on her cooking pot when it was on the fire. She also said that she would stick a hot iron on the *stryge*'s face when it came at night, so that it could be recognized the next morning. She did as she had said and, toward the middle of the night, passing through the closed door, she saw a little old woman, one of her neighbors, come in riding on a wolf and approach the child. Pretending to sleep, the mother took the iron and stuck it on the face of the old woman who ran out screaming in pain."

Until the thirteenth century, the educated rejected belief in nocturnal witches, while the populace persisted in its credulity.

The Englishman Gervaise of Tilbury who, around 1211, wrote a work for the amusement of Emperor Otto IV, considered widespread the idea that men and women flew over great distances at night, an idea that doctors, according to him, attributed to nightmares.

The nocturnal flight of certain women appeared in another popular belief, as shown by Norman Cohn. Early in the tenth century, Réginon, former abbot of Prüm, prepared a guide for ecclesiastical discipline in which he provided the text of a canon destined for great success, entitled *Episcopi*. This canon turns up again in many later writers, including Burchard of Worms: "Have you believed or have you participated in a superstition in which wicked women, minions of Satan deceived by diabolical fantasies, claim to indulge? At night, with the pagan goddess Diana, along with a crowd of other women, they ride on animals, cover great distances in the silence of deep night, obey Diana's orders as though she were their mistress, and place themselves at her service on certain specified nights. If only those witches could perish in their impiety without dragging many others to perdition! In fact, many people who have been induced into error believe that these night rides by Diana really exist, and they separate themselves from the true faith and fall into the error of the pagans by believing that there can exist a divinity or a goddess other than the only God."

Burchard goes on to say: "Who is there—except in dreams and nightmare—who has been drawn out of himself and seen while asleep what he has never seen in a state of wakefulness? Who can be so foolish and so stupid as to imagine that these fantasies, the fruits of imagination, take on corporal form?" It is noteworthy that in this case, Burchard is speaking of a belief not in cannibalistic witches of the night, but in women subjects of a supernatural queen who leads them through their nocturnal flights. Burchard sometimes names this queen Diana or Herodias, sometimes Holda.

In fact, in the early Middle Ages, a kind of cult of Diana survived, in which she appeared as goddess of the moon, lover of the night, bearing some resemblance to Hecate the goddess of magic, who was accustomed to fly through the air at night followed by unquiet souls. Diana was identified with Herod's wife Herodias, the instigator of the death of John the Baptist.

Holda, on the other hand, played an important role in German folklore up to the nineteenth century. She usually lived in the air, but she also spent time on earth, where she took an interest in agriculture. She was accompanied in her nocturnal travels by the souls of the dead. Women believed that they joined this procession which, far from being deadly, turned out to be beneficial.

The same superstitions existed in France and Italy. Guillaume d'Auvergne, bishop of Paris in the first half of the thirteenth century, reports that, according to some of the faithful, spirits in the form of women and girls went through the woods and came into houses, led by Lady Abonde. If the inhabitants had given them food and drink, they were granted an abundance of material goods. And so, foolish people left their cabinets open at night. According to Jean de Meung, writing in *Le Roman de la Rose* around 1280, many people stupidly imagined that on certain nights their souls wandered in the company of Lady Abonde and got into houses through hidden holes. In the early fourteenth century, the records of the inquisitor Jacques Fournier provide testimony about a link between the *bonnes dames* and the souls of dead ancestors. According to one witness, the heretic Arnaud Gélis had told him "that at night he went with the *bonnes dames*, that is, with the souls of the dead, down roads and through deserted places, and they sometimes went into houses, especially nice clean houses, and drank the good wine they found there."

This belief in nocturnal travels provided material for anecdotes. An *exemplum* by Étienne de Bourbon presents a wealthy and naïve peasant. One night, bandits dressed as women invade his house and go dancing through it. To cries of "Take one, give back a hundred," they take everything of value. When the peasant's wife protests, he interrupts her and orders her to hold her tongue. "These are good people," he exclaims, "they will return a hundredfold what is ours."

Thus, two old popular beliefs in nocturnal travelers coexisted. Of course, as we have seen, the educated elite denied their existence. Demons could of course incite humans to sin in their dreams, but imagining that dreams were reality and that one could take part in nocturnal flights was contrary to the true faith. Before the thirteenth century, however, the Church did not severely attack such beliefs.

This was not true thereafter. Gradually, the *bonnes dames* were replaced by people who were known, and it was imagined that these were demons who had taken on human form. One could see these demons even when awake, so that fantasies that haunted the minds of foolish old women became reality. The result was that participation in these gatherings was no longer a matter of imagination but involved a genuine association with demons.

The clerics, who no longer made a distinction between nocturnal witches and "ladies of the night," covered both with a single condemnation. John of Salisbury, an Englishman who lived for a long time in France, wrote as early as 1156–1159 in his *Polycraticus:* "It is said that a certain woman who glitters at night, or Herodias, or the mistress of the night, summons meetings or assemblies, whose participants share in various banquets. . . . It is also said that little children are offered to the lamia [*stryges*]; some of them were dismembered and greedily devoured, while the mistress took pity on others and had them returned to their cradles." Nocturnal banquet and bloodthirsty orgy are ingeniously and closely linked together, but John of Salisbury concludes that only foolish and ignorant people can believe in such fables.

In the fourteenth and fifteenth centuries, certain clerics who also assimilated the two fantasies into one imagined that groups of witches held a sabbath at night, paid homage to Satan, and had sexual relations with him. The witches' sabbath was no longer a deceptive dream; it was from now on considered a reality.

On August 20, 1493, counselors in Fribourg, Switzerland heard the statement of a witch: "Very unhappy that her husband beat her, she went off at night into a wood on a rock and began crying out to God or the devil to help her. There then approached her a being black in color who was named Satan; he asked her what she wanted, what was the cause of her sadness. She answered that she was in sore distress, for her husband constantly beat her. Satan then told her that if she would believe in him, take him for master and deny God, he would comfort her and her husband would no longer beat her; then she denied God, took Satan for master and paid him homage, kissing his ass and giving him three hairs.

"She confessed that thereafter she frequented with others an assembly which met during a period of two years in an old castle. Their master Satan summoned them to this assembly twice a week, on Wednesdays and Fridays, and gave them sticks on which they rode. And if by any chance they did not want to come, he beat them severely, and when the time to leave arrived, they rode on those sticks to return home.

"When she and her accomplices participated on the said days in the assembly, and when they were all together at midnight, they began by dancing and eating well, and then their master Satan brought them food, and one of them cooked it.

"Once, one of her accomplices embraced a young pregnant woman and squeezed her so hard that she gave birth to a son who was not baptized. Soon after the child's burial, they secretly disinterred him, brought him to their assembly, and roasted and ate him. And they ate several other children who came from they knew not where, but who had not received baptism, for they had no power over baptized children.

"When they met, they had carnal relations, but not against nature."

In a recent work, beginning with the appearance of the image of the witches' sabbath in the western Alps in the second half of the fourteenth century, Carlo Ginzburg distinguishes two traditions that are both different and closely linked. On the one hand, constructed by inquisitors and secular judges, is the idea of a plot fomented by a sect; on the other, beliefs of shamanistic origin—shamanism is the religion of certain populations of Siberia and Mongolia—rooted in popular culture, like nocturnal flight or transformations of people into animals.

WEREWOLVES

The theme of lycanthropy, the transformation of a man into a wolf, appeared as early as Niceros's narrative in the *Satyricon* of

Petronius during the reign of Nero. Presenting his story as true, Niceros reports that he went out at night with a soldier. In a cemetery by moonlight, the soldier turned into a wolf and fled howling. A wound in the neck allowed him to resume human form.

From the positions set out in the canon *Episcopi* through the works of Saint Thomas Aquinas in the thirteenth century, the Church officially considered erroneous any opinion attributing metamorphosis to any but a divine source. Burchard of Worms condemned those who believed that fairies "had the power to decide a man's fate from the moment of his birth and that whenever he liked, this man could change himself into the kind of wolf popularly known as a werewolf, or take on any other form."

However, the Middle Ages generally accepted the existence of werewolves. In the early thirteenth century, Gervaise of Tilbury attests to the diffusion of the belief. "I only know that, among us, it happens daily, human fate being what it is, that some people are transformed into wolves with the changes of the moon." Lycanthropy was a very widespread phenomenon, particularly in England. "In fact, in England we frequently saw men change into wolves when the moon was shining." And, as evidence, Gervaise recounts several stories, including that of a soldier, Rimbaud de Pinet. "Having become a wanderer and a fugitive in the country, he traveled alone, like a wild animal, remote wooded places. One night, stirred by a very great fear, changed into a wolf by the force of mental disturbance, he inflicted such damage on the countryside that he forced many peasants to abandon their dwellings. In the form of a wolf, he devoured children, but he also tore up adults with the bites of a carnivorous beast. Finally, seriously wounded by a woodsman, he lost a foot to an ax blow. It was thus that he recovered his human form." This metamorphosis is presented here as being real, and Gervaise refers only to a kind of madness, without mentioning God or the devil. The consciousness of the thirteenth-century cleric was divided between the popular and the clerical conception—the latter tried to explain the metamorphosis in a rational and Christian manner, using Saint Augustine's theory of "illusory metamorphosis." But Gervaise does not really take a position, taking shelter behind the words of others.

In his *De Universo,* written around 1240, Guillaume d'Auvergne repeats Augustine's thesis. Subjected to the demon and in a deep sleep, the consciousness is neutralized. The demon then takes on the appearance of a wolf. When he awakes, the man believes he has engaged in massacres. The text thus shows the two levels of belief: popular belief, which accepts the old idea of the transformation of a man into an animal; the clerical interpretation, which considers the phenomenon to be an illusory metamorphosis. The "realist version" seems to win out in the late fifteenth century with *Le Marteau des Sorcières.* In any event, night and moonlight are essential components of lycanthropy.

FROM IMAGINATION TO REALITY

The light of the moon permits the creation of an atmosphere of strangeness, a movement into unreality. Twilight is an excellent moment for drawing the reader into a fantastic world; as the sun sets, it transforms the landscape. On two occasions in *Le Roman de Laurin,* twilight is related to an enchantment. Thus, at the end of a hard day, knights glimpse a castle on the horizon. They try to reach it to spend the night, but the castle retreats as they advance. "They rode until nightfall, and the further they went, the more distant it remained." Unable to reach the inaccessible castle, they stop in a meadow near a wood. "The moon rose soon thereafter, and they could see more clearly through the air." Then in the moonlight, there is a battle between white knights and red knights. The travelers want to take part in the battle, but the blows they give and those they receive are unreal. The moonlight is echoed by the sparks from horseshoes so that the whole landscape seems illuminated. It is worth noting the parallel between the light of the moon and the light racing along the ground which together manifest the struggle between red and white, the evil and the good, hell and heaven. At midnight, the vision suddenly disappears.

In connection with the stars, the moon can stimulate an atmosphere of love. In *Aucasin et Nicolette,* an anonymous work of the late twelfth or early thirteenth century, in the hut that

Nicolette has built for him, Aucassin, lying on his back, "looks through a hole and sees the stars in the sky, and he sees one brighter than the others, and he begins to speak." This vision inspires in Aucassin a romance to the star:

Little star, I see you,
The moon draws you to her,
Nicolette is with you,
My young friend with blond hair.
I think that God wants to take her
So that she may make the light of evening more beautiful.

Moonlight can also have a spiritual dimension. In Adenet le Roi's *Berte aus grans piés* (c. 1280), the heroine awakens near midnight and thinks that it is day because the moonlight is intense. In this natural framework, Berthe pronounces a vow of poverty and obscurity. However, from the fourteenth to the seventeenth centuries, because of the emphasis placed on witchcraft and Satanism, the dominant culture showed a certain suspicion toward the moon which, linked to the night, thereby seemed troubling or indeed maleficent.

Noble travelers, moreover, did not like to sleep in the open at night. In the thirteenth-century prose *Lancelot*, one night, Lancelot, a knight of the round table, arrived with a companion at a hermit's hut. "Come into my dwelling," offers the hermit, "for night is falling; before you have gone two leagues in this forest, which is great and dense, it will be dark; you will have to lie down beneath a tree or on the bare ground, and neither you nor your horses will have anything to eat."

The imaginary force of the forest is linked to its size but also to its opacity, and this increases with the darkness of night, so that fear takes command of those who have to cross vast spaces unable to perceive real or imaginary dangers. In *Berte aus grans piés*, the heroine, a victim of slanders, wanders at night in the forest of Le Mans. At first she believes herself endangered by wild beasts. They are only fantasies, but panic brings about a confusion between real and imaginary perils. As night begins to fall,

Berte takes refuge in the very lair of the wild animals. Two robbers arrive and try to rape her, but she manages to escape.

A kind of complicity seems to be established among animals, plants, and all of nature. Wind, rain, and cold join with wild animals and dangerous tree branches to make Berte's nocturnal wanderings even more difficult. Her wandering follows a dual pattern: spatial, marked by flight through the forest-labyrinth; temporal, indicated by the terrors of night preceding the relief of dawn:

> Oh, night, since you will be long, I must greatly fear you
> And when day comes, may God be my help.

In a sense, Berte relives the experience of Philip the Good, duke of Burgundy. Reality and the imagination coincide.

• • •

> Now the hungry lion roars,
> And the wolf behowls the moon;
> Whilst the heavy ploughman snores,
> All with weary task foredone.
> Now the wasted brands do glow,
> Whilst the screech-owl, screeching loud,
> Puts the wretch that lies in woe
> In remembrance of a shroud.
> Now it is the time of night
> That the graves, all gaping wide,
> Every one lets forth his sprite,
> In the churchway paths to glide.

So says the fairy Puck at the end of Act V of Shakespeare's *Midsummer Night's Dream*.

The night frightens, by its darkness and by the dangers it conceals, and it generates violence. The Bible confirms this feeling, as the Old Testament of God the dispenser of justice demonstrates. "When thou makest darkness and it is night, all the beasts of the forest come forth" (Psalm 104). "The pestilence stalks in darkness" (Psalm 91). It is evil-doers who hate the light: "The murderer rises before daylight / to kill some miserable wretch. / The thief prowls by night, / and in the darkness breaks into houses. / The seducer watches eagerly for twilight" (Job 24). One must thus pray to the Lord when night comes and ask for his protection against the terrors of the night (Psalm 91).

The New Testament of Christ the savior expresses the same idea. Jesus, who declared: "If you walk after nightfall, you stumble" (John 11), confronts "the reign of darkness" (Luke 22); at his death, "a darkness fell over the whole land" (Matthew 27). And the men of the Middle Ages, who were afraid of dying suddenly and going to hell because they did not have time to repent—the "birth of purgatory" dates from the twelfth century—knew that "the Day of the Lord comes like a thief in the night" (1 Thessalonians 5).

Popular consciousness—but the proverbs that reflected it were derived from learned culture—did not really denigrate night, for it brought wisdom. But what was praised was not the darkness, but the pause it provided for reflection. And indeed, the proverbs complain bitterly against night "black as anything." They fear its snares. "Night, love, and wine, each has its poison and venom." Repeating the biblical image, they depict it as the domain of evil-doers. "Good people like the day and the wicked the night." And yet, the period of night is not composed entirely of negative aspects.

PART TWO

Man or Night Tamed

CHAPTER 3

Techniques

SAVORING LIGHT

"[N]octurnal symbols do not manage substantively to get rid of diurnal expressions: night is often given value in terms of illumination," writes Gilbert Durand in *Les Structures anthropologiques de l'imaginaire*. And light is indeed experienced as a positive value. Before showing how medieval man with various methods and techniques tried, not to domesticate—the term is too strong for this period—but to soften night, it is thus important to grasp how much he appreciated light.

In a kind of compensatory effect, the Middle Ages demonstrated a pronounced taste for flashy colors. At least the upper classes, who had access to such gratifications, loved precious stones, gold studded with jewels, silken cloth glittering with gold and silver, shimmering colors. While blue is now the preferred color of more than half the population of the West, red, chosen by less than 10 percent of our contemporaries, seemed to the Middle Ages to be the most noble of colors. (Blue won out over red starting in the thirteenth century. As for black, its rise dates from the end of the fourteenth century and from the fifteenth century.) A color of luxury—certain sumptuary laws restricted it to the aristocracy—and of celebration—in rural society, women were married in red until the nineteenth century—red evokes fire and, more mystically, the fire of the Holy Spirit, the Pentecost. In some languages, in Russian for example, "red" and "beautiful" are synonymous. In churches, the population deeply appreciated the magnificence of vestments and liturgical objects and the polychromatic brightness of the stained glass windows.

"What constitutes the perfection and the beauty of material things," asserted Robert Grosseteste, chancellor at Oxford and bishop of Lincoln, in 1235, "is light. . . . Light is the thing whose presence engenders the greatest joy." Light also joined the beautiful to the good. "Metaphysically, God is light in its pure state and, to the extent that things are luminous, they are not only noble, they are divine."

Literature shows this love of light, for example, in the description of precious materials whose brilliance adds to the brilliance of the gold in which they are set. In the brightness given off by Durandal, the sword of Roland:

> Oh! Durandal how bright and brilliant you are!
> How you blaze and glitter in the sun!

In the sunlight streaming over the army of Charlemagne:

> The evening is light, the day remains radiant,
> And in the sunlight the weapons glitter,
> Halberds and helmets glimmer and blaze,
> And the shields all painted with jewels,
> And the spears, the golden banners.

The pleasant spot, a *topos* of medieval literature, restricting ourselves to its essential elements, is made up of a meadow—or a garden or an orchard—a stream, flowers, birds, and both sunlight and coolness. This landscape is inconceivable outside a morning in spring.

Unable to attain this luminous ideal, the men of the Middle Ages attempted to reduce the darkness which constituted its antithesis. To this end, they tried to arrange for daylight to illuminate their buildings and living quarters, for lighting to reduce the density of the dark, if not in the streets, at least in their houses, and for fire, while providing heat to diminish the darkness.

Building Construction: Darkness and Luminosity

Available techniques and materials did not allow the construction of buildings like our own. While light was appreciated, night had to be allowed daily to invade churches and houses. There was a certain ambivalence between sought-for light and imposed darkness.

In the Merovingian era, attempts were made to construct light-filled churches, as Gregory of Tours testifies. As many windows as possible were cut into the walls of the nave, allowing light to enter from dawn to twilight—the difference is obvious between this conception surviving from antiquity and that of the succeeding centuries in which worshipers preferred a mysterious half-light to too much brightness. In poor churches, a canvas or cloth on a wooden frame was placed in front of the window to prevent the entry of air. In significant buildings, blocks of open-work marble were used, or stained-glass windows, probably rather small. Illuminated by the sun, they aroused the admiration of the Christians assembled for prayer. Contemporary writers emphasized this brightness, which permitted contemplation of the interior decor of the building.

Much later, the gothic was characterized not only by verticality but also by illumination. To the warmth provided by lower and darker buildings, the Middle Ages then preferred the light bestowed by the high windows of the cathedrals. And stained glass, which the French were so adept at making, according to the monk Théophile (eleventh century?), author of a *Répertoire des divers arts,* one of the best technical manuals of the Middle Ages, embellished these windows and glistened in the light of the sun.

But what a difference there was between the imposing cathedrals with their polychromatic stained glass reflecting the glory of God and the often dark houses crowded around them. Let us examine the houses of the late Middle Ages.

In cities could be found cottage-style houses—usual in the countryside—consisting of a single room with multiple uses. It was easy to build, since it was made from mud, wood, and thatch. But it turned out to be uncomfortable because, aside from an unavoidable promiscuity, it lacked openings and hence lacked light. It was hard to keep a fire going in the fireplace which drew badly at certain times of the year because of climatic conditions.

The house of an artisan or small merchant possessed a minimum of comfort. But its gable on the street and one or more stories supported with corbels and projecting outward over one another had the defect of limiting openings to a single door and one or two windows and of reducing the light in an already narrow street. In pillared houses, which were less common, upper stories were not corbelled, but rested on supports of wood or stone. The breadth and the lighting of the street were still further diminished.

Moving from the city to the countryside, let us consider Dracy, a little Burgundian village that was deserted in the fourteenth century. On the west, Dracy backed up against a cliff, the back wall for the houses of the highest level. Since the site was terraced, the west walls of the intermediate and lower houses were thus concealed by the walls of the terraces. In addition, the houses were attached, or closely spaced, so that the north and south walls had no openings. Thus, only the door at the front allowed light to enter. And this door, judging by the arrangement of the sills and the existence of keys, was probably a full door. These were therefore very dark houses; and since they had two rooms opening directly off one another, the back room was even darker than the front. The only houses with slightly more light were located at the edges of the village: windows, incidentally set at a sharp angle, had been constructed.

Thus daylight entered the houses only in the morning and only reached the front room; in the afternoon, a sort of half-light prevailed. Technical considerations—openings were points of weakness in the walls—and the desire for protection from the cold can also explain this situation.

The openings were small, and it was therefore important to arrange for them to let in as much light as possible. The best means was to use glass, but glass was expensive. In 1324, in Paris, a square foot of clear glass cost two sous, of colored glass, three sous. In 1410, a square foot cost six sous in Ghent. The glass used was thick and made up of small diamond shapes which the glass-maker assembled on site in leaden frames. Since repairs were frequent, only the rich could afford such a luxury. In 1381, a glass-maker from Arras spent forty-seven days in a castle belonging to Philip the Bold, duke of Burgundy, redoing a large window and four small ones in the chapel, as well as five windows in the great hall.

The nobility appreciated this material that was able to hold night at bay. For example, consider Mahaut, countess of Artois, for whom Master Otto, a glassmaker from Arras provided clear glass and "glass painted with images" for her castle of Hesdin. A large order was given to the same glassmaker in 1307 for the castle of Lens; he had to make and mount the glass for twenty-six windows. The relatively narrow openings of the thirteenth century were more and more replaced with wide windows, and the height of some of them was increased.

Master Jean le Sauvage provided colored windows for the openings of establishments built by the countess: the hospital of Hesdin, the monastery of Sainte-Claire, the convent of la Thieul-loye in Arras, and the charterhouses and the hospital in Gosnay. A letter from an agent of Mahaut notes that 259½ feet of clear glass and 247¼ feet of colored glass were used in Gosnay. On receipt of this letter, the recipient paid Jean le Sauvage sixty-three livres and nine deniers, which corresponds to two sous per square foot of clear glass and three sous per square foot of colored glass.

As we have noted, repairs were frequently necessary. For example, in 1343, a worker from Béthune worked for a long time at the castle of Aire, where he had to restore all the windows to the state they were in at the time of Mahaut. "To redo all the windows of the great hall, of the chapel, of the bedrooms of my lord the duke and my lord of Boulogne, and all the windows of the castle, both in the chapel and elsewhere which were in very bad condition, glass and color being similar to the originals, with coats of arms and images, a contract was made with a worker from Béthune named Jehan As Coquelès, following the orders of my lord the duke."

But what did glass-covered windows look like? Only iconography can give us some idea. Generally, the opening contained a fixed panel of glass with lead lattice work. The panel was in one piece or reinforced by vertical or horizontal bars. The windows might be supplied with an interior shutter made of wood. A second type was the mullioned window, that is, with fixed frames. Most important was the frame piece that separated the upper from the lower part of the opening. Both could be fitted with leaded glass with or without an interior shutter, or remain empty with an interior shutter. It happened that the lower part contained movable glass panels.

Because of its variable thickness, and because it was mounted in small diamonds, glass offered little transparency, but it did allow light to enter until twilight. In the face of night, buildings, through their openings and the use of glass, in some sense offered passive resistance. Lighting, on the other hand, was an active element.

Lighting

We are used to moving through city streets day and night without any difficulty. Streets illuminated by lampposts leave few areas of darkness. In the Middle Ages, the situation was quite different. The streets were not illuminated, which did not necessarily prevent the inhabitants from going out. But to do so with any safety, it was wise to be accompanied with servants carrying torches. At most, there was sometimes a dim light coming from candles placed at their windows by the residents. In Venice, however, in 1397, the Lords of the Night set up lanterns in the Rialto, and in 1450, the Ten required the maintenance from nightfall to the fourth hour of the morning of four lamps under the portico of the Cloth Merchants of the Rialto as well as two others in the street leading to the Rialto Nuovo.

For a street not to resemble a dark alley, important events like a visit of great personages had to occur. The municipal authorities then took measures. On December 25, 1519, on the arrival of the queen mother in Poitiers, the inhabitants were ordered to hang lanterns at their windows and to place "blazing candles" in these lanterns. The order stood until the court's departure.

Motives of security also required that streets be lighted. On September 11, 1542, the mayor of Poitiers declared that, "to put an end to thefts and exactions that habitually occur in this town, it is necessary to establish order, to assemble *centeniers* and *cinquanteniers* and from now on to have lights in windows to make it easier to prevent thieves and robbers from running away, and to lower awnings to keep thieves from hiding under them." He also forbade people to go about the town at night without light and to carry swords, daggers, or weapons of that kind. But this was already the middle of the sixteenth century.

After curfew, then, every resident with common sense stayed home where he had some meager ways of confronting the darkness.

Methods barely changed throughout the Middle Ages. In the Merovingian era, aside from candles, lamps were used in family homes as well as churches. Some with chain supports were hung by a rope from the ceiling of the room or hall. These lamps consisted of a container for oil and a wick, often made of papyrus. They were sometimes made of clay by local artisans and in that case were found usually in lower-class homes. Aristocratic houses also used candelabra, from which were suspended lamps or candles, which were put to use on special occasions. At other times, slaves stood near the master's table holding candles which produced smoke that was unpleasant but inevitable. Mentioning the cruelty of Duke Rauching, Gregory of Tours provides some details in passing. "If a servant was holding a candle before him while he was having a meal, as is the custom, he had the clothes stripped off his legs and put the candle out on them." Gregory elsewhere notes that it was dangerous not to have light during meals, because darkness fostered assassinations. "While he [Theudégésile, king of the Goths of Spain] was at table having supper with his friends and was very cheerful, the candles suddenly went out and, struck by an enemy sword as he was reclining, he gave up the ghost."

To remove the burned part of candle wicks, they used either tweezers or simply their fingers.

In some abbeys in the Carolingian era, tenant farmers were required to supply wax and tallow. Fish and whale fat were collected. There were even specialized establishments, like the villa of Saint-Wandrille that had to procure 200 pounds of wax, 180 of oil, and eight hogsheads of tallow, or that of Bitry, a dependency of the abbey of Saint-Germain-des-Prés, the only obligation of whose inmates was to supply twenty-two pounds of wax or eight gallons of oil.

At the time, wax was used mostly in churches. It was made into candles that were burned before the altars or the tombs of saints. Houses made do with birch-bark or pine torches. The abundant light in churches—the church in Aniane was illuminated by seven golden candelabra, seven silver lamps set in a ring, and seven lamps placed before the altar—provides a simple explanation for the wonder of the worshipers.

All these means of illumination can be found not only in documents. They have left physical traces, and archaeological digs have provided more precise notions of how light was used, particularly in villages. For example, the careful excavations of Ms. Demians d'Archimbaud in Rougiers have brought to light the techniques used in a Provençal village around the thirteenth century.

Illumination consisted of lamps and chandeliers. Oil or tallow lamps had an open container with a spout. They were hung on hooks set in the wall or on a stand that could be moved by means of a suspension rod.

Some chandeliers had rods and candle rings, others bowl-shaped containers. The rod and ring chandeliers, placed on a stand that was probably made of wood, or inserted between stones, were made up of a tapering vertical rod of variable length, extended on the other side to form a ring into which the candle was set. Different models have been found, some very primitive, others more carefully made. For example, in one, a ring in the middle of the rod seems designed to prevent the candle from sinking too low, and two short arms two centimeters from the candle ring functioned perhaps to support some object or to make it easier to install a base.

The bowl chandeliers also had several models, differing in the size of the bowl and the material—iron or copper plate covered in iron. Without feet, they were probably set on a wood or stone base. The candle was fixed by means of a long thin ring or a square prong.

These were simple candles used by peasants. It is interesting to observe the meagerness of illumination. The rings were small, half of them having a length of no more than 1–1.1 centimeter; the tallest was 1.7 centimeter. This can be related to the difficulties encountered in making wax and tallow candles.

The relatively hard wax candles were probably designed for bases with prongs. Tallow candles had a wick made of rushes or hemp, dipped and redipped in fat until the desired thickness was reached. Resin was sometimes used, but the material was most frequently beef or mutton fat, mutton fat being plentiful in the Mediterranean region. In short, the light was rather minimal, which perhaps explains the concentration of illumination in certain rooms.

The Rougiers excavations have also produced the remains of a lantern discovered in a cave used for keeping chickens. The base is made of a circular sheet of copper about twelve centimeters in diameter, with a turned-up edge reaching at most two centimeters in height. The edge has nine rivets used to fasten vertical iron strips designed to hold thin sheets of horn necessary to protect the light from the wind. The wax or tallow candle had to be set inside in a candle ring. Lanterns are mentioned in some documents as early as the beginning of the thirteenth century, but they were luxury items. Illumination was thus relatively rare, but this was the Mediterranean and people lived mostly out of doors.

What was the cost of this illumination? Guillaume de Murol, a lord of Auvergne, who lit his castle with tallow candles, spent ten livres on lighting out of total expenses of 682 livres. It is difficult to estimate the significance of the budget devoted to the struggle against darkness. We may merely note that his average annual medical expenses were only three livres, but Guillaume, who died at ninety, had a healthy constitution, and for minor ailments affecting members of his family, he relied on not very costly prayers and incantations. The costs incurred for the marriage of his eldest daughter Dauphine in 1412 were a hundred livres. In the middle of the fifteenth century in Tours, a laborer had to work half a day to earn enough for a pound of tallow. And wax was priceless.

With respect to monastic life, the Rule of Le Maître (first third of the sixth century) called for lighting at bedtime a small oil lamp, that soon went out when the fuel was used up. As a result, the sleeping quarters were in complete darkness throughout the night, so that, if the need was felt, the monks had to speak rather than use sign language. They awoke in darkness. In winter, the oil lamp or a larger one was not lit until after nocturn to permit reading in the sleeping quarters. Although these quarters remained sunk in darkness, the entry to the monastery seems to have been permanently lit up.

The Rule of Saint Benedict (530–560) sets out important modifications to these provisions. The sleeping quarters were to be lit up all night until morning. Thus "everything will be done in the light." It was thus possible to keep to the rule of nocturnal silence. Benedict absolutely forbade speech, which was penalized. Monks no longer awakened in darkness.

Fire

There was another way to fight the darkness. Fire, as we have seen, could be a calamity, as in the conflagrations recounted by the chroniclers. One night in 1395, burning pieces of wood thrown into the Rhône landed on boats stopped near the arches of the pont d'Avignon and set them on fire. Another night in 1406, some scoundrels set fire to the school of Saint-Germain-l'Auxerrois and the hôtel de l'Écu de France, and the blaze spread very rapidly.

But fire also burned in fireplaces. Every peasant house had a single hearth which was used to cook food, to illuminate, and to warm and comfort the living, the light of the fire dispelling often imaginary fears.

Illumination appears to have been a secondary function, although the light provided allowed one to pick out the shadows and to move around without banging into things. And this function was far from needless in houses that had few and narrow openings—the builder wished to prevent the entry of cold air or, in Mediterranean regions, was concerned with keeping the house cool, and glass windows were too costly for peasants—and limited illumination. In Bucato, in Italy, even though the furniture left in place after the brutal destruction of the houses was abundant, excavations have uncovered only one or at most two oil lamps made of terra-cotta for each house.

Associated with this domestic fire were the bonfires that were frequent signs of celebration at the time. We shall return to them in considering nocturnal pleasures, but they too, in a playful fashion, helped to fight against the darkness.

What is striking is the modesty of the techniques permitting an escape from, or rather a lessening of darkness. Glass, not very widespread, more translucid than transparent, did not let in very much light. Illumination, both costly and rudimentary, appears to have been minimal among the peasants who made up the immense majority of the population. Fire, whose principal purpose was to heat food and the atmosphere, provided only pale light.

Light provided reassurance, but in a time when imagination created fear of the greatest dangers, often unreal, it was also necessary to fight against violence, frequently associated with night. The public authorities tried to resolve this problem with the watch and the rear watch.

PROTECTING AGAINST VIOLENCE

At night, towns—but also the countryside—harbored many dangers: internal with the troublemakers who prowled the narrow streets and readily broke down the doors of houses to loot or attack women alone; external, particularly in wartime, and especially during the Anglo-French conflict that lasted so long at the end of the Middle Ages.

Prevention

Repression predominated over prevention. Nevertheless, measures were taken—and repeated, since they were seldom obeyed—to prevent violence. It was recommended not to go out at night, that is, after curfew, without a valid reason. Those who had to risk venturing out of doors were asked to carry torches and candles.

Police regulations called for such precautions, for they facilitated the identification of walkers in the night and allowed them to be seen from a distance. In 1431, the archbishop of Lyon ordained, "Let no one be so bold or daring to go about at night after the great *seral* of Saint-Nizier without carrying lights, on pain of being put in prison and of paying sixty sous of Tours each time he is found to have done so." Patrols were thus required to arrest anyone disobeying these rules. It was thus that the provost Arthaud de Varey imprisoned Humbert Chappuis in November 1462 when he was found around the eleventh hour of the night without light and armed with a dagger. Even before knowing the reasons for his behavior, the sergeants saw him as a suspect because he was outside at night.

In 1413, shortly after the entry of the duke of Berry into Paris, when the bourgeois learned that some of his servants had attempted to assassinate one of them, they got permission from Charles VI to carry on armed patrols at night in the streets of the capital in order to guarantee their safety. The following week, a royal order prohibited any person, whatever his rank, from going armed at night in the city. Only the bourgeois were exempted from the rule and were even authorized to arrest the offenders and put them in prison. This concession, according to the monk of Saint-Denis, greatly displeased the courtiers.

There was thus an obligation to be unarmed, for otherwise the slightest verbal dispute could degenerate into homicide. A regulation in Troyes in the fifteenth century—but the same prohibitions were found in other towns—declared, "Whoever, whatever his condition, carries in town knives, swords, daggers, or prohibited sticks, on pain of losing them and paying ten sous penalty, except for royal officers who alone have the right to do so." A 1478 regulation concerning the town of Rennes indicated that all residents were forbidden to be in the streets of the town and the environs after nine at night without lights. It was also forbidden for all "mechanics and laboring men" and other residents to carry day or night "daggers, swords, short swords, sticks or other iron, except for cutting their meat," except for the police, and gentlemen and their servants. Likewise, the residents did not have the right to assemble or to fight among themselves.

Similar measures were taken in Dijon, Strasbourg, and Poitiers, where the situation was worsened by the influx of aggressive students who "are day and night in the public streets, a danger to those going by at night and to others." By 1427, the community of Poitiers therefore asked the king to install chains to block certain streets. In the early sixteenth century, these chains were at Saint-Porchaire, at the Pilori, at Saint-Étienne, and at the Jacobins. Their keys were in the keeping of the most prominent local bourgeois, because they had been taken from their former keepers who had misused them. This guard was not to everyone's taste, since one of the bourgeois asked that the sergeants be given the duty of locking the chains on Friday night and opening them the next afternoon.

Despite the vigilance of the night patrols, in the course of 1406, a troop of unauthorized people tried to get into the hôtel de Nesle belonging to the duke of Berry. Repelled by arrows, they fled on the Seine toward the royal hôtel de Saint-Pol. This provoked a riot among the people, who believed that someone wanted to carry the king out of Paris by force. The next day, the duke of Burgundy, after putting the malefactors to flight and calming the people, ordered the Parisians in the name of the king to forge a great iron chain that would be stretched at night across the whole width of the river so that no one could secretly enter the city by boat.

In the early fourteenth century, the town of Amiens took a series of steps intended to protect its ramparts. Thus it was forbidden "on pain of a fine and imprisonment, to cross the ditches of the place by day or night, to scale the walls, to break the doors, windows, or locks of the towers and the sentry boxes." "Any boatman who takes any person across the Somme at night, to bring him into or take him out of the town, will be punished as an enemy of the town." "All persons who own boats on the Somme are ordered to bring them within the fortifications before sunset, on pain of being punished as enemies of the town and losing their boats."

Legislation governed foreigners, required innkeepers to note their names, and to turn troublemakers over to the authorities; there was particular surveillance of those without work, who inspired deep distrust. Since prevention did not resolve the problem of violence, means had to be devised to repress it.

The Watch

The public authorities in every age have been concerned with ensuring the safety of residents, particularly in cities where they are gathered in large numbers. In the Merovingian era, groups were charged with watching at night and making rounds, for at night in the city a person would rarely be seen on the streets, and then he was accompanied by an escort carrying torches or lanterns. Or else they were brigands.

Fires, which were frequent, set entire neighborhoods ablaze. Panic seized the residents, who willingly helped one another, but they lacked resources and discipline. Gregory of Tours reports that one night in 585, in early twilight, an inhabitant of Paris, after lighting a light, went into his store, took oil and other things that he needed, and went off leaving his light next to a small barrel of oil. This house was located near the gate leading to the south. The light provoked a fire, the house was destroyed, and others adjoining it caught fire. As the wind was blowing, the flames spread through the city and the blaze began to reach another gate where there was a shrine to Saint Martin. The man who had built it high with intertwined girders, trusting in the Lord and the saint, took refuge with his family and his goods inside the building. As the blaze got closer, swirls of flame rose in the air, but when they lapped against the walls of the shrine, they immediately cooled down. Nevertheless, the crowd that had gathered round called to the man and his wife, "Flee, poor people, since you can still escape. The flaming mass is already falling down on you, burning sparks and coals are falling like rain! Leave the shrine or you will perish in the fire." But the man and his wife showed no emotion. And, concludes Gregory of Tours, so great was the miraculous virtue of the blessed bishop that he saved not only the shrine and the house of his disciple, but that he prevented the flames from damaging the neighboring houses, and the blaze that had begun to rage subsided on one side of the bridge. On the other side—perhaps, according to some commentators, the north bank of the Seine and thus the île de la Cité, but the text is too imprecise to be certain—the fire consumed everything with such violence that only the river put an end to its progress. However, neither the churches nor the houses attached to them were burned.

Aside from the miracle, it is obvious how quickly fire could ravage a city. Therefore, people who went through the streets at night had to be very careful, not only about the risk of robbery, but also about fires that were frequent at the time and remained frequent throughout the Middle Ages.

Risks could come from the watchers themselves. In 595, Clotaire II issued an order against the people in charge of the night watch, who connived with thieves and allowed them to escape. When a theft has been committed at night, he decreed, those who are on guard in the neighborhood will be personally responsible if they do not arrest the thief. If, while trying to escape from them, the thief is seen in another neighborhood whose guards, if warned, also fail to arrest him, then the loss due to the theft will fall on them; they will in addition be penalized with a fine of five sous; and so on from neighborhood to neighborhood up to and including the third.

Such rules were probably seldom obeyed, since, shortly before his death, in 813, Charlemagne ordered that if one of the people responsible for the watch failed in his duty, he would be punished by the count or the first magistrate by a fine of four sous.

At night, in fact, the temptation was strong to leave thieves alone, for fear of an injury or, worse, of becoming an accomplice to share in the booty. However, we have little knowledge of the organization of urban policing in the high Middle Ages. It was not until the reign of Saint Louis that more precise regulations were put in place. In the meanwhile there was significant urban development, and subsequently the problem of security in cities was more acute. The monarchy responded by organizing, although in an incomplete manner, the watch, the rear watch, and the guard.

To defend itself, in addition to the guard made up of armed notables set at the gates during the day, the city relied on the watch, which was carried out unarmed at night, on the ramparts, on a tower of the castle, or in a watchtower. In Tours, as in many other cities, a watchman armed with a trumpet and a banner gave the alarm in case of fire or when a troop appeared on the horizon, and indicated with his banner the direction from which the danger approached. The *Chronique de Bertrand du Guesclin* presents a very vivid picture of the life of these watchmen. For example, when the town of Châtellerault was besieged by the troops of the Constable in 1370:

> There was a tower that was tall and great,
> And in it there was a watchman watching.
> To wake the watch he often cried:
> "Watch the foot of the wall! go everywhere watching!
> Soon it will be day, I see it dawning
> We will go eat some tripe
> For surely I have never been so hungry."

> So spoke the watchman.
> But the others sleep.
> They do not answer; instead they snore.
> Already at the foot of the wall I mentioned
> There were more than thirty Frenchmen
> Who were speaking aloud and said when they heard him:
> "We will keep watch everywhere, we are not sleeping;
> We really want to eat that tripe."

> When the watcher heard the French,
> He looked at the ditches, he heard the wood rustle
> And the great trunks fall
> That our people had silently sawed.
> They fall in the ditches, here twenty, there thirty-three.
> Then the watch knows
> That the French are in the ditches
> And gives the alarm:
> "Treason! Treason! lords, to arms at once!"
> Then the English take to arms.

The watchers took up their duty in the evening, when the guard came to an end, with a certain ceremoniousness. Indeed, the gatekeepers, noblemen who had watched over the city and consequently over their possessions in the course of the day, locked the gates with keys that the mayor had given them in the morning and that they returned to him at night.

The people of "low degree" then took over. Arriving at their post at the moment when the gates were closed, they climbed to the parapet walk on ladders whose feet in many towns were protected by a locked barrier. Thus, the watchers, who were by no means volunteers, would not be tempted—or more precisely, would not be able—to abandon their post under cover of darkness. Installed in sentry boxes, suffering in winter from cold and bad weather, they waited more or less patiently for night to pass and for the guard to come to liberate them in the morning.

To overlook the watch, there was a rear watch, or *rereguet*, which did not confine itself to that task but went through the streets by torchlight to prevent hooligans from getting into mischief. At every crossroads, the rear watch came to a halt, listening for the slightest suspicious noise, trying to determine whether some quarrel had broken out. When they reached the gates, they verified that they were locked and climbed the ramparts to make sure that the watch had not gone to sleep or abandoned their post.

In 1438, Jehan de la Roche, seneschal of Poitou, decreed that the lord of Bressuire was "authorized, by reason as well as by the custom of the country, to constrain and force all the inhabitants of common condition waking and sleeping in his said land and domain of Bressuire to keep watch and guard at his said fortresses both by day and by night." But this did not mean that the inhabitants were personally obligated to perform the service of the watch. This fell on households, not on individuals. There was a cleavage between the poorest who were established on the ramparts and the people of middling condition who watched over them. In general, each middling household had to supply a man between eighteen and sixty for the watch, the rear watch, or the guard. Widows were held to this obligation. Peasants in the area who came seeking protection in a castle had the same duties as the inhabitants of the castle domain. It was in fact common to find refugees inside fortresses. One evening in 1385, after supper, at the hour of sunset, the laborer Pierre Pascaut went to the fort of Beauvoir "where he was accustomed to go at night for greater safety."

At Pentecost in 1265, in the presence of the king, the Parlement de Paris declared that the inhabitants of the domain of the bishop of Paris would be required to keep watch just like the other bourgeois, when request was made of them by the provost of Paris or by the knight of the watch—called in the document "guardian of the city"—even though this was contrary to the bishop's claims of exemption. At Chandeleur in 1270, the Parlement also ordered that all the bourgeois living in the bishop's palace as well as those throughout the jurisdiction of the Temple, within the city or outside the walls, would have to keep watch like the other bourgeois of Paris.

This watch was above all a matter of the king's jurisdiction. A decision of the Parlement de Paris of May 19, 1363, dismissed the bishop's claim that he could have an armed watch kept by his bailiff and by his officers and sergeants on the eve of the Assumption of the Virgin Mary in and around Notre-Dame. The provost of Paris maintained the right to be informed and to punish anyone who violated the regulations on this point. If the bishop thought it appropriate to have officers seeing to the preservation of the riches in his church that night, he could do so, on condition that the officers keep their arms under their cloaks, and that they not show them if they were on guard duty or on their way home.

However, not everyone took part in the watch. The notables who guarded the gates during the day were exempt. So were the royal officers, as well as the fiscal and legal officials. But when Jean de Berry returned to Poitiers in 1373 and learned that the officers of his household, claiming exemption, refused to take part in the guard or the watch, he ordered the mayor to require all the inhabitants, including his officers and servants and the clergy, except for the nobles and the Franciscans and Dominicans, to fulfill this duty.

The clergy were required to take part in the watch and the guard, but they could purchase a replacement. The inhabitants of church lands attempted to avoid service outside the domain of which they were dependents. In 1367, for example, the men of the priory of Saint-Denis-en-Vaux, who acknowledged that they belonged to the jurisdiction of Poitiers, were obliged by the lieutenant general of the seneschal of Poitou to take part in the watch and the guard and to help repair the walls of Poitiers. Like the other inhabitants, they had to keep "watch at night on the walls of the said town." But one fine day, they refused. Their prior declared that they were not compelled to perform this service, for they were men and subjects of his priory, a member of Saint-Denis en France, under royal charter. At the request of the mayor of Poitiers in 1391, the king ordered that they be compelled "to go to keep the said watch or have it kept at night, each one in turn, by order of the mayor of this city." After an appeal to the Parlement, the mayor backed down, but in 1418, he appealed to the dauphin Charles, the king's lieutenant, who reinstated the 1391 orders.

The members of certain crafts also attempted to be excused from the watch. Once again the Parlement had to intervene to resolve complaints that were not always justified. On All Saints' Day 1264, it ordered that the clothmakers of Paris would keep watch like everyone else, whether the provost of Paris ordered it in person or by proxy. Similarly, at Pentecost in 1271, it ordered that the moneychangers, the goldsmiths, the clothmakers again, and some other bourgeois who claimed to be exempt from the watch, were not in reality and had to fulfill that function, whether or not the provost of Paris was present, considering that its purpose was the general safety of all the inhabitants of the city.

Special cases did exist. For example, in 1431, the *coutres* of the cathedral chapter of Poitiers, whose function was to ring the bells on the hour and to watch over the cathedral day and night, were given a special dispensation from service on the watch by the king. But exemptions and dispensations could vary as a function of the political situation. Easy to obtain when the country was at peace, they became much rarer in time of war. When the situation required, it was important to have enough manpower to warn of the approach of enemies.

It sometimes happened, although rarely, that the watch gave rise to genuine competition. When Philip the Good, duke of Burgundy, was staying in Utrecht, the council decided to organize an efficient and attractive watch in front of the prince's dwelling, a large and spacious monastery. The lord of Croy, in charge of the watch on the first day, had command of two hundred lances, not to mention the archers who stood before the duke's residence; a marvelous bonfire lasted through the night, illuminating the surroundings. The men at arms were in a large refectory in front of Philip's bedroom in order to prevent any attack. What a pleasure to hear the trumpeters, buglers, and fiddlers who never stopped playing all night, reported the chronicler Chastellain. The leaders of the watch on the following days carried it out with similar ceremony.

The fifth and final watch, on Monday, the night of Saint-Laurent, was assigned to the lord of Sempy, who surpassed all the others. When the time came to go to the assigned place, this lord assembled all the men in his charge in front of his house, men at arms and archers from both Picardy and Hainaut. The procession set out led by a squire on horseback carrying his master's banner; then came the archers two by two with a large number of torches. They thus went to Philip's dwelling, and their approach greatly pleased him; there were eight or nine hundred archers, helmets on their heads, bows drawn and arrows fixed as if to say, "Who wants to fight?" Then came the lord of Sempy, alone in front of his mounted men at arms, riding on a large and handsome steed covered in velvet, fully armed, with his captain's staff in hand, and surrounded by four torches. Every man at arms was accompanied by a page carrying a torch and a valet armed with an ax, so that there were as many torches as men at arms, 200 or 220, not counting the archers' torches. After going through the town to the sound of trumpets and bugles, they arrived in front of the duke's residence. They kept watch through the night, the men at arms in the hall and the archers outside in the great square beneath the windows.

The security of the capital, the largest city in the kingdom, the home of the richest men of the age, but also the city with the greatest number of bandits, was a major problem. Although the ramparts apparently protected the city from enemies, the people living inside did not know whether they should fear the residents of other neighborhoods. They did not know them, and yet they could not decently approach them with initial hostility. When the duke of Orléans was assassinated in 1407, an investigation was opened, and it was discovered that the murderers, about fifteen of them, had been able to find lodging in the rue Barbette without awakening suspicion. Even after the closing of the gates, it was possible to get through the ramparts for an assignation in the ditches with a woman of easy virtue or to escape from the police after a misdeed.

Under these conditions, security was a matter of great concern to the municipal authorities. Assigned by day to the sergeants of the Châtelet, it required specific measures at night. Several royal decrees show that the night guard was first a duty of the crafts, but they were assisted by a royal guard made up of mounted sergeants and armed foot soldiers. In December 1254, Saint Louis indicated that the inhabitants of Paris, to ensure the safety of their persons and their goods, to remedy the evils and accidents that occurred every night, such as fires, robberies, violence against and abduction of women, and removal of furniture by tenants to spite their landlords, had asked him to allow them to set up a watch at night. The members of a certain number of crafts promised to undertake it at their own expense, taking turns for three weeks each, and this was granted to them. The same decree indicated that in addition to the watch by the crafts and to make the city more secure, there had long been in existence another watch, maintained and paid for by the king, made up of twenty mounted sergeants and forty on foot under the command of the captain of the watch. He directed and led his men through the streets of the city all night in order to visit and strengthen the craftsmen's watch.

In 1364, when the general situation seemed much more difficult than a century earlier, Jean II the Good provided a very explicit and precise description of the organization and mission of the watch. The monarch began by recalling that from time immemorial the watch had been carried out every night by the crafts, each in turn, in order to take care of the protection of the city, of the relics in the Sainte-Chapelle, of the bodies of his predecessor kings, of the prisoners in the Châtelet, of the bourgeois, and of goods and merchandise against any accidents due to fire, murder, theft, abduction of women and girls, and other wicked actions. Every craft was required to take the watch every three weeks. If an artisan failed in his duty, the officials of the watch would replace him with another man at his expense. In addition, to make the city even more secure, the kings maintained at their expense another watch made up of twenty mounted sergeants and twenty-six foot soldiers, under the command of the captain of the watch.

After leading his troops through the streets of Paris all night, the captain prepared a report of captures. He then returned to his residence on rue Perrin-Gasselin. Toward Christmas 1456, François Villon speaks of the captain in these terms in his *Lais:*

> I bequeath *The Helmet,*
> And to the sergeants on foot who walk with care
> Groping around the merchants' stalls,
> I leave two lovely rubies, and *The Lantern*
> In the street named *Pierre-au-Lait;*
> Sure! but I'll have the *Three Lily* cell
> If they take me to the Châtelet.

Villon bequeaths to the captain a "helm"—quibbling on the term, for there was a tavern with that name at the Baudoyer gate—that is, a helmet considered as a sign of nobility. The function indeed required that its holder be a knight.

After recalling the decree issued under Saint Louis, with the difference of twenty-six instead of forty foot soldiers, the king provided very precise indications on the financial conditions of the function. The captain of the watch received ten Parisian sous in wages every day, and twenty livres a year for his cloaks; the mounted sergeants two sous each; and those on foot twelve Parisian deniers. In addition, two assistants called clerks of the watch were entrusted with recording the names. Their daily wages were twelve deniers each, and every day, they notified the craftsmen who were supposed to take the watch to come in person— or to send a replacement—to a spot in the Châtelet assigned for that purpose. The captain, the mounted sergeants, and the foot soldiers also had to come to the same spot to be registered by the clerks of the watch. If an artisan was missing, he was replaced with another watcher at his expense; he was however excused if his wife was in childbirth, if he had been bled that day, if he had left the city on business, or if he was over sixty; but the clerks had to have advance notice. As for the captain, the mounted sergeants, and the foot soldiers, those who were absent lost their wages for their night service. Once the names of those present were recorded, the clerks distributed the craftsmen as follows: six on the pavement outside the grill of the Châtelet to prevent prisoners from getting out through the gates; six around the Châtelet to prevent them from climbing down with ropes or any other means and from receiving help from the outside; six in the courtyard of the Palais de Justice, going up and down all night, in order to guard that place and its holy relics; six in the Cité near the Madeleine; six in front of the fountain of the Saints-Innocents; six under the pillars of the Grève; six at the Baudoyer gate; and the others at crossroads or places considered suitable by the clerks. All of them were on watch throughout the night, with the weapons that they possessed.

As for the members of the royal watch, they were required to leave the Châtelet as soon as the curfew bell had rung and to walk all night through the streets of the city and the suburbs, to visit the craftsmen on watch, and to ask them if they needed help or if anything had happened. Thus, the bourgeois guard, distributed in various neighborhoods, especially near prisons, could not abandon its post, which lent it the name of "seated watch," while the royal guard was required to make constant rounds to keep watch over the city streets and to arrest malefactors or anyone going armed after curfew, in short to make certain that the capital was calm and safe.

The organization of the watch resembled in many ways the organization described for Paris. Command of the royal castles was assigned to lord captains. In the case of large domains, these captains were assisted by a lieutenant, sergeants (one of whom was sometimes known as sergeant general), permanent guards, clerks, and servants. Clerks performed administrative functions similar to those of the Parisian clerks.

The service of the watch, the rear watch, and the guard was regulated by an ordinance from the captain. Under the authority of the ordinance and the regulation, the sergeant organized the work. Generally, he summoned the men who were to take part in the watch in person at home or after Sunday mass. Sometimes the priest would inform his parishioners.

Every household, as we have seen, had to supply a man for the watch, the rear watch, or the guard. In general, those of low degree were in the watch, the middling sort were assigned to the rear watch, and the richest were in the guard.

How many men were needed? Calculation is difficult, depending as it did on population, but also on the political situation. In 1452, Berthomé Hubert, former tax commissioner for the town of Bressuire and its dependencies, reported that a census carried out in 1447 indicated 900 or 1000 "subject to tax, who are men and subjects of the said jurisdiction, but he says that he does not know if they are all subject to the watch, because some of them, men of the *hospitaliers*, say they have the privilege of not taking part in the watch." According to Jehan de Boysmoreau, priest in la Forêt-sur-Sèvre around 1421, the inhabitants of the jurisdiction had to supply eight men to the castle of Bressuire for the night watch, four for the rear watch, and two for daytime guard duty. Thus, fourteen men were needed every day. It is true that an anonymous hand has written in the margin, "but it must be remembered that this was in wartime."

If we assume that each man had to serve once a month, the monthly requirement was for 420 men, of whom 240 were assigned to guard the castle at night. Even with those who were exempt, the subjects of the jurisdiction could easily supply the services of the watch, the rear watch, and the guard.

On October 12, 1464, the duke of Brittany organized the guard of the castle and town of Clisson. Eighteen men were on watch every night. Seven belonged to the jurisdiction of Clisson, the eleven others did not, but because of the situation were temporarily compelled to fulfill that function. Assuming one tour of duty each month, 540 men were needed to guard the town at night. The rear watch required four men and four soldiers. By day, each of the two gates was guarded by four men and two soldiers. In Annecy in 1476, one guard by day and two at night mounted watch at each gate. Thus, more men were needed at night than during the day.

The frequency of service does not appear to have been set with great precision at the outset of the Hundred Years War. When hostilities flared, the inhabitants who had taken refuge inside fortresses did not grumble at long and frequent nocturnal duty, for their existence was at stake. But during truces, they showed much less enthusiasm. They had little desire to "wake the whole night, from which they lost their work the next day," for their need for rest made it impossible to do their usual work; and when they did not fulfill their watch duties, they were reluctant to pay the fine for absence. The kings of France tried to deal with this difficulty by intervening frequently to fix the length of service. Finally, on December 1, 1451, in Poitiers, Charles VII decided that every subject would have to be on watch only twelve times a year, that is, once a month, but those who had lesser obligations could not have them increased, according to a decree of April 1479.

Every household was thus obliged to provide a man for the watch, but difficulties sometimes arose. Some households, of widows for example, might be without men, others contain men unable or unwilling to perform the service. There were legal procedures to avoid the watch, namely, replacement, exchange, and subscription.

- *Replacement.* This was a matter of finding someone able to perform the service in place of the absent man. The ordinance of Caboche even tried to institutionalize the practice, since it permitted a son to replace his father, a servant to take the place of his master, and more generally any man having the necessary abilities to fulfill the functions of another. The ordinance, which we know was of brief duration, codified well-established practices. Around 1392, Colin Ayraud, "as valet and servant of Regnaut Alizea de la Chavonnière, stood watch for several nights in the castle of Bressuire." Often, paying a certain sum of money was enough to find a replacement. But the money had to be paid, or else suit was sometimes brought by those who had stood watch and had not received the reward promised for carrying out their task.

- *Exchange.* Less frequent, this consisted in an exchange between people belonging to the same jurisdiction or to neighboring jurisdictions. For example, Hugues Moricet, a cattle worker in Lezay, would normally stand watch in the castle of Lezay, while Jehan Brun owed the same service in Le Marais. They changed places, because Moricet lived near Le Marais and Jehan Brun near Lezay. Of course, authorization of the captains turned out to be indispensable, but they usually agreed when the replacements seemed able to perform their functions. However, replacement and exchange had the drawback of involving strangers. Captains therefore sometimes preferred to choose replacements themselves, obviously at the expense of the absent men.

- *Subscription.* We have previously observed that toward the middle of the fifteenth century the jurisdiction of Bressuire was able to supply more men for the watch than protection of the castle called for. In such circumstances, the lord tended to ask for a sum of money, in place of the watch, from the men whom he did not need. Thus a part of the population was obliged to subscribe, to pay a fee to the lord. In 1421, the subscribers in the jurisdiction of Bressuire each paid twenty sous, a bushel of oats, and a pair of chickens. To limit abuses, in a decree of December 1, 1451, Charles VII decided that absence would be compensated for by a sum of ten deniers of Tours. Since the same document prescribed monthly service, the annual subscription amounted to ten sous, and after the 1479 decree to five sous.

The men of the watch considered up to this point remained within legal bounds. They paid for a replacement, changed places with a neighbor, or were forced to subscribe. Some, however, tried fraudulently to avoid service on the watch. If their machinations were discovered, they were obviously penalized.

The decree of 1364 of Jean the Good devotes a long section to fraud, proof that if it was not universal, it was at least relatively frequent. It states that when mounted sergeants become aware that some men of the watch have gone to bed or about their own business, they are allowed to imprison the other members of the watch group so that a report could later be made to the provost. This order had not been carried out for a certain period because of the bad conduct of two clerks of the watch, Pierre Grosparmi and Guillaume Pommero, who took money from the men who owed guard duty to exempt them. Since then, standing guard had been "discontinued," both by the craftsmen and by the sergeants on horseback or on foot, which had brought about many disorders that obviously had to be brought to a halt. The king therefore, wishing to restore tranquility in his fair city of Paris, ordered that the previous regulations be applied. Grosparmi and Pommero would be dismissed and replaced by other clerks, with wages of twelve deniers a day each, and they were required to swear allegiance to the provost of Paris and the captain of the watch. The clerks would advise the men who were on watch to be in the Châtelet before the hour of curfew, and they could not be excused from that obligation, except for the reasons already mentioned, and on condition that they made known the cause of their absence. Each of the clerks would have a large paper and would record on one the names and nicknames of the craftsmen, and on the other the captain of the watch or his lieutenant, and the sergeants on horseback or on foot. Once that was done, they would distribute the men of the watch from the crafts in the manner already indicated and the sergeants on horseback or on foot according to the orders of the captain or his lieutenant. In case of the absence without legitimate reason of a sergeant on horseback or on foot, they would put someone in his place, and the replacement would receive the absent man's twelve deniers. And because several had been found carrying out a false watch, it was required that the watch, both mounted and on foot, present itself in summer at the hour that curfew was rung in Notre-Dame, and in winter at nightfall; at that time the watch would be expected to leave the Châtelet. If the royal watch, going through the streets and squares supposed to be guarded during the night, found one of the craftsmen's watch absent without a legitimate reason, his companions would be obliged to state the names of the defaulters so that they might be punished the next day by the provost of Paris. The captain, or a competent person in his place, would be on duty every night; and the sergeants on horseback or on foot who failed to appear for the watch would lose the wages due for the night on which they were absent. The clerks would give the names of defaulters each month to the captain, and he would pass them on under seal to the treasurer of Paris. The clerks were forbidden to take money for exempting a man of the watch, under penalty of a charge of misappropriation.

Defaults showed up in every region. They resulted in a fine, except for the cases enumerated in the 1364 decree, and provided sufficient notice had been given. These fines for defaulting could be more or less heavy. In Chauvigny in 1369, there was a sliding scale: two sous and six deniers for missing the watch, five sous for the rear watch, and seven sous for the guard. But all towns did not apply the same scale. Royal decrees themselves exhibited a similar variety; thus the charge for default set in 1424 at two sous and six deniers was only five deniers in 1479.

Fines were designed to pay for replacements. But many captains held on to them, and these profits sometimes were used to pay them, in whole or in part. Some of them even used extortion on defaulters. In 1463, the captain of the Marais took a silver cup from Pierre Girart because he had not done his duty; Girart paid his debt and recovered his cup. The king was obliged to decree severe measures "because the captains of several cities, castles, and fortresses have caused great prejudice to the people, because they have taken and raised exactions in the form of ransom, because of the watch." In December 1373, Charles V ordered the captains of his fortresses to swear that they would no longer tolerate such profits and would return all their seizures, and "they will take as a fine for defaulting only fourteen deniers in coins worth four Parisian deniers, which will be used to pay other men of the watch, without the captains receiving any profit."

Sometimes, the men charged with ensuring the tranquility of their fellow citizens disturbed public order. In a decree during the week of Brandons in 1311, the Parlement de Paris sentenced Pierre le Hatecourt, a mounted sergeant, to dismissal, a fine of twenty livres, and a year in prison in the Châtelet for having subjected a bourgeois to violence.

On July 9, 1413, between eleven and midnight, as the guard was keeping watch according to its custom around the residence of the duke of Guyenne, the captain of Paris went up into the living quarters, and finding the duke in the midst of a ball, stigmatized his conduct, which he called scandalous. Then he blamed the Sire de la Trémoille for being responsible for such behavior. Insults, a brawl. The captain, named Léon de Jacqueville, received three knife blows in the chest. Then the men of the watch, informed of the events, and that Georges de la Trémoille had called the Parisians villains, rebels, and traitors, came running like furies, sword in hand, got into the building by forcing the doors, and they would have massacred several lords had the duke of Burgundy not calmed them.

In these circumstances, the watch became a practice that was less and less tolerated by the inhabitants who in some cases ended up by rebelling. The men of Archigny refused to stand watch in the castle that the bishop of Poitiers owned in Chauvigny or to pay the fines for absence. The captain, along with a few soldiers, went to their parish and saw about fifty inhabitants in a meadow. As he addressed them, they insulted him, and blows were exchanged. In the struggle one of the rebels was killed.

In a less violent register, men of the watch tried to escape from their obligations or at least attempted to make them less onerous. Some spent the night, or part of the night, playing cards or boules. On a bitter night in the winter of 1418–1419, instead of wandering through the icy streets of the town, the rear watch of Bressuire chose to play cards in the home of Nicolas Aureyau. As for Jehan Verdier, saddlemaker, inhabitant of the same town, one night in 1417, he simply went home to bed instead of standing watch at Juilleau tower.

It goes without saying that, when they discovered such behavior, the men of the counter-watch intervened, sometimes very forcefully. In Rouen, they confiscated the weapons of a sleeping member of the watch, if it was a first offense; after a second offense, the man was thrown to the bottom of the wall (unless the document can be interpreted in another way, and they threw not the man but his weapons off the ramparts); on the third offense, he was brought before the municipal authorities. But such practices were not current in all regions.

In Paris, the results were not very convincing. Service on the watch was very ill tolerated and default was frequent—moreover, there were complaints about having to inform the captain of the reason for an absence, because a wife would be exposed to danger during an absence at night—as was fraud. And yet the capital was divided into sectors, at the head of which were *quarteniers, cinquanteniers,* and *dizainiers* charged with seeing to the execution of measures taken by the municipality, which, in a sense, the members of the watch represented. The security of Parisians was thus not ensured in a strict fashion. *Le Bourgeois de Paris* even notes humorously that, to complete his rounds, a captain of the watch named Gautier Rollart, had three or four fiddlers go before him playing their instruments, seeming to say to the malefactors, "Run away, I'm coming."

There were weak results in Paris, and yet the capital was well endowed compared to other cities, but the insufficiency of personnel did not permit really rigorous supervision. Security did not seem to be in the hands of a really professional structure; it relied above all on the structures of the neighborhood and the family.

We can add that in wartime, when the city was under siege, the men of the watch—like the gatekeepers during the day—were incapable of defending it. At night they could only repair the breaches made by the enemy during the day, and they were of use only because of their numbers. They turned out to be unable to use bows or artillery pieces. They did nothing but warn the inhabitants when they saw something suspicious in the environs. When this signal corresponded to a serious danger, the authorities sounded the alarm, and men subject to mobilization went to their assigned places. When insecurity was persistent, the watch and the rear watch tired men out and prompted them to give the alarm rashly. The crowd then streamed into the street, armed, not really knowing the reason, and it was difficult to get people to return home. On the other hand, when calm persisted, attention relaxed, men refused to carry out a hard duty, and they were no longer able to confront a possible danger.

Cities were thus rather badly guarded, so that some attacks happened by surprise—admittedly, often with the help of traitors living in the city—and brigands had no qualms about robbing or killing good bourgeois who were imprudent enough to leave their houses for dark, narrow, and often unsafe streets.

Furthermore, fires of the time were as frequent and as intense as those of the high Middle Ages. The watch could give the alarm for accidental fires, or even for criminal ones if they were individual acts. Of course, it could do little when enemies penetrated the city by surprise and set fire to houses to spread fear and panic among the inhabitants as they destroyed their belongings.

Penalties

Night, as we have seen, played a major role in the imagination. Whether or not violence really occurred, the fear caused by darkness led to severe penalties against nocturnal offenses. Night was thus an aggravating circumstance. Malefactors were not merely infringing the rules of public order; acting under cover of darkness, they were demonstrating their evil intentions, their deep perversity, and premeditation. Speaking of the private life of Louis d'Orléans, brother of Charles VI, *Le Bourgeois de Paris* declares that it was shameful by day as well as by night, but goes on to say that at night it was a greater sin.

The judicial authorities therefore sentenced criminals who acted by night more severely, providing for special treatment. The law of the Visigoths had already done so for anyone who killed or stole a horse, a cow, or any other animal at night or in secret. The treaty that established a division of jurisdiction between the lord of Yzeron and the archbishop of Lyon included a particular clause relating to crimes committed at night, the fines for which were to be shared between the judicial authorities.

The accused tried to show that the crime with which they had been charged had not been committed at night, thereby indicating that it was an aggravating circumstance. At Easter 1308, the Parlement de Paris issued a decision concerning a dispute between Conrad Bouvel, a merchant from Florence, on one side, and the provost of Paris and the captain of the watch on the other. It involved a seizure by the watch from Bouvel of three bundles of weapons. Bouvel maintained that the seizure had taken place by day. The provost and the captain asserted to the contrary that the bundles had been taken during the night, as Bouvel was having them transported out of the kingdom. Since the investigation showed that the seizure had taken place in daylight, the court released the weapons.

Jean Gérond, a *macelier* in Lozanne, convicted of having stolen an ax, confessed the theft—unavoidably since it had been found in his house—but he asserted that he had taken it during the day. Jean Combes was accused of having bought stolen firewood from an accomplice. He admitted the facts, but specified that the transaction had not taken place at night but during the day. In fact, had he admitted that the sale had taken place at night he would thereby have confessed his knowledge of the illicit source of the firewood.

"Night has no shame," says the captain to the Jouvencel. And, indeed, at night it was easier to conceal one's identity and to play on people's terror. The monk of Saint-Denis reports that one night, under cover of darkness—this happened in 1382—the doors of the houses of the richest bourgeois of Paris were marked with various signs, which justifiably increased their terror, especially because they did not know if the perpetrators were internal insurgents or external enemies who had made the marks for easy recognition of the best opportunities for looting. The same author states that civil laws legitimate killing those who destroy knighthood, highway robbers, and anyone found in one's house at night.

The notion that night is an aggravating circumstance was persistent. Dealing with a robbery committed in 1829, the royal court of Nîmes issued the following decision: "Considering the reasons the legislator had to characterize robbery at night as a crime, while it would be a misdemeanor without that circumstance. . . . It is easier for a thief to steal at night; the darkness of night, the silence of night, encourage it, in concert with the rest which the other citizens are taking at this time, along with the threat to life incurred by the owners of stolen goods, if they surprise the thief in the act and want to stop him or merely recognize him and prevent him from carrying out his theft."

OBSERVATION

The techniques for taming the night mentioned up to this point relate to the material realm. They were supplemented on the intellectual level by the scrutiny given by the men of the Middle Ages to nocturnal phenomena.

Study

In an age when miracles seemed to be natural, when reason left room for imagination, people were struck by the wonders that could indeed occur by day just as much as by night. To them, these phenomena contained a symbolic message.

The *Chronique du règne de Charles VI*, written by a monk of the abbey of Saint-Denis, notes that a week before the uprising of the Maillotins in 1382, day and night could be seen a brilliant globe of fire flitting from door to door above the city of Paris. On July 10, 1396, toward the fourth hour of the night, in the bishopric of Maguelone, a comet of considerable size and extraordinary brightness glowed in the sky, while five small stars rotated around it and collided with it several times. After this kind of battle, there appeared a man of fire, mounted on a bronze horse and armed with a lance shooting flames; he struck the comet and suddenly disappeared.

In the middle of the night, men at arms in garrison in Guyenne were awakened several times by a noise. Looking at the sky, they saw armed horsemen engaged in battle. Troubled, they sent the son of the master of the crossbow men to the king of France to report the phenomenon and obtain an explanation. Then experts of obvious merit and deep science declared that the prodigy that had occurred in the Maguelone region foretold the deposition of the pope by the king and the clergy—this was the period of the

Great Schism when the Church was led by two popes, one in Avignon, the other in Rome—while the second foretold wars and massacres. The monk of Saint-Denis, for his part, declares that only God knows the explanation for these supernatural phenomena; however, he goes on to say that, when history is consulted, similar prodigies have always foretold great events.

On June 17, 1406, between six and seven in the morning, just after sunrise, a dense cloud coming from the north spread rapidly over the whole surface of the ground and so darkened the sun that for around a half hour the brightness of day was changed into deep night. Astrologers had predicted the day and hour of the eclipse, and asserted that the phenomenon foretold something extraordinary. The bad weather that followed and disorders of all kinds that appeared in the heavens justified their predictions, for a week later, furious winds came up and a frightful storm broke, containing hail of the size of goose eggs.

These prodigies, to which men were sensitive throughout the Middle Ages—we could cite many examples drawn from the *Gesta Francorum* by Gregory of Tours—suggest a few remarks. People were attentive to anything that went on in the sky, and certain phenomena seemed all the more terrifying because they occurred at night. Considering the last example, it seems that not only did the imagination play a role, but science was not absent. Astrologers—in this case we might say astronomers—predicted the day and hour of the eclipse. They appear to have been genuine scientists in the current sense of the term. Obviously, the consequences they drew from the phenomenon demonstrate that they did not yet possess the scientific rigor required of present-day scientists.

In any event, the sky was observed at night as well as by day. In what manner did men of science talk about the night? The sky could be a subject of serious study; the *Images du monde* had increasing success from the twelfth century on. Authors gave the sky more space than the earth, like Gossouin, who devoted thirty-six chapters to the sky, almost twice as much as the nineteen devoted to the earth, in the three books of his *Image du monde*, the first version of which, in three parts, was composed in 1246. The world may have been compartmentalized, but it was open above, so that the inhabitants of cities and monks in their cloisters could every day contemplate half the canopy of heaven. Night appeared much more spacious than day. Gossouin presented a picture of the wise looking at "the firmament that turned around the whole world and moved" and watching "many nights and many days" to see "the stars that rose in the east and started moving above their heads. . . they thus watched many nights and were not bored, they thus found much joy in seeing the firmament turning so magnificently."

Scientists and scholars scrutinized the stars and their movements, but travelers also observed them to show them the way. Indeed, everyone watched the sky, for, without clocks, it was a way of telling time as well as seeing the coming weather.

This is how the writers of the thirteenth century explained the alternation between day and night. The sun rotating around the round earth illuminated only one hemisphere. The earth, much smaller than the sun, generated a conic shadow in space. If you could see stars only at night, this was because in daylight their weak light was annihilated by the brightness of the sun. The stars resembled candles set behind a large fire.

The sky and the stars influenced the things of this world.

> The sky and the stars are
> The instrument of nature above
> By which it works ceaselessly
> As God wills . . .

The influence of the stars was recognized, as was that of the moon on the system of humors and on the tides.

The dialogue of *Placides et Timeo*, a late thirteenth-century prose encyclopedia, is instructive. The sun is the only source of light; when the sun is not above us, it is night; the way in which it illuminates the moon, which varies according to its position in relation to that body, explains the different phases.

"Placides: What? the sun is, in this world, the only source of light. And yet fire is light.

"Timeo: Not at all. All light comes from the sun. The earth, in itself, is dark, and the animals living within have no eyes. The same is true of water which does not light up the air at night. Air does not illuminate: shut yourself up in a vaulted room without windows. Nor is fire light in itself; in fact, out of the presence of air, it is unable to illuminate, and nothing is blacker than smoke; the truth is that fire has the property of putting solar light in reserve better than the other elements."

Two passages in the *chanson Aye d'Avignon,* an anonymous *chanson de geste* composed *c.* 1200, manifest an interest in the course of the stars. There is a navigator who relies on the stars:

> They are all Saracens . . .
> They have come by sea, navigating by the stars.

And there is a young Frank, captured and raised by a Saracen king who has inculcated in him some notions of astronomy. From practice, we move to theoretical knowledge.

> Ganor the Arab feeds the child well . . .
> The king has him learn
> Chess and the tables
> And the course of the stars.

In both cases the Saracens, whom *La Chanson de Roland* presents as skillful nighttime navigators, are the source of this examination of the sky.

But the stars, the sun, and the moon had first of all a utilitarian function, since they permitted the measurement of time. In *Berte aus grans piés,* the heroine gets lost in the forest of Le Mans. Thanks to the moon, she can keep track of the passage of the days. The clever leader able to predict bright moonlight can use it to fight the enemy. In *Le Roman de Laurin,* the marquis de Narbonne is defending the town of Marques and thinks that the rising of the moon will allow him to attack the king of Syria: "The moon is full and it will rise. Let us make a sortie for we can cause them injury."

The eye, which made sight possible, could be compared to the sun because it, too, was thought to emit rays. The great period of ophthalmology in the Middle Ages occurred between the ninth and eleventh centuries, with centers in Baghdad and Cairo, and later in Salerno and Toledo. Hunain ibn Ishaq, who was active in Baghdad in the ninth century, was the most renowned scientist. Beginning in the eleventh century, treatises written in Arabic were translated into Hebrew and Latin. Thereafter, compilations and commentaries proliferated.

Although the anatomy of the eye was well known, its physiology was much less so, and the treatises contain many errors which were to last until the eighteenth century. The crystalline lens was considered the essential organ of vision, the place where the image took form. The other elements of the eye had the sole purpose of serving and protecting it, just as the sun and the planets rotated around the earth to supply mankind with light and the sense of time. The second error was the belief that a visual spirit formed in the brain was carried by hollow nerves to the crystalline lens. There it blended with light coming from external objects, and thus vision was created.

Ibn al Haytham, known in the West as Alhazen (965–1039), attempted to demonstrate that light did not come from the eye. Experiments proved that rays that moved from objects toward the eye created vision, and not the reverse. As Marie-Thérèse Lorcin notes, his work had little influence. For Western scientists, the eye emitted something, thereby creating vision. It therefore had an active, not a passive role.

The sky was considered more with wonder than with fear. Guillaume de Conches compared the stars to precious stones set in gold. Gossouin de Metz spoke of "sweet melody" and "some used to say that little children heard this melody when they laughed in their sleep."

Representation

What procedures did artists use to evoke night? The creation of day and night described at the beginning of the book of Genesis, and the biography of Christ, who was born, was betrayed, and died at night, made it impossible to evade the question of night.

The liturgical drama that flourished in the tenth and eleventh centuries came directly from the mass. In the church, worshipers

became spectators and contemplated a series of scenes unfold-
ing in places that had taken on material form; the crypt became
a tomb, the altar a crèche.

In the crypt or the chancel of the church, natural light was
very limited, and fire therefore burned all the more brightly. This
fire that glowed or went out, and the veil that hid or, on rising,
revealed the cross were the essential scenic devices. Putting out
the lights one by one during the Good Friday service permitted
the creation of darkness, symbol of the death of Jesus. The cross
open to view and then covered by a veil had the same meaning.

In the semi-liturgical drama that flourished in the second half
of the twelfth century and in the thirteenth century, staging
became so complicated that it had to be moved from the chancel
or the nave. The stage of the sacred theater and of the secular
theater coming into being at the time was no longer inside a building, so that representation of the night turned out to be much
more difficult.

In the open air and in daylight, realism was excluded. Additional light had to be used symbolically. In *La Passion du Pala-
tinus*, a mystery play of the fourteenth century, one of the four
knights set by Caiaphas around the holy sepulcher to resist the
resurrection of Christ is paralyzed by the light given off by the
angel sent by God the Father to deliver his Son from death.

A scene might be considered nocturnal to the extent that it
contained a reference to darkness or to a nocturnal source of light
like moon or stars. The record of expenditures for *Le Mystère de
la Passion* performed in Mons in 1501 indicates that after the per-
formance a piece of cloth used to represent the sun and the moon
had been sold for twenty-two sous and two deniers. Pieces of cloth
and curtains could be used to symbolize both light and darkness;
for example, a half-white half-black cloth could represent God's
separation of light from darkness at the creation of the world. But
it was language that was best adapted to handle the nuances of
the nocturnal. Characters mentioned the darkness surrounding
them, called for light, or declared their intent to look for it. A
single element—black dye or the moon—was enough to confirm
the text. On the psychological level, there was evidence of a grow-

ing desire for realism in the representation of night in both theater and painting.

Pictorial representation of the night evolved in the course of
the Middle Ages.* At first, night took on the appearance of an
allegorical figure standing near the principal figure. For example,
in "Isaiah's Prayer" from the *Psaultier de Paris* (tenth century),
Nyx appears in the form of a woman wearing a violet dress and
carrying an inverted torch. Above her head haloed in midnight
blue floats a veil symbolizing the nocturnal vault of heaven. The
colors manifest the presence of night, which in the Middle Ages
was not represented in black but in blue, dark, to be sure, but
clearly distinguishable from black. Indeed, the term used was
"midnight blue."

Paintings representing night long contained symbolic elements. In an illumination by the Maître des Heures of Boucicaut
and a collaborator, Saint Christopher is represented leaning at the
door of a house holding a lantern. Only the lantern and the starry
sky suggest darkness.

From the Carolingian era on, all miniatures place the cross of
the Crucifixion between the sun and the moon. The burial in the
Très Riches Heures du duc de Berry contains crepuscular lighting with the moon. The same manuscript contains a splendid
nocturne in the arrest of Jesus with a scattering of stars in a steel
blue sky and perhaps above Christ's halo a shooting star taking
the place of the moon.

The clouds of night were a first attempt to give material form
to darkness. They appear, hiding the sun and the moon on either
side of the cross during the Crucifixion in several works by the
Maître des Heures of Boucicaut.

Painters and playwrights seemed to develop in tandem.
Largely free from the constraints of realism, their imagination
accepted a night in which objects were seen as in daylight. Indeed,
painters such as Jean Yvonnet and Jean Fouquet were given the
task of making sets for some plays.

---

* Profound thanks to Mme. Danièle Alexandre Bidon, who was kind enough to send
me many slides which it is unfortunately impossible to reproduce in this book.

But while playwrights did not know how to resolve the conflict between nocturnal action and the daylight of the stage, painters discovered shadow and its pictorial virtues, and they tended toward realism by making the painting darker, emphasizing contrasts between shadow and light, and hiding what night concealed. In the fifteenth century, the *Dream of Constantine*, a fragment of *The Legend of the Cross* by Piero della Francesca, and an illumination by the Master of the *Livre du Coeur d'Amour épris*, which represents Love giving to Desire the heart of the sleeping René d'Anjou, provide good illustrations of this remark. In both cases, there is a sleeper wearing a nightcap and an artificial source of light located in the painting: a radiant angel descending through the air on the left and extending a hand to Constantine, a night light on the lower right providing low-angled light.

Nocturnes dealt above all with the life of Christ, birth (the Annunciation and the Visit of the Shepherds) and death. In his *Rational des divins offices*, Guillaume Durand (c. 1230–1296), bishop of Mende, places great emphasis on the darkness at the death of Christ. He writes that "the sun reddening because of the sin of mankind was covered with darkness during the passion." It is noteworthy that all painters in the late Middle Ages cast darkness not only over the arrest and death of Jesus but also over the flight into Egypt—was this a helpful night?—and the Resurrection.

Darkness is sometimes absolute. For example, in a miniature from the *Livre du Coeur d'Amour épris*, two men are speaking; only the armor of one of them and the horse's harness glow by the light of the moon.

Wonder

Were the people of the Middle Ages sensitive to the beauty of the night? Iconography and literature suggest that they were.

The manuscript of the *Coeur d'Amour épris* contains an image of an early morning sun still enveloped in the darkness of night. The early fifteenth century has remarkable examples of dawns with radiant rising suns.

The dominance of day and the value placed on light did not prevent writers from sometimes celebrating night with great intensity, as in these two nocturnes from *La Chanson de Roland.* The poet describes the Saracen fleet sailing toward Spain by night.

> On the high prows, at the top of the masts,
> The carbuncles and the lanterns are numerous:
> From above they cast such light
> That all night the sea is more beautiful;
> When they reach the land of Spain,
> The whole country is lit up and glowing.

Beauty of the sky is described purely for its splendor, with no concern for any marvel. Later, during the night when the city of Saragossa is taken, the brightness of the moon and stars seems to be in concert with the conversion of the pagans to the light of Christianity.

> Day goes off and night has fallen;
> The moon is bright and the stars glitter.
> The emperor has taken Saragossa. . . .
> The king believes in God and wants to serve Him,
> And his bishops bless the waters,
> And they lead the pagans to the font. . . .
> . . . Night goes off, bright day appears

CHAPTER 4

Activities

N̶ight, given over to sleep, ought not to have been disturbed by any activity. And yet—aside from nocturnal violence—it was at least partially filled with both work and diversion.

WORK

Schedules

In principle, all work was prohibited, in particular because the artificial light of candles posed the risk of making mistakes and thus badly serving clients. *Le Livre des Métiers* by Étienne Boileau, provost of Paris toward the end of the reign of Saint Louis, makes this explicit. For example, "beaters of silver and gold cannot work at night, for the light at night is insufficient for them to ply their trade well and truly." There were royal decrees along the same lines. Nevertheless, it should not be imagined that the city was dead at night and that, loyal and obedient, artisans abandoned their workshops as soon as curfew was rung to go home to eat and sleep. To begin with, the regulations of a certain number of crafts did not include a clearly formulated prohibition. Others were authorized to carry out absolutely necessary nighttime work. Finally, there were those who violated the regulations.

Bakers had to deliver fresh bread and brioches in the morning, and surgeons had to treat the injured even on Sundays. Ovens for glass making could not be allowed to go out in Venice or in any other city with that industry. A letter of remission from 1476 referring to a glass-making operation located in Bichat in Poitou shows that this kind of work never stopped. Eight years earlier, when he was thirteen or fourteen and employed as a worker in this glass-making business belonging to Étienne Fouet, François Simonneau worked at the oven day and night. One day around prime, François dropped a large piece of wood that he was bringing to feed the fire on the head of Marquis Musset who was dozing near the oven.

The glovemakers of Poitiers were fined for working at their craft at night, but they had permission to dry their hides and to "prepare them with lime."

In addition to necessity, there were the privileges enjoyed by important personages who had no wish to wait. No goldsmith could work at night, except for the king, the royal family, and the bishop of Paris, or with the permission of the masters of the craft guild. This provision of *Le Livre des Métiers* was repeated by Jean II the Good in August 1355.

In 1431, a Parisian artisan returned home around eight or nine at night, perhaps because of urgent work that had to be finished after curfew, unless "the said petitioner who had been earning his living" had decided to stop at a tavern and stay for a while.

It is not always simple to establish a distinction between daytime and nighttime activity. In principle, work began at sunrise or an hour later and ended when the lights were put out, that is, at curfew or when compline was rung. But there was a great variety of situations. Curfew was rung at six in winter, at seven in summer. Various criteria were adopted to establish the boundaries of daytime work. From Easter to Saint-Rémi, tannery workers set the rising and the setting of the sun as the limits of the working day for summer, and for winter, the moment when there was not enough light to distinguish a denier of Tours from a denier of Paris. Regulation and practice were thus less rigid than might at first appear.

It is true that craft guilds themselves sometimes requested authorization to work outside the bounds of the legal day. Surprisingly, this was especially the case for the workers. Lengthening the work day allowed for overtime and thus for higher wages. An edict of Arras of 1315 indicates that a commission including delegates of both master clothmakers and fuller workers authorized the latter, at their request, to work "longer days," in order to obtain "higher" wages. To be sure, to justify this decision, reference was made to an increase in the weight and the dimensions of fabric. But was it not rather a means for workers to fight against price increases and the loss of purchasing power of wages because of the currency changes of Philippe le Bel? It is rather surprising to note that this king permitted work at night. On January 19, 1322, Gilles Haquin, provost of Paris, confirmed these edicts, citing the following passage: "Item. Of the crafts of Paris who say that according to their old records that no one may work at night . . . that they may work day and night when they see that it will be good."

As for the masters, they were just as concerned as their workers with the length of the working day. As Jacques Le Goff has shown, to counter the workers' cheating, they tried to regulate that day. For this purpose, work bells, *Werkglocken*, were installed. For example, in 1335, Philippe VI de Valois allowed the mayor and magistrates of Amiens to "ring a bell that they have hung in the belfry of the said town which is different from the other bells" to indicate "when the workers of the said town and its environs would go each working day to their work in the morning . . . and also in the evening, when they should leave their work." The problem was particularly acute in the textile trades in which wages made up a significant proportion of production costs. Indeed, places in which cloth making played a lesser role did not have such a bell.

The length of the working day—and hence the problem of night work—was thus at the heart of relations between bosses and workers. The former, who now saw working time precisely set by the bells, tried to lengthen it.

In 1467, the master glovemakers informed the king that they had to stop work at four or five in the afternoon in winter, at a time when demand was greatest and expenses highest. They requested authorization to work from five in the morning until ten at night. The king accepted the arguments and granted their request. To convince Louis XI, the glovemakers also noted the idleness of the workers! "With this their apprentices and workers are idle and by this apply and occupy themselves, during this time when they have no occupation, from the said four or five o'clock until the next day, with various games and dissipations, and hardly want to apply themselves to do well, which is the interest of the commonwealth." It can indeed be noted that the authorizations given in the late fifteenth and early sixteenth centuries reflect a longstanding situation. The shoemakers who asked for permission to work by candlelight in 1514 asserted that the prohibition of night work had not been respected for many years in the trade.

Night work might also be related to the worker's situation. An employer had more effective ways of pressuring a worker hired for a long period than one hired by the day.

Conflicts

While it was in the interest of employers to lengthen the working day—at least to the extent compatible with the workers' good physical condition—the workers generally did not share this aim, preferring to spend the evening resting, in a tavern, or with their families. Hence there were conflicts. Particularly explicit was the one between the clothmakers and the fulling workers. In 1251, the two sides reached an agreement providing, among other things, that the workers would observe the traditional working hours.

In 1256, to prevent misunderstandings, it was agreed that four arbiters, two for the masters and two for the workers, would have the duty of watching over the condition of the guild—*Le Livre des Métiers* indicates that the workers had their *vesprée*, that is, that those who were hired for the day left their work at the first sound of the vespers bell from Notre-Dame during *charnage* (the time of year when meat could be eaten), and during fast times at the sound of compline. But twenty years later the workers informed the king that the masters made them work late at night, which was harmful to their health—"they said that the masters kept them too late from their *vesprées*, which was dangerous for them and greatly to the peril of their bodies." The masters retorted that they were merely following a regulation of Blanche de Castille. It was then provided—to avoid any misunderstanding—that the workers would obey this regulation to the letter, requiring them to work until twilight when they would cease all activity, and the masters had to release them.

Above all, it was a question of knowing at what time work came to an end. According to the Polish historian and political figure Bronislaw Geremek, at the time of their complaint, in 1277, the workers were having difficulty finding employment, so that the masters took advantage of the situation by abusively prolonging the working day.

The same problem was at the heart of the dispute between the master cloth-cutters and their workers in the fifteenth century. In 1407, the workers complained to the civil tribunal of the Châtelet "because of the night hours which they [their masters] force on the workers of the said craft." The masters were not violating the regulations, since the statute of 1348 provided that the working day began at midnight in winter. The workers were thus protesting as much against the regulations themselves as against the practices of their masters. After a suspension, the conflict resumed and reached a preliminary resolution in 1411. The statute of the cloth-cutters was upheld, but the workers had the right to a half-hour meal break at nine in the morning.

The master cutters were not satisfied and did not accept the 1411 judgment, on the pretext that it did not provide for sanctions. A further judgment, dated June 1415, following a trial before the provost of Paris, then prohibited night work in winter and set the limits of the working day in that season, that is, from November 1 to February 2, from six in the morning to five in the evening, or nine and a half hours of work, since a half hour was deducted for lunch and an hour for dinner. That is to say that night work was practically prohibited. The text of the judgment makes reference to the frequent disputes that broke out between masters and workers on the subject of the end of the working day.

In case of an infraction, the masters had to pay a twenty-sou fine, the workers ten sous. In short, modifying the 1348 statute, this judgment favored the workers by prohibiting night work.

It seems, however, that the masters did not respect this ruling over the course of the following years. Another document of August 1489 declares that work in winter must not begin before six in the morning nor end after seven at night. This was a retreat from the 1415 ruling; in winter, night had fallen by seven. Indeed it is possible, given the use of the expression "no longer than," that the masters sometimes kept their workers beyond these hours. But the conflict was still not at an end. In January 1490, the Parlement de Paris declared, among other orders, that workers were obliged to work beyond the hours set by the earlier statutes. That is to say that their attempts to avoid night work finally failed.

Conflicts were not limited to the capital nor to the textile sector. For example, between 1383 and 1393, the vineyard workers of Sens and Auxerre conducted a struggle before the Parlement de Paris against their ecclesiastical, noble, and bourgeois employers to shorten their working day. In this case, it was probably not merely a matter of getting some time to rest, but also of being able to work on their own land. A July 1383 decree of Charles VI for Sens in fact declares: "They abandon their work and leave between noon and nones or thereabouts, in particular long before the sun has set, and go to work on their vines or to do other work, and there they toil and carry out as much work as or even more than they have done for those who pay them; and what is more, in working for their employer, they pace themselves, without completing their task, in order to be more vigorous and less tired to work where they do after they have left."

In this case, we are dealing with artisans close to the land but connected to the town by their profession. One might say that the question of night work did not arise in the countryside. There was no question of working in the fields at night. On the other hand, at home by candlelight, peasants, and even more their wives, could complete minor tasks which, not occupying their minds, allowed them to amuse themselves at the same time.

In short, even though the condition of the workers was not as miserable as that of the unfortunate weavers of silken cloth imagined by Chrétien de Troyes around 1168,

> And we are in great poverty,
> But riches from our virtues
> Go to the one we work for.
> We wake a great part of the night
> And all day to earn them . . .

it is nevertheless true that too frequently in the Middle Ages the working day had in reality no fixed limits. To be sure, statutes were enacted. Bells at work represented progress, but the employers had control over them. The church tower or belfry clock, however, made it possible to verify the time.

In this period when social legislation was embryonic, relations between employers and workers depended above all on a way of being; and masters could have very diverse attitudes according to their temperament or their thirst for wealth.

In a somewhat paradoxical way, unemployed workers vitalized certain neighborhoods before the start of the working day, for example in squares like the place de Grève in Paris, where day laborers were hired: "that all manner of people, men and women, who are accustomed to do or carry out work or labor . . . go before sunrise to the usual places where workers are hired, to hire themselves out," declares a decree of 1354.

Activities other than craft work, ordinarily done during the day, could take place at night, like hunting and fishing. To be sure, both, and particularly hunting, were leisure activities for aristocrats. But they also had, particularly in the case of fishing, some degree of utilitarian purpose. It was a matter of obtaining food, and night was sometimes a propitious time to do so. An act of Charles the Bald of 869 mentions that the monks of Saint-Evre de Toul will have the right to use the bishop's fishery in Pierre two nights a week. The same authorization was granted by Otto I in 947. A miniature in the *Livre du Coeur d'Amour épris* represents a nocturnal scene of fishing on an islet.

Thus physical work did not entirely stop at night. This was all the more true of intellectual work. Jean de Garlande (c. 1195– c. 1272), a professor in Toulouse and Paris, enumerates in his dictionary all the tools needed by every member of the university guild in the thirteenth century. He mentions in a prominent place "a night lamp with tallow and a candle holder, a lantern."* Studies at the university in Poitiers began at six in winter and, from mid-March on, at five with the daily lecture of the titular professor. A serious student would have to rise early and at night he continued to work by candlelight.

Notaries who practiced their profession in France by pontifical privilege were authorized to work after curfew, so that the young scribes employed in their offices sometimes remained bent over their scrolls very late at night. Legal activities were thus carried out at night in towns, while hoodlums prowled the streets in search of mischief, and monks or pious laymen gave thanks to God, or people amused themselves.

Distractions

Nocturnal activities included leisure as well as work. Nighttime distractions seem to belong to two categories. Some are nocturnal by definition, like evening gatherings and bonfires; others prolong daytime enjoyments, like parties.

Evening Gatherings

In the country, women liked to get together in the evening to gossip while carrying out minor domestic tasks, in particular in the écraignes of which Tabourot des Accords gave an invaluable description in the sixteenth century. "In all the land of Burgundy," he writes, "even in the good towns, because they are populated by

---

* "Alone at night, with a book illuminated by a candle—book and candle, dual island of light, against the dual darkness of the mind and the night" (Gaston Bachelard, *La Flamme d'une chandelle* [Paris, 1961], p. 54).

many poor winemakers who do not have the means to buy wood to defend themselves against the rigors of winter, much harsher here than in the rest of France, necessity the mother of the arts led to the creation in some out of the way street of a small room or building made up of several poles stuck in a circle in the ground, the upper parts bent, so that they have the form of the top of a hat, which is then covered with many clumps of earth and with manure so well mixed as to be impenetrable. In this room, between two poles, on the side best protected from the wind, a little opening one foot wide and two feet high is left as an entryway, and all around are cloth seats so that several people can sit down. There, generally after dinner, the prettiest daughters of these winemakers gather with their distaffs and other work; and they stay there until midnight."

A document of 1390 makes earlier mention of these meeting places. On the Saturday after the last Christmas at around two in the morning, several young men went to Combertroux to enjoy themselves with the marriageable girls and the women spinning yarn in the *écraignes,* as was the custom in the winter for the young bachelors of the town and its environs. They went into an *écraigne* then, but young men of the village waited for them to come out and a brawl ensued.

Jacques Fournier, responsible for investigating the Cathar influence in the Pamiers region, questioned many male and female peasants in the region of Montaillou. His inquisition records are invaluable for an understanding of the life of the inhabitants of a village in the Ariège.* They vividly show how evenings were spent in the Pyrenees region. Here are some examples.

The first evening took place in Ascou, near Ax-les-Thermes. Raymond Sicre, who had just quarreled with his wife, went out to take a look at his flock. In the house of Pierre Amiel, who lived with his mother Rixende, he saw lights, so night had just fallen. Indiscreet, Raymond went in and listened without being noticed. The conversation was about dinner:

---

* See Emmanuel Le Roy Ladurie, *Montaillou, village occitan de 1294 à 1324* (Paris, 1975).

"I greatly fear," said Rixende to one of her guests, "that the bread I have made will not be to your liking, for we women of the mountains do not have fine sieves, nor do we know how to knead good bread."

"Not at all," replied her guest, "this bread is good and it has a fine appearance."

"If you like it, I am delighted."

"This cheese is good and pleasant," said another guest.

Since the guests also appreciated the fish, Rixende explained: "The man who brought them to me this evening gave me great pleasure, and Galharde, the wife of Guillaume d'Ascou as well, for she gave the oil to fry them in. She did it in secret; she is the best of women, but she is afraid of her husband."

"She is indeed a good woman," agreed a guest, "but her husband is a lout; this very evening he really bothered me."

"Yet he's a good man," retorted Rixende, "and he is very helpful."

And Jean Peyre Amiel added that he was a good neighbor who didn't go looking for quarrels.

"If Guillaume doesn't do any harm, that is a fine way to be," replied one of the guests, offering a carafe to Rixende. "Will you have something to drink?"

"No," she replied, "there is enough wine in another carafe. Don't worry about me. But serve yourself as you wish."

The conversation changed subject; it turned to the problems of the church.

"It would be good for the people of Ascou and Sorgeat to have a church of their own. They wouldn't have to go down to the church in Ax-les-Thermes."

"I don't agree. It's better that the people of Ascou have only the church in Ax. Otherwise, expenses would increase. In any case, the priests of Ax and elsewhere do not teach the people of Ascou as they should."

An opinion shared by another guest.

"The priests teach the people very little. Not even half the people of the village go to their sermons and understand something of what they are saying . . ."

These are the elements of an evening gathering in a little village in the Pyrenees in the early fourteenth century. Food is tasted. Neighbors are talked about in praise, sometimes in blame. They mention the absence of a church and they move on to a critique of the priests of the nearest parish—the two guests sitting on a bench in front of the fire were Cathar missionaries. Leaving his observation post, Raymond Sicre did not hear the rest of the conversation, but it probably moved on to talk in favor of Catharism.

In San Mateo, in the home of Guillemette Maury, a former inhabitant of Montaillou who had fled her village to escape the Inquisition, long evenings were spent by the fire after the evening meal. In addition to the hostess and her two sons, when they were not watching the flock, there were friends and relatives, *parfaits* who were passing through, and various other people, like beggars or wool carders working in Guillemette's shop.

They discussed varied subjects: the Cathar religion when they felt confident; other subjects when guests of the evening were not trusted. For example, they talked of former heretics, relations with the Inquisition, or more simply a son's marriage or the condition of the animals. In principle, the evening ended when the fire was banked, but some continued talking until cockcrow.

In Montaillou itself, Jean Maury, the pastor's brother, liked to gather friends and relatives at his house. A *parfait* attended, which drew the attention of the Inquisition. But aside from this presence, the evening passed in an ordinary way. For example, in 1307 or 1308, the participants in one evening were Jean's father and mother, his four brothers, his two sisters, and two *parfaits* who had arrived in the early evening. Jean Maury was twelve at the time; he recalled the scene in 1323. After taking care of the sheep, he came into the kitchen to join the others already there. At dinner, only the adult men, that is, the father and the eldest son, sat at the table with the two *parfaits*. The mother and two daughters served them. The younger sons ate near the fire. The simple meal included round loaves of bread and cabbage in oil. The men then sat on a bench; the mother, considered impure because of her sex, sat on another bench at some distance from the *parfaits*. The young children went to bed and were not present for the adults' discussions. However, Jean Maury did not leave the room immediately after dinner and was able to hear his father and one of the *parfaits* speak. He was then put to bed well before the evening reached its peak. In addition to his young age, it is worth noting that Jean had to get up early to take the sheep to pasture.

These peasant evenings in Montaillou took place by the light of the hearth. Only the bedrooms, outside the kitchen, sometimes required another light, supplied by a torch or a candle, for a call of nature, unless a full moon made that unnecessary. Evenings in Montaillou resembled in many respects those of other regions, but had a few characteristic traits—the role of the Cathar religion in the conversation, the limited consumption of wine.

Les Évangiles des Quenouilles presents old women who talk about everything, life, love, death, in the course of the long evenings between Christmas and Candlemas. They mention many recipes, more or less magical, which sometimes have night as an ingredient, in all some 230 popular beliefs widespread in Flanders and Picardy in the late fifteenth century.

Some of these beliefs have to do with the devil, incubi, or werewolves. While on Monday evening, the six neighbors meet between seven and eight, on Tuesday they get together as early as five. There, Dame Transeline du Croq, an adept of geomancy and a priest's concubine—"the priest of the town heard her confession day and night"—indicates in particular exorcisms to avoid the company of the devil or of incubi. "Whoever leaves at night a seat or stool with the feet above [that is, whoever has not turned over her seat before going to bed], so long is the enemy [the devil] riding on the house." "She who fears the nocturnal visit of the *quauquemaire* [incubus] in her bed, let her put an oak seat before a good fire and, if the incubus arrives and sits on it, he will not be able to get up before daylight." (See chapter 2 above).

The moon played a major role in these popular beliefs. On Wednesday evening, Abonde du Four, prostitute turned madam, teaches that, to win at a game of dice, you have to sit facing the moon. On Friday evening, Gomberde la Fae, suspected of heresy and a discreet procuress, declares that small children are conceived in the absence of the moon, for men then usually have a "lack of marrow." We also learn that, to obtain health and happiness, we must greet the moon when it is new, full, and waning.

Other maxims take up family problems. Whoever wants to have a son must conceive him in the morning, a daughter in the evening or at night. The superstitions presented in *Les Évangiles des Quenouilles* were sufficiently widespread to be part of conversation. Thus the ecclesiastical authorities, who were especially afraid of indecency, looked on these evenings with a certain degree of suspicion. A mandate of 1493 concerning the diocese of Saint-Brieuc attests to this. "Already in a previous synod, to put an end to inept and scandalous abuses that were very often occurring in meetings of the spinners, we had forbidden these meetings in our town and in the whole diocese, subject to the penalties decreed in the statutes of that synod. We know that this prohibition has been violated several times. This is why we specially renew those statutes, and we again prohibit all our subjects of whatever estate to hold these meetings of spinners, with dances, follies and excesses, to attend one or to appear at one, on penalty of excommunication, and for each transgression a fine of ten livres applied to our charities. We especially reserve the power of absolution for these penalties and we refuse it to any priest or chaplain."

These evenings were apparently not always confined to conversation, since young bachelors came to meet girls and women. The mandate, indeed, did not grant to simple priests absolution for the offense committed by meeting at night. Such commands had little effect, for evening gatherings continued to occur. In the eighteenth century, the civil authorities were concerned with them, apparently with no greater success.

We cannot conclude this survey without referring to death watches. Corpses, like young children, were the concern of women, who washed them and then watched over them. A dead man did not remain long under his own roof, rarely more than a day and a night. Certain testators—in the Comtat Venaissin—asked urgently that they be watched "a full night," "the night following the death." The formulas indicate that burial took place quickly. Why did the Church hurry burial? It perhaps wished to limit the wakes, because practices incompatible with Christian dignity, like feasts or dances, were involved. In Flanders, prohibitions of banquets were frequent, providing negative evidence of their existence.

Why then were wakes asked for? Funeral meetings bringing together friends and relatives around the dead go back to very ancient times. It happened that the testator anticipated a meal for "those who would watch over him." The meeting there appeared secular, for no mention was made of the clergy. But the requests for wakes in the Avignon region coming from well-to-do city dwellers, particularly from widows, were linked to religious considerations—a wish for a more imposing liturgical apparatus, desire for a mass said in front of the body.

Bonfires

Medieval society, whose members worked all day in the fields or in workshops and normally stayed home after nightfall, had one very common method of providing amusement in the darkness against which the fight was so difficult. These were bonfires, which were lit on both religious and secular occasions. It is legitimate to speculate that some were lit purely for the purpose of pleasantly prolonging a day that one was reluctant to see coming to a close.

The bonfire was associated with the feast of Saint John, June 24. A letter of 1407, referring to a little village in the Saintonge region, describes how the villagers prepared it. The day before, "several people living near the castle or fortress of the said place . . . went to make and build a fire as is customary for the solemnity of the said feast . . . at the crossroads before the said castle." One of the villagers pulled up a wooden fence and put it on the fire, enraging the owner. In the evening, the petitioner, who was tending the fire with a stick to keep it burning well, quarreled with the complainant and struck him.

In 1426 in Paris, there was such a great flood on the night of Saint John that, while the fire was burning well and people were dancing, the river extinguished it; logs that were not entirely consumed were then removed from the fire and burnt at the foot of the cross on the place de Grève. According to tradition, in 1438 on the same spot a great fire was lit on the night of Saint John by the authorities, on one side the king's daughter Marie, a nun in Poissy, on the other the constable Arthur de Richemont.

The custom was thus very widespread. The accounts of Isabeau de Bavière indicate that the queen gave four sous to a poor man on the day of the Saint John fire in L'Hay near Paris.

On June 24, certain herbs took on special virtues; these were Saint John's herbs. In *Le Dit de l'Herberie*, which is the dialogue of a charlatan, Rutebeuf, a poet who died around 1285, mentions these plants, in particular artemisia, with which, he says, "women make a band on the night of Saint John and make it into a hat to put on their heads," because they think it an effective remedy against certain illnesses. *Les Évangiles des Quenouilles* teach: if you have a recalcitrant husband who does not want to give you enough money, take the first node of a stalk of wheat, picked close to the ground on the night of Saint John, and put it through the keyhole of the chest, and it will open without fail.

But let us return to the bonfires, or more broadly the festivals of fire. Flames rose in the night throughout the year, new fire on the night of Holy Saturday, torches of the Brandons on the last Sunday of Carnival, candles at Candlemas. This fire glowing in the darkness represented Christ, the savior of humanity, but it was also the sign of beneficent forces more powerful than evil. Happily wasting wood for heating which was so important at the time was a way of dismissing the grayness of everyday life and the haunting worry of having enough money to eat. Moreover, fire warmed the atmosphere and made it possible to stay outside a darkened house without the risk of catching cold.

But bonfires were not lit only at particular times of year. They illuminated any occasion as a sign of popular jubilation. *Le Bourgeois de Paris* mentions them on many occasions. For example, in 1430: "On the twenty-sixth day of April 1430, the authorities of Paris had great fires lit, just as at Saint John in the summer . . . and informed the people that it was for the young King Henry, who proclaimed himself king of France and England, who had landed at Boulogne, he and a great horde of mercenaries, to fight the Armagnacs, who were nothing to him."

People danced around these fires. The monk of Saint-Denis recounts that when Isabeau de Bavière entered Paris in 1413, the whole population greeted her with transports of delight and showed its joy "with dances, songs, and fires" that lasted all night. In the late Middle Ages, in Boigneville, near Gallardon, the inhabitants "and other people roundabout have the custom, each year on the Sunday of Brandons, to amuse themselves and to dance toward evening and to have lanterns made of wisps of straw set on a stick and to light them on fire, calling them *brandons*." On this same day of Brandons, near Troyes, after supper fires were lit "next to which the good people had the custom of gathering and dancing, and children and servants would jump over the fires when they had died down." In 1382, on the night of Saint John in Arras, boys and girls did the *carole*, a dance or a solemn march accompanied by choral songs. Documents suggest that it was done by forming a chain, a ring, or most frequently a procession of people solemnly advancing by twos or threes. The only difference between a religious procession and the *carole* was the spirit in which it was done, for the *carole* songs were songs of love. Bonfires were probably the occasion for other kinds of dances. Boys and girls together around the flames illuminating them would *baller*, jumping more than dancing in an atmosphere full of excitement and even with an erotic charge.

Let us conclude with the solemn reception in Ghent of Philip the Good, duke of Burgundy, as Chastellain recounts it in his chronicles. Fire occupied a predominant place in these solemnities. From the time he went through the first gate of the city, the duke found the streets hung with red cloth and torches lit on the roofs all the way to the door of his house. Crossing a large bridge over the Lys, he could see a vessel in the middle of the river "and low down on the boat all around the outside were installed two hundred torches all lit up burning in the water, and on board similarly as many as could be fastened." The mast rose in the middle, the rigging entirely decorated with torches like stars in the sky, and in the middle of the mast hung a shield with the duke's arms full of torches, so that the castle seemed ablaze. Not far from that could be seen a house entirely covered, roof, walls, doors, and windows, with "glistening" gold, and filled from top to bottom with torches. The large, spacious slaughterhouse was so full of torches that nothing else could be seen; the richly decorated fish market had the same appearance; the belfry full of lit torches could be seen at night from five or six leagues away and seemed completely ablaze, because of its height and its bulk, and this blaze lasted for three days. "That night, everywhere in the city there were the most sumptuous fires that had ever been seen until now and the light of the torches persisted everywhere until dawn." The same spectacle recurred the next day, and the third and fourth days up to Friday, with men and women singing, dancing, and making night into day.

Maying

May "planting," which was very widespread, involved hanging a branch at a girl's door. Young men often went to cut this branch at night, sometimes creating problems, because landowners were afraid that their trees would be devastated. In 1393, in Saint-Amand-en-Pevèle, a young man who cut a *buysset* in the petitioner's mother's garden on the night of May 1 created an uproar. In 1380, some young men in Crécy-sur-Seine went one night to cut wild roses in Pierre Penon's garden; he asked his chambermaid for his bow and arrows to chase off the intruders. A document of 1405 concerning the village of Buchy, in the Caux region, provides more precise details. On Saturday, the second of May, several young men were gathered in one of their houses; they asked the girls who were present if, the next day, they could wear May branches, and the girls agreed. That evening after sundown, they went into a wood, cut two branches that they placed in a garden, and then went off to drink barley beer while waiting for dawn.

A curious person would sometimes ask one of the *esmayeurs* which girl was to receive his branch. The question was asked in 1431 of a young man of the Ponthieu region who, on the night of Saint James and Saint Philip, had gone to look for a May branch in the town of Lanches. The petitioner answered that the questioner had only to follow him to find out. The other man got angry, setting off a quarrel.

Similarly, on Wednesday, the eve of Corpus Christi, young men from Saint-Satur went to gather roses in the gardens of the town in order to make hats, following the custom of the young men of the town, according to a letter of remission of 1392.

Festivities

Great aristocratic festivities took place not only by the light of day, when there were spectacles, particularly tournaments. but afterward when fine ladies and gentlemen joined together for supper, which began, depending on the season and the region, at an hour more or less distant from sunset. The meal was followed by dances that lasted late into the night. Festivities sometimes lasted for several days.

One of them, in the reign of Charles VI, can be compared to the din made by the young at second marriages. Because of its conclusion, it is known by the name of the *bal des Ardents.* "There were all sorts of masquerades and dancing to the sound of instruments till the middle of the night. Alas, no one knew that all this merrymaking was going to end in a horrible tragedy."

Among the queen's ladies-in-waiting was one particular favorite named Catherine. Isabeau de Bavière had great affection for her because she was of German origin and spoke German like the queen. The king decided to have her marry a rich German lord and for the occasion wanted to make a display of great splendor. The many illustrious guests assembled at the hôtel Saint-Pol where the wedding was to be performed.

The bride had been widowed three times, and the lords wanted to mock this new union. The monk of Saint-Denis writes that, "in several places in the kingdom, there are people who are foolish enough to believe that it is the height of dishonor for a woman to remarry, and in such a case they indulge in all kinds of licentiousness, disguise themselves with masks and costumes, and subject the bride and groom to a thousand humiliations."

The king, persuaded by the advice of some of his courtiers, decided to indulge in this diversion. He took five of them with him, and they dressed from head to foot in flaxen clothes, with pieces of tow stuck on with tar. Then they put on masks, came into the hall in their disguises, and began to run in all directions, making obscene gestures, emitting horrible shouts, and howling like wolves. Their movements were no less indecent than their shouts; they frenetically danced the *sarrasine*.

One of the guests, paying no attention to the damage he might cause, threw a burning brand at one of the actors. The inflammable clothes of the dancers were immediately set ablaze. The victims cried out horribly and ran around in confusion. Flames rose to the ceiling; liquefied tar flowed down their bodies and attacked their flesh. These torments lasted for nearly a half hour. In trying to put out the fire or to tear off their clothes, they burnt their hands to a cinder. The lower parts of their bodies were also consumed by flames.

The count of Joigny expired in the arms of the men carrying him off. The Bâtard de Foix and Aymeri de Poitiers died two days later; Hughuet de Guisay survived for three days. The only ones to escape death were the king and the lord of Nantouillet. As soon as the latter felt burning, he rushed into the palace kitchen and jumped into a tub full of water. The duchess of Berry saved the monarch from death by covering him with her dress.

Not all festivities unfolded so dramatically. For example, for the feast of Saint-Denis in 1389, on returning from a journey to Normandy, Charles VI decided to take some rest and to offer his wife splendid festivities. They were made up of three parts: the knighting of the two sons of the duke of Anjou, Charles and Louis; jousts and diversions; and the celebration of a Requiem in memory of Du Guesclin. They lasted for several days, but only the "diversions" took place at night.

On Monday, toward the ninth hour of the day, the king, who had chosen twenty-two very valiant knights, invited them to prepare to enter the lists. They jousted until nightfall. After supper, the ladies and damsels granted the prize of valor to two knights whom the king rewarded with rich presents. The rest of the night was spent in dances and masquerades.

The tourney of knights was followed on the second day by the tourney of squires. After supper, the ladies granted prizes to the winners of this contest as well. On the third day, the last day of jousting, knights and squires entered the lists together, and the best were rewarded in the evening.

"The fourth night put an end to the dances and the excesses that followed them. It must be said that the lords, making night into day, indulging in all the excesses of the table, were led by drunkenness into such disorders that, with no respect for the presence of the king, several of them profaned the holiness of the religious edifice and gave themselves up to libertinage and adultery."

If we look at the entry of Isabeau de Bavière into Paris on Sunday, August 20, 1389, a pretext for magnificent festivities that lasted through Friday, the pattern of the days seems similar. For example, on Tuesday, thirty knights fought until nightfall; among them was the king. Then, at sunset, they left the field—the champ Sainte-Catherine. The queen of France was led to Saint-Pol where the ladies' banquet was held. Dances and festivities lasted until sunrise. The ladies and the heralds granted one of the jousting prizes to the king.

If day was reserved especially for sporting challenges, virile exercises, at night it was the ladies who took the lead, for they granted rewards to the most valiant lords. Lords and ladies then came together as equals in the dance.

Let us move from Paris to the Burgundian states, the scene of sumptuous festivities. The feast of the Pheasant on February 17, 1454, also began with jousts, but the essential element was a banquet, in the course of which Duke Philip the Good attempted to persuade the knights to join a crusade to recapture Constantinople from the Turks.

After admiring the delicacies, the participants were led to their places by the marshals of the court. When all were seated, various spectacles were presented. At the moment when the feast reached its peak heralds at arms entered the hall and behind them came the king of arms of the Golden Fleece. In his hands he bore a living pheasant, wearing a very rich golden collar, encrusted with precious stones and pearls. Golden Fleece said to Philip that it was customary at great feasts to present to the lord a peacock or another noble bird, so that he might make useful and valuable vows. The duke then gave Golden Fleece a writing indicating his vow to help Christendom. The lady representing the Church thanked the duke and encouraged the guests to do as their master had done. Then she withdrew on the elephant that had brought her in. As soon as she left, nobles on all sides began to make vows and to put them in writing. But, as the feast risked going on too long, the duke ordered a halt; everyone who wanted to commit himself by a promise would give their vows to Golden Fleece the next day.

Everyone got up from the table and the delicacies were removed. Through the great door entered many torch bearers, followed by players of tambourines, guitars, and harps, and behind them came a lady wearing a white satin dress. On her white shoulder was written in golden letters "Grace of God." She was accompanied by twelve knights, each one leading a lady by the hand. The knights were wearing crimson doublets. The ladies were in crimson satin dresses trimmed in fur. Grace of God led the twelve Virtues before the duke to whom she handed a parchment and presented the young women; they were Faith, Charity, Justice, Reason, Prudence, Temperance, Strength, Truth, Generosity, Diligence, Hope, and Courage. Then she withdrew, while the Virtues remained for the diversions "and began to dance in a masquerade and to make good cheer."

During the dance, the masters of arms and the heralds, along with the gentlemen, asked the ladies and damsels who had jousted best that day; the prize awarded to Monseigneur de Charolais was bestowed by Mademoiselle de Bourbon and Mademoiselle d'Étampes. He kissed them according to custom, and the assembly cried in a loud voice "Montjoie!" Wine and spices were brought in in gem-encrusted cups. Charolais announced a joust for the next day. Toward two or three in the morning, the duke and his court retired.

These sumptuous festivities—sometimes with people of more modest estate as spectators—thus took place partly at night, with a banquet followed by dances. In addition to the *carole*, they danced the *tresque* (farandole), the *trippe* (a dance like the jig), the *vireli* (a turning dance), the *coursault* (a kind of gallop), and the *baler du talon* (a dance in which the heel was stamped on the floor). The dances might take on the character of spectacles. They then had a more dramatic aspect, like the scene of the chain of flowers described by Jacques Bretel in *Le Tournoi de Chauvency*, a poem narrating festivities organized in 1285. Four knights promenaded a lady to present her to the audience. Then they let her play with a crown of flowers that she held in her hand. She had a dialogue with the minstrel, who chose a knight in the audience and commanded him to go to the lady. She accepted the gallant and took him by the hand.

The duration of supper and ball varied from one festivity to the next. At the marriage of Charles the Bold and Margaret of York, sister of the king of England, on Sunday, July 3, 1468, the meal did not end until three in the morning, because of the abundance of delicacies, and so the ball did not last long.

Some of these festivities, in which the aristocracy played an essential role, had popular counterparts. When Isabeau de Bavière entered Paris, not only the nobles, but also more modest people, joined in the festivities. Decorating the streets of a city and lighting it at night required the assistance of many people. Guilds also played a role in public festivities as evidenced by these lines from a rhymed chronicle:

> The great waxen light [supplied by the guilds]
> Throughout Paris remained alight
> For three whole nights.

Taverns

Festivals were relatively rare. They did not erase the daily tedium following long and sometimes arduous work. Men, and particularly young men not eager to return to their dark rooms and solitary beds, went to taverns. Christine de Pisan considered drunkenness and love of pleasure the besetting sins of workers. The masters wishing to lengthen the working day emphasized, as we have seen, the moral effect of the measure: young apprentices would no longer have time to get drunk in taverns.

"Everything for taverns and women," wrote François Villon. Taverns were indeed a great success in a period when, if we are to believe Guillebert de Metz, Paris had more than four thousand of them. They were found especially at the gates of the city and in densely populated quarters: the place de Gréve, les Halles, the place Boudoyer, rue Saint-Jacques. They were identified by the branch of greenery and especially the hoop that were part of their signs.

The tavern was one of the principal sites for male sociability, even at night. To be sure, a decree of 1350 prohibited innkeepers from admitting drinkers after the Notre-Dame curfew had rung, but contemporary documents very frequently mention drinking parties and nocturnal games interrupted by the watch. The fact was that after their work day artisans and peasants liked to spend some time in a tavern, at the risk of getting drunk and enduring a wife's reproaches when they returned home.

For young men without wives to greet them—even harshly— the tavern had many attractions. A cleric familiar with the institution enumerated its comforts:

> Are you hungry? There you will eat;
> Are you thirsty? There you will drink;
> Are you cold? You will warm yourself;
> Or hot? You will cool off.
> In taverns, to be brief,
> You will find food and drink,
> Bread, wine, fire, and sweet rest,
> Sound of tankards and pots,
> Of cups of silver and of plates.
> And when you leave, you stagger,
> And you are sometimes so joyful
> That tears come to your eyes
> Larger than pear pits.
> But, really, it's only from drinking!

Gambling

Drinkers ruined themselves in these taverns. "They go off naked as animals," writes Rutebeuf; in fact, they left their clothes as payment. "They've gambled everything, drunk everything." But was there more gambling in the evening or at night than during the day? The letters of remission indicating the time of day of gambling attest to a clear preponderance of references relating to meals: 39 percent after dinner, 27 percent after supper. Gambling was most frequent in the afternoon or early evening. Since the time of meals varied, play after supper—eaten between four and seven—could take place before or after sunset. In any event, notations referring to nighttime properly speaking amount to only 5.7 percent. Night does not appear to have been very propitious for gambling, but this may have been due to the actions of the authorities. Following the pattern of measures taken by Louis de Tignonville, the bailiff of Troyes, who in 1395 prohibited dice playing day or night, many regulations did the same. Others prohibited it only at night. In Langres in 1307, a police regulation prohibited all gambling after curfew. The watch could even enter houses to see whether the rule was being respected. In Arras in 1470, games of dice were also prohibited "at night after the last bell," but this prohibition did not extend to the men of the watch. The public authorities wished to prevent gambling that could not take place normally because of inadequate light. They intervened not exactly against gambling but against cheating.

Love

The occasion of sin, love was also a pretext for feasting. Chambermaids enjoyed themselves with students in the cellars while their masters and mistresses were sleeping; toward midnight they would happily eat delicious cheese pies and drink pints of wine. And Villon quietly reminded them of the "game of the donkey," an animal celebrated for his sexual vigor.

Much more innocent were the men who went by night to sing under their ladies' windows:

> I also find in my sight
> Another group of madmen
> Who wander the streets at night
> Stretching their necks like cranes
> And looking into windows
> So they might see the beings,

The ones whom they love.
Alas, poor unfortunate fools
Are you not quite deceived
Mad, distracted, and demented,
To stay, as long as night lasts,
Exposed to rain, to wind, to cold,
Teeth chattering in your throat
As loud as a blacksmith's hammer?
You have to struggle hard to sing
For at best you hum.

All this time, the beloved is quietly sleeping or, worse, is in bed with another:

Is it not truly laughable
To hear singing in the street,
Pleas addressed to her whose bare body
You hold lying in your arms, soft and white?

But if the singer's constancy was rewarded, he could taste conjugal love.

Marriage was the occasion for diversions, some of which took place on the wedding night. A public act, marriage—including the first lovemaking of the young bride and groom—was in fact a matter of interest for the whole community. It seems that the young people of the country took pleasure in disturbing the tranquility of the newly married by calling on various customs.*

In Dreux in 1390, a royal sergeant marrying off one of his children entrusted a dressmaker of the town with organizing the festivities. Late, after the departure of most of the guests, several weavers came to the spot where the wedding had taken place, and making a great noise asked for the right of proclamation, claiming that it belonged to them. The petitioner refused and added that they had not earned it because they had not sung. The same

---

* These customs are described by R. Vaultier, *Le Folklore pendant la guerre de Cent Ans d'après les lettres de rémission du Trésor des Chartes.*

year in Roissy, in the jurisdiction of Paris, toward the second hour of the night, several apprentices were drinking in a tavern to the "stripping bare" of a bride, according to custom. But since the father of the bride who had promised to pay for the celebration, two or three pints of wine, did not come soon enough, one of the young men went to find him and got into an argument with him. Things sometimes went more smoothly. In December 1425 near Chartres, a vineyard laborer aged about twenty-five told the following story. The Sunday before the feast of Saint Andrew, the petitioner and a companion were eating supper together in Chartres, and then decided to go to see if the banns were being sung for a carter of the abbey Saint-Père of Chartres who had gotten married that day. They went to where the wedding had taken place and found a certain number of young men gathered to obtain the banns. To get them to leave without causing him any trouble, the young groom gave them six breasts of chicken, a quart of wine, and three loaves of bread to go off and drink together.

The wine that was given out was called for by the village workers from the groom, sometimes before nightfall. The following example mentions the wine of the bedding, here asked for by the wedding guests. On Sunday, January 25, 1428, Jehan le Bailly, a poor laborer, left his village near Reims with four companions to go to a wedding. They ate dinner and supper in the company of other guests and decided after supper that it was appropriate to go to the bride's bedroom to ask for two jugs of wine *"pour le vin de couchier."* Jehan le Bailly and three friends went upstairs where they found the bride, her father, and a few other people, and asked for the two jugs. If they didn't get them, they said, they would prevent the bride from going to bed. When they were refused, a brawl broke out.

In origin, an obligation due to a lord by a husband, the right of the first night became a right owed by a groom to his companions. In January 1391, near Chaumont, after eating, drinking, and dancing all day at the wedding of Michel Bergier and Oudote, "at night after the supper of this wedding, around two in the morning," a certain Chrestionot had a discussion with other young men about who had the right to the first night payment owed by the groom. Each one claimed it as his. To disqualify two of them, it was pointed out that one was already married and the other was not from the village. Similarly, in 1396, young men from a place called la Grève went to Montierender to ask a winemaker for his first night payment, because he had just married a girl from La Grève. The groom led them to a barn, had them sit at a table, and gave them bread, wine, and cooked meat. While they were eating, he sent for the bailiff's lieutenant and a few sergeants and told them that five young men would not leave him in peace and wanted his first night payment. It seemed that he refused to give money, preferring to pay in wine, which cost him little.

When night had fallen, the guests would leave the festivities, leaving bride and groom, if not alone, at least with close family. Women would lead the bride to the nuptial chamber. Relatives, friends, and neighbors would attend on her. One of the *Cent nouvelles nouvelles* enumerates the phases of her going to bed: undressing by the women—reverse of the morning dressing—followed by a lesson of sexual education. If the young bride was ignorant, the husband had to be able to "control himself carefully." Masculine experience in this domain seems to have been indispensable, judging by *Les Évangiles des Quenouilles:* "When a young virgin man marries a virgin girl, the first child they have is usually mad."

Documents attest to the custom of going to listen to the "happiness" of the couple. A young man from Pitres, in the jurisdiction of Rouen, went at nightfall "as a diversion to listen outside the house of the said groom to the 'happiness' of him and his bride, intending no harm, but wanting the wine." Instead of wine, he got hot water.

"But believe me that at that moment the unfortunate lady uttered a very strong and very harrowing cry that several people heard very clearly; they thought, in truth, that she uttered that cry at the moment when she lost her virginity, since that is the custom in this kingdom"—in reality she was giving birth. The gentlemen of the house where the groom was living then came to knock at the bedroom door and to bring the *chaudeau*—the *chaudeau* involved visiting the bride and groom in the course of the wedding night with a warm and comforting drink, generally made from highly spiced wine. The one of the *Cent nouvelles nouvelles* that recounts this scene notes that the husband refuses to open. The gentlemen then threaten to break down the door, because the *chaudeau* is getting cold. The groom finally gets up and lets in the men, who ask him if the *chaudeau* has been earned. The table is set and everyone sits down to drink to the health of the couple.

When there was a second marriage, the young men of the village would perform a charivari. In the Nivernais in 1441, Jean Bergier le Jeune and a widow named Agnès decided to solemnize their vows. After the proclamation of the banns in the parish church, around nine at night, several young men of the parish went to their house, for the two fiancés "had a joint household." Armed with basins, *fressouoirs* (frying pans), and horns, they began "to sound the said horns, to strike the said basins and *fressouoirs* and to make a charivari." The pregnant fiancée could not stand the noise, and a brawl ensued. Through this charivari, the young men perhaps intended to show their disapproval of a widow remarrying, but also of a couple living in apparently marital fashion. This *aubade* ended in a quarrel, but this was not always the case—and only charivaris that ended badly were recorded in letters of remission. A friendly arrangement must have been frequent. In the region of Sens in 1402, young men had always made a charivari for those who married a second time. That year, there was the rare windfall of three widowers who had decided to remarry. Thus the young men, numbering about thirty, assembled on the Thursday after the feast of the apostles Peter and Paul, around the hour of nones, and then walked through the town banging on pots and pans, and made charivari for the three widowers, following the local custom. Afterward, they all went together to have supper with the fiancés at a tavern. We know the story because a quarrel broke out when it was time to pay the bill.

Sometimes these demonstrations were very large. In 1478, law clerks, the clerks of the seneschal, and schoolboys in Toulouse decided to organize an enormous charivari because of the fifth marriage of Dame Catherine Aligonne, who was more than eighty years old. Because of her four previous widowings, she had managed to accumulate an enormous fortune. Her fifth husband was not yet forty. The wedding, celebrated quietly, was soon public knowledge. The law clerks then decided to give a nightly concert for Dame Aligonne. Since she did not want to make the payment that was customary in such cases, they left rotting carcasses at her door. The husband and wife sued, and the case went to court. The Parlement required Dame Aligonne to pay.

The charivari had its rules: it was forbidden to molest the fiancée; it took place at night, after sunset, and was carried out with horns and copper utensils; young bachelors organized it, and the local authorities sometimes granted them the right to make a din. In contrast, the Church was hostile to these demonstrations, since it saw them as a mockery of marriage. Young people seemed to be an element opposed to deviance in matrimonial matters, for marriage with an old woman would be sterile and young women of an age to conceive would lose a possible husband.

A literary text, an addition to the second *Roman de Fauvel* (fourteenth century), describes in a curious and precise way a scene of this kind, noting in particular that the organizers are in disguise.

> They are heavily disguised.
> Some have put their clothes on backward,
> Others have put on large sacks and monks' habits.
> Some held a great pan,
> One a hook, grill, and pestle, and the other a copper pot
> And all of them acted drunk.
> Some had cow bells,
> Sewn on their thighs and buttocks,
> and above them large bells,
> Others drums and cymbals
> Large instruments that were squalid and dirty,
> Clappers and rattles
> And the cries were so great and the notes so high
> That they can't be described.

The text suggests some resemblance to the *maisnie Hellequin*. The fantastic visitors who appear in Fauvel's palace prefigure the "madmen" and "fools" of the following century. Wedding night uproars of this kind survived in the French countryside until the nineteenth century.

Hence, the length of the work day did not prevent distractions at night, on Sundays, and during religious or secular festivals. Not infrequently, daytime celebrations continued into the night.

The count of Foix Gaston Phebus, for his part, led a nocturnal existence. He dined with great ceremony at midnight by the light of torches. During his stay in Orthez, Froissart had to get up and go through winter cold to the castle to read a few pages of his *Meliador* to the prince after his meal.

Night was nevertheless devoted above all to sleep.

CHAPTER 5

Rest

ight was normally devoted to sleep.* Sleep is a requirement of human nature and, with the exception of willing or unwilling night owls, ordinary mortals took their rest at night. But in what settings and in what way?

MATERIAL ASPECTS

The Bedroom

The room in which people slept had different characteristics according to period, region, and social category. Modest houses had a common room furnished with a fireplace around which all interior activities took place. But what designated the bedroom, which in contemporary civilization is the room designed for nightly rest?

In the feudal era, the distinction between bedroom and other rooms was not clearly marked. Rooms were not assigned to a spe-

---

* On this subject, see my article "Dormir au Moyen Age," forthcoming in the *Revue belge d'histoire,* with references to sources and secondary works used.

cific use, but were quickly adapted to the wishes and needs of the inhabitants.

Around 1120, Arnould, lord of Ardres, had a wooden house built, a carpenter's masterpiece, containing three levels. On the first level, the ground floor, were storerooms and granaries. On the second level were located the living quarters, the lodgings of the house servants, "then came the great bedroom where the lord and his wife slept; next to this, an enclosed room was used as a bedroom or sleeping quarters for female servants and children." In a part of the large bedroom was a separate chamber, where early in the morning, at night, in case of illness, or to warm the servants and the children who had been weaned, it was usual to light a fire. The kitchen was also on this level. "On the upper floor of the home they had installed high bedrooms; in one of them, when they wished to, the sons of the lord slept, in the other, because that was fitting, his daughters; in other rooms, the men of the watch, the sergeants assigned to guard the house, and the guards, always ready to intervene, sometimes dozed." No trace of a room distinct from the large room of the second level has been found. This room must therefore also have been used at the same time as a reception room.

How can this confusion be explained? In the palace of the counts of Champagne in Troyes in 1777, a wall separated the conjugal bedroom and an area containing a platform for the lord set higher than the seats for the guests at banquets. Instead of contrasting reception room and bedroom, it is therefore better to speak of a central room surrounded by little bedrooms. The document concerning the lord of Ardres clearly shows the existence of a bedroom–living room and a series of smaller contiguous rooms.

In the late Middle Ages, peasants, the majority of the French population, lived in houses that differed from region to region but were in the end all variants of a classic pattern: living quarters of two rooms, one containing the hearth and the other functioning as a bedroom, to which were added buildings for the livestock.

In Montaillou, the central part of the house was the kitchen. Bedrooms were adjacent to this room or one flight up. Raymonde, the daughter of Pierre Michel, described the house where she lived in Prades-d'Aillon, a village near Montaillou, in this way: "There were two beds in the lower room of our house: my mother and father slept in one, the other was for any passing heretic. This lower room was next to the kitchen, connected by a door. My brothers and I slept in a bedroom next to the kitchen, which was in the middle."

In the countryside, very varied noble houses ranged from the great fortified castle to the small manor resembling a peasant house. Jeanne de Chalon, a noble Burgundian lady, lived in a solid house in Ligny. A large farmhouse, it was designed primarily as a residence. In the midst of the common land was the noble lodging: a tower with three rooms below and three rooms above. Next to the large common room where meals were eaten was the vast bedroom of the owner; next to this bedroom was a wardrobe. Above the common room was a bedroom, the only room on the upper story that was well furnished. The tower contained five other small rooms. In the late Middle Ages the bedroom was distinct from the "living/dining room."

In cities, the basic plan sometimes resembled that of rural houses: a front room designed for work or family use—in the latter case, since it had a fireplace, it was used for eating and sleeping—and behind this room a kitchen, and possibly a bedroom. The frequently vertical division of a building would place the bedroom one flight up—the ground floor containing a spacious work place and a small kitchen. This bedroom, generally not closed off, functioned as a living room and the sole bedroom, unless there was another similar room another flight up.

But what a difference there was between the hovel of a poor working woman and the home of a great personage. The mistress of one bourgeois, a poor girl who worked as a wool spinner, had nothing "but a bed and a blanket, her spinning wheel and a few domestic implements." In contrast, the home of Pierre Sureau, tax collector of Normandy, well known because of an inventory of 1435, was a three-story building with six bedrooms, not counting the one for clerks and servants. In these rooms there were no tables and few chairs, a sign that they were designed for sleeping. Thus, while modest houses made no separation between social and private life, in bourgeois houses rooms were given particular uses. The hall became an antechamber, and other rooms were divided into bedrooms and reception rooms. Higher in the social scale, the upper nobility provided a certain number of rooms for each member of the couple.

In the hôtel Saint-Pol, Isabeau de Bavière had her private apartment. Her living room was four and a half by four *toises* (a *toise* was six feet), her bedroom four *toises* by four. The queen also had a wardrobe, a large cabinet, a small cabinet, a gallery twenty-four *toises* long, not to mention a large and a small chapel. The principal rooms were matted; rugs of braided rushes covered the wood floors.

The author of *Le Ménagier de Paris* gives his young wife valuable advice concerning the care of the conjugal bedroom that is to welcome the husband on his return from his travels: the husband will be "lying comfortably, in white sheets, with a white nightcap, well covered with good furs and satisfied with other joys and frolics, liberties, loves, and secrets, which I conceal."

In winter, the husband will have a good fire without smoke "and lying comfortably between your breasts, well covered, enchant him there"—that is, give him pleasure.

In summer, the good wife will make certain that the room and the bed have no fleas, which is possible to accomplish in different ways. With the help of platters coated with birdlime or turpentine and a lighted candle set in the middle. By spreading a cloth rubbed against the nap—or lamb skins—in the room and on the bed; the fleas will alight on the cloth and be unable to get off, so they can be carried away on the cloth. By putting cotton batting on the straw and the bed and when the black fleas land on it, they can be immediately seen and easily killed. But the most difficult is to get rid of fleas in blankets or furs; for example, they have to be put in a tightly closed sack and, without light or air and tightly confined, the fleas will perish. To avoid having mosquitoes land on the sleepers' faces and viciously biting them, you have to get up and burn hay to make smoke, which will chase them off or kill them. A mosquito net can also prevent these insects from getting near.

If there are many flies, take small tufts of fern and attach them to strings; flies settle on them and you can throw them outside. Similarly, it is good to close up the bedroom before night-fall, leaving only a small orifice open to the east; as soon as dawn comes, the flies will leave through this hole which you will then block up. A mixture of milk and hare gall will kill them. The same result can be achieved with the juice of crushed raw red onions. You can also kill them by hand with small shovels. Windows well sealed with waxed cloth or parchment will keep them from getting in. The bedroom will thus be able to provide a restorative nightly sleep.

But it was not always possible to sleep at home. In the late Middle Ages, poor students tried to find a room in a college. Most of the time, the master divided them in pairs, an older and a younger one. He kept in his possession a key to the room, which usually had to remain open. Comfort improved with time. In his will in the fifteenth century, Jean Pluyette declares that the scholarship students he mentions will be lodged "where there is a fine fireplace in a well-aired room and not on the Bièvre."

On journeys, if you were not housed by a relative, friend, or acquaintance, you had to stay at hotels or inns that were sometimes of poor quality. The most favored or wealthiest got a bed; the others slept in a common room. There was always a crowd at the Écus de France, the Étoile, the Dauphin, or the Trois Rois.

In the late Middle Ages, the clientele of the inn of la Couronne in Aix-en-Provence contained between 20 and 32 percent of merchants from one year to the next among those who can be identified. Mule drivers and other carriers lodged elsewhere. In this hotel that was probably of a relatively high standing, the percentage of clerics was between 27 and 32 percent of those identified; they included priests as well as monks and mendicant friars. The abbot of Saint-Victor of Marseille stayed the evening when he was hunting boar. Administrative and judicial requirements explained the presence of a certain number of court personnel and agents of the regional government, from 16 to 18 percent. Nobles sometimes stopped off at this spot during a long journey. Most of them—from 17 to 22 percent of the clients identified—were Provençal. They came to Aix for the same reasons as the count's agents and were, of course, accompanied by servants. Thus this hotel had a generally regional clientele who came because Aix played the role of a capital city. The majority of these travelers stayed for only one day. Some merely allowed their animals to rest, others arrived at night and left the following morning. Most came on horseback, alone or with one other person.

It is difficult to determine the cost of lodging, since the innkeeper's "bill" was not itemized and services were grouped together. "For one man and his horse, five *gros*"; this was the average price for a day. Sometimes, however, certain details were provided. A bed cost between two *patacs* and a quarter of a *gros*. As a term of comparison, a meal, morning or evening, cost one *gros* and two *patacs* (according to Noël Coulet).

Some establishments might give rise to a degree of anxiety. In his memoirs, the young Platter recounts how, traveling from Basle to Montpellier at the age of fifteen, he spent a night in a miserable inn located in the midst of a forest. He sat at a long table in the company of beggars and Savoyard peasants with troubling faces, eating roast chestnuts and black bread and drinking cheap wine. Fortunately, after staring fixedly at the travelers' weapons, the locals started drinking and went off a little drunk to sleep before an outside fire.

Letters of remission obviously emphasize problems that were frequently caused by the lack of privacy: thefts and quarrels. A letter of February 1470 recounts the adventure of Jean Taillebeuf, a young cloth merchant from Melle, aged twenty-five, who stopped at the hotel of Lucas Rateau, where he was accustomed to stay, along with four other merchants. After supper, they took care of their horses and then returned to the room where they had eaten and talked until it was time to go to bed. Then two other men coming back from a wedding arrived. Rateau decided that four would sleep in one bed and three in another, which the five merchants refused to do. A brawl ensued.

Not everyone could pay for even a modest room at an inn. People therefore often camped at night in the fields, gathering together if the situation seemed dangerous, for example in time of war. In any event, they had to confront bad weather, which seemed to be no obstacle, judging from these lines by a fifteenth-century poet: "Who hasn't slept in the wind and rain / Is not worthy company."

In the same period, Michault Taillevent recounts his adventures in Beauvaisis. Overtaken by night, he has to sleep on the ground, with only a bush for a bed.

> Then he looks at his bed all made,
> That had for only curtains
> Nothing but thistles and thorns,
> And the bed of hard earth,
> The pillow thick roots,
> And brambles for a blanket.

Silence reigns, but Michault is not comforted. His ear is cocked for fear of wolves. He impatiently awaits the sound of church bells, cockcrow, or the barking of dogs. Thus he spends the night full of anxiety, before leaving with his companions, merchants and carters . . . but bandits capture them.

Sleeping in the open air did have its pleasures. It was the occasion for amorous trysts. On July 24, 1391, Jehannette la Grosse reported to the court of the Châtelet in Paris that the preceding Saturday at around nine at night, when she was returning to Paris to sleep, where she usually did, that is, in the old houses in the ditches outside the city walls, she saw a stack of hay. Since she had no hay for the night, she approached the stack to take some. When she reached it, she saw a man she did not know, with whom she had carnal relations.

And it was pleasant to sleep under the stars in summer, when the nights were mild and you could admire sunsets or luminous dawns. "Red evening and white morning / Are the joys of the pilgrim," according to a saying.

It was not proper for churchmen to sleep in the open air. We have met some at the hotel de la Couronne in Aix-en-Provence, but these were well-to-do travelers. In any event, priests normally lived near the church and monks in their monastery.

Priests had vowed chastity, which they did not always honor. Precautions were nevertheless taken. Gregory of Tours writes that Aethérius, bishop of Lisieux, had many small beds for the priests around his own; they were thus able to keep an eye on each other. Guibert de Nogent reports that in the bedroom of Bishop Guy de Beauvais slept the young son of a knight as well as a monk from Cluny, of deep piety, and "several other personages as holy as they were noble."

The place of rest was a particular problem for monks. Egyptian cenobites had cells. Western monks originally lived in the same way. In Marmoutier, Martin's eighty companions lived separately in wooden huts or in grottos. In the Jura, cells were perhaps not contiguous at first, but they later formed a single building.

But such a system had drawbacks, particularly in Gaul where, according to Cassien, the monks suffered from the instinct of ownership. On the other hand, because of the length of services, the monks spent little time in their cells, where they were no doubt tempted to sleep rather than to watch and pray. The practice by some of them of land clearing and agriculture turned out to be hardly compatible with solitude. Hence, toward the end of the fifth century a rather ferocious reaction against this system took place. After the fire of Condat that burned the cells, Eugende had shared sleeping quarters built, which would be illuminated all night by an oil lamp. If Césaire of Arles prescribed in both masculine and feminine rules a single place for sleeping, this was because he wanted to combat the instinct of ownership. Since the monks slept in individual beds, concern with chastity was also a factor.

The dictates of the Rule of Le Maître concerning common sleeping quarters thus come as no surprise. Le Maître considers the common sleeping room a matter of course. He lays less emphasis on it as a place for shared rest than on its arrangement to facilitate surveillance by the provosts. Elsewhere, the emphasis is placed on the arrangement of beds, set up so that the abbot would be able to monitor the behavior of monks during siesta and sleep. While in the legislation of the Eastern Emperor Justinian monks watched each other, here that task was entrusted to the hierarchy.

It thus seemed that the dormitory had won out and that the problem to resolve was that of cohabitation, the provosts having to sleep near their ten charges and the abbot at the center of the community. At all times, the provosts were charged with nocturnal surveillance, which can be explained by the material conditions. Lighting was not permanent; as a result, the abbot, in the center of the room, could not be aware of the attitude of all of his monks, while the same thing was not true of the provosts lying in the midst of their men. The abbot always monitored the monks at the time of going to bed—but, as we have seen, less rigorously than the provosts—in summer during siesta, in winter after nocturn, in Lent during prayers. This organization presupposed small communities since it involved a single dormitory.

The Rule of Saint Benedict deserves presentation in some detail because of its importance. Benedict brings together a certain number of notations that are scattered in Le Maître. Like the latter, he prescribes a single dormitory, but exceptions are foreseen if the number of monks grows too large. Groups of ten will then be distributed in different rooms, singly or in pairs, and the elders will watch over their members.

While Le Maître provides for leaving the dormitory in complete darkness, so that the monks, in case of need, are obliged to talk to one another, Benedict provides for permanent illumination. As a result, his Rule strictly prohibits any speech in the course of the night, on pain of punishment. And waking does not take place in darkness. In addition, the younger monks' beds are not grouped together but mixed with those of the elders. It seems that Benedict in this rule is less concerned with the problem of chastity than with the possibility of laziness on waking.

Although the dormitory had become the norm in the sixth century, cells did not disappear. The Council of Tours in 567 had to reiterate the rule of the dormitory and the individual bed, which suggests that the dormitory had not yet won out in Gaul.

In any event, the appearance of the dormitory in the early sixth century is a phenomenon of some importance. The cell made the cenobite's life a solitary existence, devoted to contemplation. Sleeping in common meant a renunciation of that ideal to struggle against the instinct of ownership and against impurity. The dormitory would be a palliative measure. It should however be added that well before its appearance, the cell had been transformed to the extent that the community of prayer and work left it only the role of bedroom.

Of course, the Benedictine Rule was not always exactly observed in the course of the Middle Ages. If separate rooms were prohibited at Cluny, the numerous reiterations of this prohibition show a rather widespread laxity. In 1263 in Mont-Saint-Jean—to observe the rule while simultaneously violating it—small rooms with doors that could be locked were installed in the dormitory. The Visitors ordered the abandonment of this system, which nevertheless turned up in Eauze in 1403 and in many other places. Watch had to be constantly kept to make sure that the monks slept in common. On a single occasion, in 1386, the order appeared less strict, with reference to the priory of Saint-Victor in Geneva, which then contained nine monks. As the Visitors had noticed that they slept in separate rooms in the dormitory, the chapter ordered that a large opening be made in each cell to facilitate surveillance.

Throughout the Middle Ages, the supporters of the common dormitory put forth the same arguments to justify their position: a monk who has made a vow of poverty and possesses nothing during the day should live similarly at night; sleeping in common fosters chastity because monks watch each other; finally, since demons appear especially at night, monks gathered together can fight more effectively against them. Permanent light created a favorable climate morally and spiritually. Peter the Venerable insisted on this point. If a monastery did not have sufficient resources to maintain light simultaneously in the church and the dormitory, he ordered that the lamp lighting the sanctuary be carried at night to the dormitory. For, he added, you are the children of light.

The dormitory required nine candles a day, or sixty-three a week. With a pound of wax, you could make three candles in winter, four or five in summer. This illumination presented various advantages. According to Richard de Saint-Ange, it symbolized light, allowed the monks to take care of needs without difficulty, and improved surveillance.

This last element was a matter of very strict concern for the hierarchy. In 1386, the general chapter ordered the priors of Saint-Victor in Geneva and of Contamine to make the rounds of the dormitory every night, and then to lock the door and keep the key. They even recommended that the prior of Saint-Victor in Geneva have a solid lock made, so that no one could come in or go out.

There remains the case of those on the margins of society. Hospitals, which were not limited to the treatment of the ill, had above all the aspect of a refuge. They had a certain number of rooms, like the Hôtel-Dieu in Paris which had four rooms and 279 beds, and a delivery room with twenty-four beds.

Prison cells were far from attractive. According to a fourteenth-century document, there were in the Châtelet—a fortress overlooking the bridge allowing access to the île de la Cité—several prisons that were more honest and honorable than others. But many names were far from prepossessing, like *Death*, the *Ditch*, the *Well*, *Barbary*, or the women's prison called the *Griesche* (the harsh).

The Bed

The bed was the most important piece of furniture in the room where people slept. Writers frequently enumerated the objects needed by a couple, and the bed generally occupies first place among them. For example, Eustache Deschamps in his ballad "for the newlyweds,"

> For your household you need
> Between you, newlyweds,
> Mattress, cushions, bed, and straw.

And Gilles Corrozet, in his *Blasons domestiques* of 1539, celebrates first the bed, then the bedroom, before moving on to the chair, the bench, the table, the dresser, the chest, and the stool. He spiritedly expresses his attachment to this "delicate and soft" piece of furniture, which is the "adornment of bedrooms" and, far from any erotic connotation, symbolizes the purity of conjugal love.

The medieval bed was very similar to its contemporary counterpart. It consisted of three elements: the wood frame; the bed itself which corresponds to what we call bedding; and finally the material fastened around and above the bed to protect the sleeper from the view of strangers, from light, and from drafts.

The wood frame was called *châlit* or *couche*. Generally made up of a platform of boards, it was made of oak, less frequently of pine. In addition to this planked bedstead, there was a webbed bedstead, that is, provided with straps that were periodically restretched, equivalent to our trestle bed. Some beds combined both features.

Under some raised bedsteads it was possible to slide a small bed, very useful when there were numerous overnight guests. For more ease, these little beds were on wheels. There were bedsteads that could be disassembled for transport, for example on military expeditions. Elevated bedsteads were provided with a wooden step, necessary to climb into bed. The step was located between the bed and the wall, creating a space generally called a *ruelle*, which achieved some notoriety in seventeenth-century literary circles.

On or in the bedstead was a layer of straw, the *paillasse*, on which was usually set a mattress, the *couette*, made of more or less costly material according to the owner's wealth: canvas, twill, woolen, or silken cloth, containing straw, woolen wadding, feathers, or down. In addition, there were cushions, a bolster, pillows, a pair of sheets, a blanket, and a bedspread.

Some bedsteads had wooden columns and iron rods designed to support a canopy, which first appeared in the thirteenth century. The material above and around the bed was arranged in various ways, but in the fifteenth century a cage was frequently set above the bed made up of a canopy to which were attached four strips of cloth, one for each side. This was generally of colored serge, but for the more wealthy could be made of silk or fur-lined cloth.

Some beds were very wide; they might measure one and a half, two, or even three *lés*, the *lé* probably equivalent to the space for one person, which demonstrates the custom of several people sleeping in the same bed. Saint Romain, writes Gregory of Tours, has a large bed prepared so that they can all—nine lepers and himself—lie in the same bed. In the fourteenth century, the bed belonging to Francesco Datini, a merchant of Prato, and his wife Margherita was three and a half meters wide, and next to it were a step, a seat, and a chest.

Appearances of beds varied according to social categories. The materials used and the number of sheets or cushions were certainly not the same for peasants as for lords. The bedstead indicated another distinction. Some beds had none at all, others had rudimentary bedsteads, and some were carefully built. Both documents and miniatures show a variety of canopies and curtains, or the fact that they were sometimes lacking.

A hierarchy of beds can thus be established. At the bottom was the world of the marginalized, especially the prisoners. In the Châtelet, in the cell called the Ditch, they slept on the stone floor—no bed nor even any straw—however, the jailer had to supply mats. In the prisons of Beauvais or Barbarie, lodging cost two deniers, but if a prisoner wanted a straw bed, he had to pay four deniers a night. In the *Prison aux chaînes,* a more honest establishment, to have a bed a prisoner paid four deniers a day to the jailer, but only two if the prisoner brought the bed from outside.

Having a bed was thus one of the great desires of a prisoner lying on stone and straw: "Sure, but I'll have the Three Lily cell/ If they take me to the Châtelet." Villon, imagining himself arrested for theft and taken by the sergeants to the Châtelet, identifies the prison with an inn at the sign of the Three Lilies of France, punning on *lis* and *lits,* the beds generally denied prisoners, especially common criminals.

Around 1320, the inmates of the leprosarium of Le Bourg in Narbonne slept on wooden beds furnished with coarse mattresses. For four beds they had only ten sheets, even though their state of health required frequent changes. They had only seven blankets and one *couette,* along with a few blue bedspreads. At least they slept in sheets and under woolen blankets. The comfort of leprosaria in fact depended on the social station of the inmates. To Saint-Lazare de Noyon, an establishment reserved for them, bourgeois had to bring a fully furnished bed and seventy ells of different cloths.

In the orphanages of the diocese of Paris in the middle of the fourteenth century, beds consisted of one mattress, one pillow, a pair of sheets, and one blanket. Other establishments provided two blankets in summer and three in winter. A century later, the orphans of the Lyon region each had a berth furnished with a featherbed or a mattress, a pillow, a bolster, two cloth sheets, and two blankets. The provision of a complete bed was evaluated at at least two livres of Tours. These beds were set up in a sort of dormitory, or *poêle,* next to the kitchens and heated in the winter by vents connected to the kitchen fires.

Hotels were more or less well provided. One inn in Rouen, for which we have an inventory done in 1395, had rooms reduced to the bare necessities: twelve beds and twelve candlesticks for twelve travelers. Each guest was given a furnished bed without a frame, a candlestick, two pairs of sheets, four *touailles* (towels), two pillows, and four head coverings.

From prisoners in the Châtelet to orphans in Lyon there was an increase in comfort. If the former sometimes slept directly on the floor, the latter had a mattress. The many intermediate stages between the two can be readily imagined. A miniature by Jean Bourdichon depicts a beggar lying on a straw mattress on an open work bed, with torn sheets and a wretched blanket full of holes. The *meschantes couchetes* of the common people were much closer to this than to the luxurious beds of the aristocrats.

If we go up in the hierarchy, we see that wealthy bourgeois and clergy with profitable livings liked their comfort and great lords competed in munificence. The inventory of the furniture of Nicolas de Baye reveals that this clerk of the Parlement de Paris in the early fifteenth century had at least six bedrooms, one called turtledove, another red, a third white. There were ten beds of varying widths, often two *lés*—sometimes noted as two little *lés.* The most expensive, estimated at six livres, eight sous, was a bed two *lés* wide, full of down, lined on the sides, found in the turtledove room. There were twenty-four sheets, most of flax, the others of hemp; ten blankets, generally of *pers* (blue) cloth, but one was green, another yellow, and a third vermilion; eleven counterpanes, most of them white; three mattresses, one cotton estimated at forty sous, the second stuffed with *bourre* (coarse wool) estimated at twenty-four sous, and the third only a *pail-lasse de feurre* (straw beaten to make bedding) worth only four sous; six *chambres*, that is, the material set on and around the bed, the finest including a canopy and a headboard of black cloth fringed in white and black, and three chests decorated with rings. Two finely woven sheets and four rugs completed the collection. Our clerk was thus well supplied with bedding material.

As for Pierre Surreau, tax collector of Normandy, the inventory after his death in 1435 indicates that his household then contained fifteen furnished beds with their bedsteads and chests. For this eminent personage, a normal bedroom generally contained two beds, a large one of two and a half or even three *lés* and a small one of a *lé* and a half.

Mahaut, countess of Artois, although the records of her household present relatively simple furnishings, had wooden beds of imposing dimensions with columns supporting canopies and curtains. But she also had a small bed that she carried with her on her travels. The *couettes* were carefully maintained. Since there were often not enough of them in Hesdin and Arras when the countess received too many guests, she rented them. Beds without canopies were sometimes simply sheltered by a pavilion or an *épervier*, a small tent that was easy to transport.

In the later Middle Ages, some rooms demonstrated unprecedented magnificence. Records provide many examples. In 1393, when Catherine of Burgundy married a Hapsburg, she brought with her a luxurious bedroom. "A bedroom of blue satin embroidered with the arms of Mademoiselle of Austria, provided with a full canopy, a headboard, a counterpane, curtains of *cendal*, ten squares of the same material, embroidered with the arms of the said damsel, the said bedroom also furnished with a finely woven bed cover, with four tapestries to hang on the walls, a mattress cover, a bench cover, and six squares of wool with the arms as above, and three bedside rugs to place all around, and a cover of blue cloth filled with fine vair."

Indeed, furs then played a much more significant role than in our time. They were used to make pillows and blankets or counterpanes. In 1379, the inventory of Charles V records twenty *couvertoirs* and two *demi-couvertoirs* with fur lining (while only one was lined with cloth), with fine vair predominating. Until the middle of the fifteenth century, records indicate the presence of many fur-lined blankets, sometimes all of those that are recorded. This practice is explained by the fact that the men of the Middle Ages—with the exception of certain cenobites required to sleep in common—slept without nightclothes. In addition, it was not possible to heat bedrooms without fireplaces.

There were different kinds of blankets, for children and for adults, decorated, with fur sometimes on one side, sometimes on both. In the first half of the fourteenth century, the blankets used by great personages had dimensions that varied generally between 11 and 14 square meters. But the surface increased toward the end of the century. For example, a blanket recorded in 1379 of 5.64 by 6.24 meters contained 2,128 ermines on a surface of more than 35 square meters. The largest known blanket belonged to Charles V, also recorded in 1379, and it measured 8.36 by 4.64 meters, or a fur-covered surface of 38.79 square meters. The court of Burgundy was not far behind. A lord who had twenty of these blankets for himself would obtain smaller ones, but sometimes of equal quality, for his servants, wet-nurse, child minder, or for the children. Later, blankets seemed to correspond more closely to the size of beds.

In the fifteenth century, fabrics competed against furs, which became rare after 1450. The courts of the Medicis and of King René give evidence that most blankets were now lined with taffeta, silk, or sometimes cotton.

Completely opposite to this luxury was monastic austerity. The Benedictine monk's bed normally had a sort of felt covering on top, a straw mattress (*sagum*), a cushion, and a blanket (*laena*). In Cluny, the chamber man provided the monks with bedding material. He also made sure that they received a mattress with fresh straw on All Hallows' Eve. In Cluny, *sagum* took on the meaning of summer blanket; the *laena* or winter blanket was made of a shaggy fabric or of fur. It seems that the monks of Cluny were at first permitted only one blanket. Peter the Venerable authorized two white ones or two black ones, or one of each color, but not four as had become customary. And he prohibited precious fabrics. The blankets, which were woolen in summer, might be lined with goat or sheep skin in winter. Abbot Bertrand and his successor Henri I proscribed colored blankets, particularly red or green ones, and the monks were not allowed to use flaxen sheets.

Monastic beds might nevertheless have a fine appearance, while remaining austere. In the dormitory of the priory of Poissy, writes Christine de Pisan, the nuns slept fully dressed, without sheets, on a mattress stuffed with wadding, but their beds were covered with elegant tapestries.

What has been said so far concerns only adults. Very young children obviously required for sleep something entirely different from a bed. The cradle—well studied by Danièle Alexandre-Bidon and Monique Closson in *L'Enfant à l'ombre des cathédrales* with the help of iconographic sources and to which the following paragraphs are greatly indebted—was suited for a child's size.

"For the child, you need cradle, swaddling clothes," writes Eustache Deschamps. And indeed most of the time, during the first months of life, the child lay in a cradle made during his mother's pregnancy. This is recommended in *L'Outillement au vilain*, a thirteenth-century poem. Aristocrats did the same. In 1401, the records of Isabeau de Bavière mention "a cradle for the queen's child due to arrive soon."

In the humblest classes, the eldest child's cradle was used for the younger brothers and sisters, and because of frequent births, it was never unoccupied for long. But the distribution of this piece of furniture varied a great deal as a function of social category. Of 135 inventories in Dijon, only four mention it, which is surprising when you consider the many depictions by miniaturists of bourgeois or noble interiors.

Peasants probably used mostly troughs, baskets, or hollow tree trunks. In the fourteenth century, the hospital of Saint-Jean-de-l'Estreé in Burgundy procured troughs for the children of poor mothers.

A box made of four panels of wood built to the size of the newborn appears in miniatures set on the floor. A box with bars was probably most frequent because it recalled the manger in depictions of Christ's Nativity. Simple when it was made by a father working in the evenings, it became an object of beauty when specialized artisans constructed it and added sculpted vertical posts and copper knobs.

Miniatures depict rocking cradles more frequently than stationary ones, perhaps because they were more widespread. The difference between the two types often derived solely from the addition of curved runners at the head and foot of the cradle. Longitudinal runners were rare and seem to have been confined to Italy. The sawed-off cone shape appeared only in the most sophisticated cradles.

The wealthiest circles quickly adopted the small bed. If it scarcely appears in the ninth century, this relative absence perhaps attests simply to the lack of interest of the clergy in the furnishings of childhood. In the late Middle Ages, depictions of such little beds have a more secure appearance because a swaddled child could not fall and a nursemaid was charged with watching him. Nevertheless, this piece of furniture seems better adapted for children of two or three, who could get in and out of bed on their own.

There were finally carrying cradles attached with straps to the mother's or father's shoulders. They were necessary particularly for journeys that were too long to allow for carrying the child in one's arms, or when doing agricultural work when there was nowhere to set the cradle down.

We do not know at what age children stopped using the cradle. Its dimensions varied as a function of the parents' situation. Among the lower classes, it seems to have been relatively small, for its principal function was to prevent the child from turning over and falling; moreover, when there was a risk of falling, protective straps guarded against that danger. Much larger cradles were made for little princes, for these were exhibition pieces. One *bersouère* was six feet long and nine feet wide.

The cradle, generally made of raw wood, was painted for royal children orange-red or vermilion and green. Records indicate that the little prince or princess had several cradles: one for everyday use entrusted to the nursemaid, others for public occasions. Some of the latter were occasionally covered by a white or striped canopy with the sides held up by loops: "pavilion of green and violet damask" for Marie of Burgundy, "net of green satin providing two beds for the bedroom of the royal children" around 1400. Such objects demonstrate more membership in a social category than attentiveness to childhood.

Fir, larch, cypress, and cedar were then considered incorruptible woods. Modest and aristocratic classes both used "Irish wood," aromatic and rot-free pine and fir. We should take particular note of ebony wood, used for princes' cradles from the seventh century to the early Renaissance. Isidore of Seville already thought that its black color comforted the child and dissipated his fear of the dark. Nine centuries later, in 1500, Jean Lemaire de Belges wrote nothing different. "He saw the noble cradle, which was richly sculpted and made of a black wood named ebony, very dear and much sought after, growing in the Indies, from which are made the cradles for royal children because it has the virtue of protecting them from terror."

Ebony wood was very costly. Thus, outside princely families, people satisfied themselves, at least those who were relatively well off, with an amulet made from ebony. Barthélemy l'Anglais, a Franciscan born in England c. 1190 and author of a *Liber de Proprietatibus rerum* (translated into French as *Livre des propriétés des choses* in 1372 by Jean Corbechon), notes that "it was the practice to place this wood near newborn children so that they would not be afraid of black things, as Pliny says."

Bedding was little different from presentday bedding and included the elements used by adults, that is, mattress, sheets, pillows, and blankets. It was in addition appropriate to take care that the cradle was not full of sharp and hard things, but on the contrary of materials to protect against the cold.

The mattress was probably made of rye, very widespread at the time, for the very young, who were still incontinent. Older and richer children must have used, like adults, a filling of hemp or feathers, but feathers of inferior quality. A bottom sheet, at least in aristocratic circles, covered the mattress; and though the child probably quickly dirtied the sheet, it was not often changed in the cold and dark, even if the parents had to get up to soothe the child. Bedding did not always include a top sheet. Sometimes a single folded piece of cloth could serve as both top and bottom sheet.

In short, there was generally a small white sheet and a blanket, neither of which was hemmed. The purpose of the blanket was to keep the infant warm. But how widespread was this costly item among the poorest classes? In any event, among aristocrats, and as for adults, there were luxurious blankets for children made of fur—cloth of gold lined with ermine, cloth of scarlet lined with the white of conies (rabbits). A light veil over the baby's mouth prevented him from swallowing the hairs. The miniaturists depict these blankets as blue or red to the exclusion of all other colors.

The child's head was raised by a pillow. He did not sleep lying flat because it was thought that he might suffocate from regurgitating, and at night, or even during the day, the accident might go unnoticed. *Carreaux*, little square pillows, played the same role as for adults, that is, to provide a certain comfort; the only difference was in their size.

Night Clothes

It was customary to sleep in the nude, which explains the importance of fur-lined blankets among the well-to-do to fight against the cold. Since the head was outside these blankets at night, in order to avoid catching cold it was not unusual to wear a nightcap.

This was not exactly the case in monasteries. The Rule of Le Maître attests that monks slept clothed and that they changed clothes morning and night. In addition, they were required to wear at night a different belt from that worn during the day. The reasons for such changes were essentially of a practical order. The daytime belt, with an attached knife, might provoke accidents. And dressing at night is explained particularly by a concern with chastity and speed of getting up to attend the nightly offices. These prescriptions had, moreover, been applied for a long time.

Saint Benedict also recommended that his monks go to bed clothed and with a strap or cord around the waist. But a few centuries later, the monks of Cluny wore only a nightshirt to sleep. In fact, for them, the prescription of the Benedictine rule, *they shall sleep clothed*, meant that it was fitting to keep on the piece of clothing closest to the body to hide their nakedness. As soon as nocturn was rung, the monks put on their cowls before throwing back the blankets covering their bodies.

As for young children, to their bed at night was added swaddling clothes, warm and thick fabric made of hemp among the poorest, of wool among the better off. Blankets and swaddling clothes were held down by straps of varying widths.

It has been said that medieval beds, some of which were very wide, held not only husband and wife, but also the children, friends, servants, and even strangers. This is not incorrect. A letter of remission from 1395 notes that Michaut Mestraut, from Chardonchamp near Poitiers, and Raillart have long been companions, "sleeping, rising, and working together."

Another letter from 1398 recounts the following anecdote. On the Tuesday before Lent, a young Englishman named Guillemin, a clothing worker passing through town, came into the shop of Jean Jourdain, known as d'Anjou, a dressmaker in Parthenay. Jean Jourdain hired him, and the following Wednesday, after eating and drinking in several places in town until nighttime, they went to the house of a wool carder who had lodged the Englishman the night before; but the worker and his wife refused to take him in again. Seeing that night had come, Jean Jourdain took him home and had him lie down in his bed with his wife, who was already asleep, placing himself in the middle. While he was asleep, Guillemin decided to rape the wife. She defended herself, punched her attacker, and got out of bed to look for a candle, but the Englishman went after her and put out her candle. The wife then began to scream and woke up her husband, who quickly got up and grabbed the Englishman, who had to release the wife. Jean Rousseau, a dressmaker and Jean Jourdain's neighbor, who was passing by, hearing noise, went into the house and brought his neighbor's wife home to sleep with his own wife; then he went back to calm down the two men and returned to his own home. Nevertheless, the episode ended badly, since in defending himself, Jean Jourdain killed the Englishman.

Documents and miniatures frequently show an entire family sleeping in a single bed. Penitentials allude to children smothered by their parents lying next to them. The width of beds made such practices possible.

However, efforts were made to combat this lack of privacy, principally for moral reasons. In a treatise on lust, Jean Gerson writes: "Please God that the custom were in France that children sleep alone in small beds, for so many brothers and sisters and others were together, as is the custom in Flanders." In a pastoral letter of 1496, the vicars general of Christophe de Penmarch, bishop of Saint-Brieuc, acting for their superior, prohibited "brothers and sisters and other relatives older than seven from sleeping together, that custom leading them to commit countless, infinite, and horrible sins of exceptional gravity, as many confessors have informed us," on pain of excommunication and a fine of ten livres; the same penalty was imposed on parents who permitted the practice.

Although monastic rules prescribed a dormitory, they also required individual beds. Hospitals had the same concern, and the sisters of the Hôtel-Dieu in Paris complained of being forced to put "little children, little girls as well as little boys, together in several dangerous beds in which other patients had died from contagious diseases, because there are no individual beds for these children, but they sleep six, eight, nine, ten, and twelve in the same bed, at the head as well as at the foot." And the same establishment tried to place "the seriously ill each one apart in his own bed." Hence, sleeping together in a single bed was often experienced as an imposition.

Those who could preferred to sleep alone or with a person of their choice. The presence of a manservant or a chambermaid could, however, turn out to be useful, and many bourgeois and nobles wished to have them available at night. To accomplish this, they set up a small bed in the master's bedroom or put the servants in a small neighboring room. The good bourgeois author of *Le Ménagier de Paris* recommends that his wife have her girls or chambermaids sleep near her "in a wardrobe or bedroom where there is neither skylight nor low window and not giving on the street." But this was particularly for the purpose of monitoring their conduct, for girls from fifteen to twenty are "foolish and have seen little of the world." The *Cent nouvelles nouvelles*, which devote a great deal of space to nocturnal amorous adventures, give clear evidence of this cohabitation, as we have already noted.

SLEEP

The "Sleep of the Just"

Did people sleep a lot in the Middle Ages? It is difficult to know if the men of the time spent more time sleeping than we do. However, peasants and artisans worked by natural light and they had no paid holidays, so that it is plausible to think that long mornings in bed were more difficult then than now. The author of *Le Ménagier de Paris* declares to his wife that her rising "must be in the morning," and "morning means matins." However, although he recommends that she hear matins to praise the Lord, his remarks suggest that the young wife would afterward go back to sleep. We should recall that matins and lauds coincided with sunrise.

Peasant evenings and aristocratic festivities could go on long into the night. But isn't the same thing true today? Speculation gives way to more precise information for children and especially for monks.

Children's sleep gave rise to conflicting recommendations. Some let them sleep during the day, between meals. Others argued against the practice, like a doctor in the court of Burgundy: "He should be prohibited from sleeping during the day, except during the long days of summer," no doubt so that he would sleep better at night and not trouble his parents. He recommends a night of nine or ten consecutive hours for a child younger than six: "He should go to bed at ten and sleep until seven or eight in the morning." Habits seem to have been very different in rural areas. We have seen that in Montaillou, Jean Maury, who was twelve, was in bed before the family evening had really gotten under way. It is true that he had to get up early the next morning to lead the sheep to pasture. The youngest children went to bed even before the evening meal.

According to Saint Benedict's Rule monks had to get up for nocturn, which in winter took place at the eighth hour, which, according to Benedict, allowed for resting a little more than half the night. Since night contained a maximum of eighteen hours, half would be nine; bedtime was therefore around five in the evening. Sleep was limited to seven hours (from seven to two in the morning) at the vernal equinox, when night consisted of twelve hours.

For the summer, Benedict prescribes that matins following vigils be said at daybreak. At the summer solstice, with the sun rising at four, if you count one hour for vigils, a quarter hour for a pause, and three quarters of an hour for matins, the monks must have risen around two. The monks might go to bed around ten-thirty—night fell at ten—and thus five and a half hours of sleep with, as recompense, an afternoon siesta. The second morning sleep granted by the Rule of Le Maître was impossible in summer and of no use in winter.

To wake up for the nocturnal offices was nevertheless often an unpleasant obligation. Raoul Glaber (early eleventh century) shows how the monks were tempted to loll in bed, beginning with himself. The demon whispers to him: "I wonder why you are so eager to jump so quickly out of bed, as soon as you've heard the signal, and to interrupt the sweet rest of sleep, while you could give yourself up to rest until the third signal."

But the conscientious monk was afraid of not waking in time. Peter the Venerable, the abbot of Cluny in the twelfth century, recounts the story of Brother Alger who, thinking he had heard the bell for nocturn, woke up, looked around, imagined he saw the other beds empty, and went to the chapel. There was no chanting in the chapel. He returned to the dormitory and found his brothers in deep sleep. He understood that the devil had awakened him at the wrong time so that he would stay in bed when the bell really rang. Fortunately, clocks would bring peace of mind to the anxious. A thirteenth-century instruction concerning the abbey of Villers orders that the clock be set after compline, "and then you can sleep peacefully." This would avoid the misdeed immortalized by the children's song:

> Frère Jacques, frère Jacques,
> Dormez-vous? Dormez-vous?
> Sonnez les matines, sonnez les matines.
> Ding, ding, dong; ding, ding, dong.

Saints, exceptional figures, hardly took the time to sleep. An example is Saint Dominic. According to Brother Buonviso, "it is also certain that the blessed brother often spent the night praying to God, it was a well-known fact among the brothers. The witness wanted to know where the father slept, but he could not discover a place reserved for him to sleep as the other brothers had, only sometimes he was found asleep on a bench, other times on the ground, or on the straps on the bottom of a chair or a bedstead. He lay down at night dressed as he was while walking during the day." This testimony is corroborated by, among others, Brother Rudolph and Brother Stephen, who "does not remember ever having seen him sleep in a bed; we had set up a corner for him to sleep where there was only a bedstead with a simple blanket, without a mattress and without sheets."

Troubled Sleep

Men of the Middle Ages, like our contemporaries, sometimes had difficulty falling asleep and sometimes suffered from insomnia. At first sight, it seems they ought to have been less stressed than we are, but we cannot judge former times by the standards of our way of thinking. Juvenal had already talked of the annoyance caused by traffic in Rome. Material and psychological concerns, however different from our own, were capable of troubling the nightly rest of our ancestors.

Current medical research has established that sleep disturbances fit into three categories. First insomnia, which can be defined as difficulty in beginning and maintaining sleep. Unlike someone who sleeps less than six hours a night and pronounces himself satisfied, an insomniac thinks that he has slept badly. Among those suffering from depression, insomnia grows more serious with the severity of the illness and the age of the sufferer. Troubled waking at three or four in the morning and a near impossibility of going back to sleep are frequent characteristics of depression. If we are to judge by letters of remission, suicides frequently occurred during this period of wakefulness in the middle of the night. Insomnia might also involve great difficulty in falling asleep after a long period of waiting, or sleep interrupted by frequent wakening. Many sufferers of anxiety have great difficulty in falling asleep, wake frequently during the night, and have nightmares. The elderly stop sleeping at night like other adults, but take frequent naps during the day.

Excessive sleep, much rarer than insomnia, has been noted as a temporary phenomenon among people suffering from existential difficulties or having experienced emotional trauma. Sometimes a tendency toward excessive sleep is connected to a state of depression, but in this case the sleep is not restful.

Troubles associated with sleep include somnambulism, which takes place during the first third of the night and involves mostly children, and phenomena that are grouped under the heading of nightmare: nocturnal fears of children, genuine nightmares at the end of the night bringing about an anxious awakening, and frequent nightmares or neurotic visions at any time of night.

While the poet and chronicler Jean Froissart was staying at the court of Gaston Phébus, count of Foix and Béarn, in the latter part of 1388, a squire told him the surprising story of Pierre of Béarn, Gaston's bastard brother. Expressing surprise that this lord was not married, Froissart was told that he was, but that his wife and children had left him because he was a sleepwalker. He would get up at night, even though he was asleep, take hold of a sword, and wield it in the empty air. If he did not find a sword, he would make such an uproar "that all the devils in hell seemed to be with him." In his novel in verse of more than thirty thousand lines, *Meliador*, Froissart depicts a sleepwalking knight named Camels de Camois who behaves exactly like Pierre of Béarn.

Why were these two knights somnambulists? It is all the more difficult to answer because the word did not appear until the late seventeenth century. Documents do exist, as Alain Boureau has shown, but in them the somnambulist is called a "sleeper" (*dormiens*).

Somnambulism appears in medical and theological writings in the course of the twelfth and thirteenth centuries. In the *Questions de maître Laurent*, a work showing Italian influence compiled by an Englishman around 1200, the compiler asks: "It happens that many men get up at night while asleep, take up weapons or staffs, or get on horseback. What is the cause of this? What is the remedy?" The answers to these questions are diverse, but they all contend that these nocturnal activities bear no relation to dreams.

Gervaise of Tilbury, in his *Otia imperiala*, mentions a woman from Beaucaire apparently afflicted with this infirmity. Carried off into the air one night by lamia, she invokes the name of Christ and finds herself in the Rhône "soaked up to the navel." What is novel here is the demonization of the somnambulist, which was to receive juridical sanction in the fourteenth century. The canon *Si furiosus* (1312) indicates: "If a madman, a child, or a sleeper mutilates or kills a man, he incurs no penalty for this." The somnambulist is thus not criminally responsible for his acts, just like a madman or a child. Commenting on this canon, a professor at the University of Toulouse, Guillaume de Montlauzun, recounts that one of his fellow students, an Englishman, walked in his sleep one night down to the Seine and killed a child there; then he returned, still asleep, and went back to bed.

The Middle Ages were not devoid of methods for combating sleep disorders. Let us look first at the rather special case of a young child who was unable to fall asleep or woke up in the course of the night. He then had to be rocked to calm him and to keep his crying from preventing his parents from sleeping. To be sure, not all children resembled the one that Guibert de Nogent's mother had adopted. This orphan, who was a few months old, was perfectly calm during the day, but at night uttered such extravagant cries and screams that the poor woman and her servants could not sleep in the same room. In vain, Guibert's mother hired well-paid nursemaids to stay by his side all night and shake rattles. She did not succeed in quieting the night hours disturbed by such a clamor, and she became so downcast and exhausted that she was unable to sleep. Guibert, of course, saw in the child's attitude a sign of the devil.

The task of rocking children became for some women a veritable profession, for little princes, in addition to a nursemaid, had a rocker at their service. This was an action that belonged to the maternal function, incompatible with the masculine condition. *Les XV Joies de Mariage* provides negative proof. This work recounts the miseries (the "joys") suffered by the unfortunate man who has had the unfortunate idea of getting married. The wife "makes him carry the children off to play, she makes him rock them."

Rocking from side to side seems to have been preferred to rocking from front to back, but rocking the child with a soft and regular motion was not always enough. Barthélemy l'Anglais writes that the nursemaid "amuses the child to make him sleep," or that she must "sometimes sing next to the child to give pleasure and delight to his senses by the softness of her voice." The little Burgundian princes went to sleep to the sound of veritable orchestras made up of harps, *doucines,* flutes, and other fine instruments.

Charles d'Orléans himself composed a lullaby:

> When they have not slept enough
> These little tiny children
> They wear beneath their bonnets
> Faces full of sorrow.
>
> It's a pity if they arise
> Too early the little darlings
> Who have not slept enough
> These little tiny children.
>
> May God let them rest
> Sleep on soft cushions
> For they are so graceful.
>
> Alas! Alack! Oh woe!
> When they have not slept enough.

The cradle that could easily be moved during the day when the need arose was set at night near the parents' bed, on the mother's side. She could thus pick up the baby in the dark to nurse it and put it back to bed, or rock it without getting up. Satirical works depict and laugh at nighttime troubles caused by the child's crying. For example, *La Farce du Cuvier:*

> At night, if the child awakes
> As they do in many places,
> You must take the trouble
> To get up to rock him,
> To walk, carry, and feed him
> In the bedroom, even at midnight.

The cradle protected the infant, who risked being smothered if he slept in the parental bed. Miniatures show various procedures designed to protect him from danger on those occasions when he did sleep next to his parents. The mother had more pillows, elevating her more. The child did not sleep in the middle of the bed, but on one side, so that there was no risk of his parents' suffocating him if they slid into the depression in the center of the mattress.

The child thus generally spent the night near his mother, and even in the absence of some nighttime incident, his health was a matter of concern. This could be a matter for the father, and his involvement was not infrequent. In the fabliau entitled *Gombers et des II clercs,* the protagonist "had the habit at night, when he had just pissed, to feel the cradle." The cradle might be located in the nursemaid's room, when the parents had hired an outsider to take care of the baby. In any event, the infant was not left alone; he did not have his own room.

Medieval doctors recommended sufficient sleep and considered excessive late nights harmful. They even discussed the sleeper's position, which played a not insignificant role. Aldebrandin of Siena noted that "sleeping in reverse position is bad, for it provokes many illnesses," notably "frenzy" and "the fantasies that doctors call incubi."

To calm the excited, the anxious, and insomniacs particular use was made, as Muriel Laharie has shown, of opium and plants containing atropine, whose therapeutic value was already known in Antiquity. Opium derived from white, black, or red poppies was a very effective sedative. Matthieu Platearius, a Salerno doctor (d. 1161), taught that the white poppy could be used directly. "To put a patient to sleep, make a plaster for the temples of poppy with woman's milk and the white of an egg."

But generally, "opium" was poppy juice obtained by an incision around the top of the plant and on the leaves: the liquid thus extracted was the "opium" used for external applications. According to the pseudo-Arnaud de Villeneuve, a late thirteenth-century Neapolitan doctor whose *Brevarium medicinae paracticae* was long wrongly attributed to Arnaud de Villeneuve, "opium alone, diluted with woman's milk, under the nostrils provokes unlimited sleep."

Plants containing atropine, like mandrake, *jusquiamus*, and belladonna were also known well before the medieval period. Male or female mandrake was used in the same way as opium. Practitioners used the leaf of the *jusquiamus* for external treatment, and its white and red seeds for internal treatment. The pseudo-Arnaud de Villeneuve writes that "the root of the *jusquiamus*, ground with mint and placed in a poultice on the forehead, brings on sleep." Doctors used belladonna less frequently than the other atropine plants. Similarly, hemlock, because it was "poisonous," played a very restricted role in the feudal period.

There was also recourse, but intermittently, to other less toxic plants, whose sedative or hypnotic properties were known, like wild lettuce, about which "some say that its milk puts you to sleep because of its very bitterness," peonies, valerian, violets, and many others. Thus, the quality of sleep could be improved.

We have noted that nightmares could arise at night, particularly when the sleeper's mind was troubled by cares. The old ancestral fears arose again from the depths of consciousness. But, as has recently been demonstrated, a normal individual always dreams during the so-called paradoxical phase of sleep.

*Dreams**

Pope Gregory the Great distinguishes five categories of dreams. For some he gives a physiological explanation: too much food. Others are inspired by the devil. A third kind flows from the day's cares. A fourth type comes from God, as can be seen in the Bible. Finally, a dream can be a response to a wish or a preoccupation of the sleeper. This celebrated classification can be found in many medieval writings. There was, however, a less nuanced division, which attributed dreams to God, to the devil, or to man.

The Church Fathers, like the Ancients, contrasted authentic dreams to chimeras. According to an ancient belief, false dreams appeared in early sleep, while truthful dreams occurred only after midnight. In the twelfth century, Adelard of Bath gave an explanation for this. Dreams coming before midnight have no value because of the influence of digestion.

But in general, distrust predominated. Cicero had already seen belief in dreams as a superstition: when they did not come from a bodily condition, they were nothing but a creation of the mind. And Isidore of Seville was of the same opinion. Moreover, biblical texts also express repugnance toward dreams. "All dreams are nothing but vanity," says Ecclesiastes, and Ecclesiasticus: "It is like clutching a shadow, or chasing the wind, to take notice of dreams. . . . Divination, omens, and dreams are all futile, mere fantasies, like those of a woman in labor."

Medieval writers reiterated these ideas. John of Salisbury declares that a man who believes in dreams has left the paths of faith and reason. Pierre of Blois goes further: belief in dreams puts your immortal soul in peril.

A believer must therefore mistrust dreams. An anecdote recounted by Saint Jerome illustrates the recommendation. In an epistle to the young Eustochium, Jerome tells how he took the works of Cicero on a retreat in the desert. Reading the Roman

---

* There are many references in the study by Herman Braet, *Le Songe dans la chanson de geste au XIIe siècle,* and the article by Jacques Le Goff, "Le Christianisme et les rêves" (see bibliography).

writer gave him much more pleasure than reading the Bible, the language of which seemed barbaric to him. It was then that, in a dream, God appeared to him and ordered him to give up pagan writers. He promised to do so. However, twenty years later Rufinus criticized him, for he had apparently not kept his vow. Jerome retorts that a dream does not correspond to reality. To support his assertion, he cites texts from scripture, and he provides examples to show that our dreams are made up of extravagant images or images that come from our desires alone. "How many times have I seen myself dead and lying in a tomb! How many times have I imagined myself flying above the earth."

However, other sacred texts seem to grant some value to dreams. Prophets reveal the future by interpreting them. Do we not read in Numbers: [The Lord said];

> Listen to my words.
> If he were your prophet . . .
> I would make myself known to him in a vision,
> I would speak with him in a dream.

And in Job:

> Once God has spoken
> he does not speak a second time to confirm it.
> In dreams, in visions of the night,
> when deepest sleep falls upon men,
> while they sleep on their beds, God makes them listen,
> and his correction strikes them with terror.

Thus some writers thought that divine intentions could be learned from dreams. In the twelfth century, Hildegard von Bingen, like Richard de Saint-Victor, accepted that God reveals the secrets of the future to us in dreams. This position gave rise to a difficulty: the temptation to attribute divine origin to all dreams. How could this be resolved?

The church stigmatized dream interpretation, for there were dreams that had the purpose of leading men into error. In *Les Dits de saint Pirmin* (eighth century), we can read: "Pay no attention to your dreams, for they foretell only deceptive things: adore the one God and the Holy Trinity." Many writers mention the traps set by the devil during sleep. Pierre de Blois (twelfth century) teaches that a dream is only one of the many ruses of the devil.

The better to achieve their aim, these ruses can take on the form of lies of divine origin. Indeed, there are many commentaries on this sentence from 2 Corinthians: "Satan himself masquerades as an angel of light." The second stratagem used by the Evil One turns out to be even subtler. This is the false prophet whose predictions are fulfilled so that the dreamer has confidence in him. For example, Jean Cassien speaks of a monk to whom Satan at first sent truthful dreams and who, deceived by these nocturnal revelations, converted to Judaism.

Finally, it is very difficult to determine the origin of dreams, so that Gregory concludes his discussion by urging the faithful to be very vigilant. According to Gregory and Isidore, only saints may recognize divine revelations.

The twelfth century, while the influence of the devil over dreams was in retreat, saw the development of the influence attributed to human physiology. The passage from dream interpretation to medicine and psychology was expressed in the thirteenth century by Albertus Magnus and Arnaud de Villeneuve. Further, dreams that had been thus secularized were no longer confined to the elite, but were the property of simple clergy and even later of the non-ecclesiastical population.

The autobiography of Guibert de Nogent is particularly rich in dreams, containing as it does forty-six narratives of visions, dreams, or apparitions, among which fifteen are presented truly as dreams: three concern Guibert as a child, two his mother, two his tutor, one his mother's steward, three monks, two secular nobles, and two people distant in time and space. For Guibert, a dream was both a physical and a spiritual experience that generally took place during sleep at night.

One night while Guibert's tutor was sleeping in his room, he seemed to see a venerable old man with white hair who took the child by the hand and led him to the doorway. Stopping there, he pointed out the bed to the child and said to him, "Go and find that man, for he will have great affection for you." Then he released his hand and let him go. Guibert ran toward the man, covered his face with kisses, and woke him up. The tutor was then gripped by such love that, without delay and disregarding his fear of his cousins, on whom he and his family were totally dependent, he agreed to come to live in the home of Guibert's mother.

One of the noble conspirators of Laon, an accomplice of Gérard de Quierzy, reported to him a dream that he had had the night before and that had, he asserted, filled him with fear; it seemed to him that two bears were tearing his liver or a lung from his body.

In his *Summa Theologica* in the thirteenth century, Saint Thomas Aquinas clearly and distinctly sets forth the origins of dreams: "You should know that dreams can depend on two kinds of causes, internal and external. The former are themselves either mental or physiological. a) Mental sources of dreams: the imagination represents to us in sleep those things on which we have focused our attention and our feelings in a state of wakefulness. A like cause can have no influence on subsequent events, with which this kind of dream has only a purely accidental relation. If those events occur, this is pure chance. b) Physiological sources of dreams: internal inclinations of the body produce movements of the imagination related to those inclinations: a man who is full of cold humors dreams that he is in water or snow. This is why doctors say that it is important to pay attention to a patient's dreams in order to diagnose his inner state.

"As for external causes, we also find a dual division, based on the distinction between the corporeal and the spiritual. a) Corporeal influences: the imagination of a sleeping man may be affected by the ambient air or by the influence of celestial bodies. In that case, the imaginings that appear to him in sleep are in harmony with the position of those bodies. b) Spiritual influences: it is sometimes God, through the ministry of angels, who gives certain revelations to men in their dreams. 'If he were your prophet . . . I would make myself known to him in a vision, I would speak to him in a dream' (Numbers). But on other occasions, it is demons who are at work. They make images appear in sleep, by means of which they reveal certain things to come to those who have forbidden pacts with them."

Human physiology has hardly changed, and of course we recognize that the men of the Middle Ages dreamt in the same way as those of the twentieth century. But mentalities and psychologies change over the course of time. Where our rational spirit sees only fantasies (or so we would like to think), in the Middle Ages so impregnated with religion or religiosity, it was thought that dreams might have a divine origin. Dreams and visions were not without links to the spiritual life of the faithful.

PART THREE

God or
Sublime Night

Night, despite the incitement of devils,
and beyond the limited efforts of man to dominate it,
may lead toward God.

CHAPTER 6

Visions

NIGHT, THE MONK, AND THE BEYOND

On November 4, 824, there died in Reichenau a monk named Wetti who, on the eve of his death, reported a vision that he had had. Heito, the abbot of the monastery, transcribed his account. Soon thereafter, the poet Walahfrid Strabo, abbot of Saint-Gall, composed a version in verse.

One Saturday, Wetti took a potion, but he vomited it up and began to experience disgust for food. At dawn the next day, he felt better, took medicine again, and was again overcome by disgust. But he remained untroubled and rested on Monday and Tuesday.

Since the brothers ate dinner in a cell next to his, he had his straw bed carried there to wait for the end of the meal while sleeping. He was stretched out with his eyes closed, but awake, by his own account. There then appeared an evil spirit, very ugly, with an unseeing face in which any indication of eyes was absent. Terrifying and gleeful, the spirit held instruments of torture in his hands, apparently about to torture him. There then appeared a troop of evil spirits who invaded the cell. Armed with little shields and tiny lances, they spread themselves everywhere and formed a kind of house in which to imprison him.

It was then that divine mercy was made manifest, for there then appeared magnificent and honorable men. Clothed in the

177

monastic habit, they were seated on stools. One of them declared: "It is not just for the demons to act in this way, for this
man is resting; order them to leave." At these words, the demons
scattered.

Then appeared an angel of incredible splendor and beauty,
dressed in a purple garment, who spoke to Wetti in a friendly
voice: "I come to you, very dear soul," he said. "If the Lord will
pardon my sins," answered the monk, "he will show mercy; if he
does not desire to do so, let him do what seems good to him."
This conversation marked the end of the first vision.

Night had fallen. Awakened, the monk sat up, looked around
him, and saw two monks, one of them the provost of the monastery, who had stayed to watch over him; all the others had gone
to rest after dinner. He called to them and told them what he had
seen. He was so terrified that, forgetting the gravity of his illness,
he fell to the floor and fully extended his arms at his sides, and
he asked them to intercede so that God would forgive his sins.
While he was in this position, the monks begin a continuous
chant of the penitential psalms and others appropriate to the
occasion.

When the recitation of the psalms was finished, Wetti arose,
got back into bed, and asked to have the *Dialogues* of Saint Gregory the Great read to him. After nine or ten pages had been read,
he exhorted his brothers to relieve the weariness they felt from
watching over him and to rest for the little bit of night that
remained.

The two monks moved off and settled in a corner of the cell
to doze. While Wetti too was asleep, the angel from the earlier
vision appeared and praised him for having found refuge in the
Lord, both through psalms and reading during his torment. He
urged him to read and reread Psalm 118, which describes the
nature of virtue. Wetti would obtain the favor of the Lord by acting sincerely and without ulterior motives.

The angel then led him along a very pleasing road. On the
way, he showed him mountains that were very high and of out-
standing beauty. They were encircled by a wide river in which a
countless multitude of the damned were set for their punishment, and he recognized many among them. Elsewhere, he saw

unfortunate souls subjected to all kinds of torment; many of them had received minor orders, and some even had been ordained priests. Tightly strapped to tree trunks, they were plunged into the fire; and he saw the women they had defiled bound in the same way, also plunged into the fire up to their sex. The angel told him that, two days out of three, they were struck by whips on their genitals.

"Most priests who desire terrestrial goods and fulfill secular functions," said the angel, "dress luxuriously and eat too well; they think piety is found in material wealth. They pay no heed to the good of souls, are concerned only with their pleasures, and frequent prostitutes. Thus, they can intercede neither for themselves nor for others. And yet their prayers might be of great help. But here is the recompense they have received, and they suffer this punishment because of their earlier merits."

Wetti also saw in that place a building resembling a wood and stone castle, crooked and made shapeless by the darkness; smoke was coming out of it. When he asked about this building, the angel answered that it was the dwelling of monks from various monasteries and regions, grouped together for their purgation. He pointed out one in particular, enclosed in a leaden casket until the last judgment because of the love his community had borne toward money.

This monk had been shown to a pilgrim who had indulged in excesses, toward the end of his life, less than ten years earlier; the incident had been widely reported at the time but had since been forgotten. Wetti had not heard of it. By manifesting itself on two occasions, this vision thus demonstrated that monks had to free themselves often from unhealthy habits so that money would not for them be changed into lead.

In this place, Wetti was also shown a high mountain. The angel told him that an abbot who had died less than ten years earlier had been placed on the top of this mountain for his punishment, but it was not eternal damnation. Still he suffered the harshness of the air and the discomfort of wind and rain. The angel went on to say that a bishop who had recently died ought to have tried to gain his forgiveness through prayer, for he had asked him to do so through one of his priests in the course of a vision. But the negligent bishop was not very charitable and did not come to his aid. "And for that reason, he will be unable to help himself," he said. "And where is he?" "Here he is, on another part of the mountain, where he suffers the pain that has been inflicted on him."

Wetti said that he had also seen in this place a prince who once reigned over Italy and the Roman people; an animal was tearing at his genitals, while the rest of his body was untouched. Stunned, he expressed surprise that such a man, so ardent in defending the Catholic faith and the Church—this was Charlemagne, named by Walahfrid Strabo in his poem—could be punished so ignominiously. The angel leading him immediately answered that this prince, even though he had accomplished many admirable deeds that were pleasing to God, had nevertheless given in to debauchery. "However," he added, "he is destined for the fate of the elect."

He also saw countless magnificent offerings, fabrics, silver vases, horses, fine and bright white linens. When he asked the angel to whom these objects belonged and what their appearance meant, his guide answered: "These goods were amassed by the counts ruling the various provinces; they are gathered together here so that people may see them and know that they are the fruit of pillage and greed." He went on to say that these goods would remain there until their legitimate owners resumed possession of them.

And he denounced the way of life of these counts. Some of them did not punish crimes, but persecuted men by penalizing the just, justifying bandits, and associating with thieves and scoundrels. "Blinded by the desire to receive gifts, they do nothing to be rewarded after their death. They have never dispensed justice in thinking of their future life, and even though they have to apply it freely to obtain eternal rewards, they render it only for money." The angel pointed out some who, he said, had already been judged.

Wetti also reported seeing countless laymen and monks from various regions, some saved, others damned.

The angel then led him to very beautiful places, where the vaults seemed of gold and silver and glowed so brightly and with such incredible beauty that the human spirit cannot conceive them nor words describe them. There then came forth the King of Kings, the Lord of Lords, accompanied by a host of saints, glowing with such glory and such majesty that no man with the eyes of his body was able to bear the intensity of the light.

The angel guiding Wetti said to him: "You must die tomorrow, but in the meanwhile let us devote our efforts to obtaining divine mercy." Then, going before him, he led him to a place where holy priests were gathered. "Here are those who have been crowned because of their good works," he explained. "Let us ask them to obtain forgiveness for you." They asked the priests to intercede. The holy priests arose immediately and went toward the throne; there, prostrate, they implored mercy for the monk. During this time, he stood aside with the angel. "He should have been a model for his brothers, but he was not." And the priests heard nothing more. Among them Wetti claims to have recognized Denis, Martin, Aignan, and Hilaire.

They then went to a place where there was a countless host of holy martyrs. "Here," said the angel, "are those whom a triumph has covered with glory, those whom you venerate in the Church for the honor and praise of God, those whom you must ask to intercede to obtain forgiveness for your sins." When Wetti prostrated himself to beg them, they immediately went toward the throne of divine Majesty and asked benevolence for the sinner. "If he has corrected those whom he has misled by the example of his depraved conduct and if he has brought back to the true path those whom he has led down the road of error, then all his sins will be forgiven." But how could such results be judged? "Let him bring together those whom he has seduced by his example or his teaching and led into illicit deeds, let him prostrate himself before them and confess that he has acted and taught evilly, let him ask forgiveness and beg them by almighty God and the saints not to act or teach evilly in the future." Among the martyrs, the monk claims to have recognized Saint Sebastian and Saint Valentine.

Then the angel led him to a place where there was a countless host of holy virgins, glowing with incomparable dignity. "Here are holy women. We must pray to them so that they will intercede with God." When this was said, as before, they prostrated themselves before the blessed, who immediately went toward the throne to ask for a long life. Before they prostrated themselves, the Lord appeared to them. Raising them up, he said to them: "If he teaches good things and gives good examples, your request will be granted."

After their departure, the angel began to set forth for the monk the vices in which mankind wallowed. "Mankind is allowed by its creator to give itself to the devil by means of all kinds of crimes, but nothing offends God more than the sin against nature. This is why you must struggle and show great vigilance in order not to succumb to the crime of sodomy. Not only does this very contagious disease kill the souls polluted by the coupling of males with one another, but this evil is aggravated in the case of husbands, since they lose the good of nature that God has granted them in their wives. I advise you to proclaim that publicly. And do not hide the risk attached to fornication with concubines. In fact, as long as they are degraded, they will not merit the kingdom of heaven." Wetti answered him: "Lord, I do not dare to make such statements because, by reason of the insignificance of my person, I do not feel capable of it." The indignant angel replied: "What God wills and orders you through me, you do not dare to proclaim!"

Then he began to give him various advice on mending his ways: "I am the angel sent to guard you, I who once was sent by God to Samson, about whom the *Book of Judges* speaks, from his very birth, in order to cooperate in an admirable enterprise, until Samson, softened by the pleasures of the flesh offended God because of Delilah. I then abandoned him. When you were a child, you too were very pleasing to the Lord, but then you began to live at your whim, and you displeased Him greatly; and now you must become pleasing in His eyes again by repenting your sins.

"In monasteries, the roots of vices must be annihilated for the seeds of virtue to be able to proliferate. Beware of avarice! When it reigns, it opposes poverty of spirit and closes the gate of heaven. Let gluttony in drinking and eating become extreme frugality! You must give up luxurious clothing and wear only what is needed to cover your nakedness and protect you from the cold.

Pride should give way to unfeigned humility. Some, in fact, seem to bow their heads, but they continue to raise up their hearts. In the Western regions, in Germany and Gaul, monks must be urged to imitate the humility of Christ and voluntary poverty, so that they will not be removed from the gate opening onto eternal life. God, through me, makes this terrible promise."

Sin had also grown among the congregations of nuns!

"Then where can apostolic life be found preserved intact?"

"In countries overseas, because spirits helped by poverty succeed in reaching the kingdom of heaven; no earthly obstacle stands in the way."

After saying this, he spoke several times of the crime of sodomy, and emphasized this crime against nature suggested by the devil. The monk asked him why the ravages of the plague produced so many victims. "The world," answered the angel, "has been guilty of a great number of crimes and this is the punishment for its sins. It is a sign sent by the Lord to show that the end of the world is near!"

Referring to a certain Count Géraud—prefect of Bavaria in the reign of Charlemagne—he said that he was resting in peace and had obtained the glory of the martyrs, for he had zealously undertaken the defense of the Holy Church and fought against the infidels. "He suffered loss of the life of the world, and so he participates in eternal life."

Wetti awakened for the second time; the birds were already singing at the approach of dawn. He called to the brothers who had spent the night nearby. Moved by this vision and filled with fear, he set forth all these facts for them in order and asked that, as soon as the father abbot arrived, his words be taken down in his presence. They answered that the brothers absorbed by nocturnal meditation did not dare break the barrier of silence. "Then inscribe these things in wax," he told them, "so that they will be ready when dawn appears. I fear that what I have seen and heard cannot be divulged with my dull tongue. But these visions have been granted to me with such an obligation to reveal them that I fear my silence will draw down upon me a great punishment. The intercession of the holy virgins with God to secure for me a long life has left me in uncertainty: did they intervene for the duration of eternal life or of this earthly life? If this intercession has not brought about a lengthening of my earthly life, according to my guardian angel, I will die tomorrow."

During this time, the morning hymns came to an end, and the father abbot came with some of the monks to see him. When he came close, Wetti asked to have a private conversation with him. All the others left, and the abbot remained with four monks. The tablets on which the two monks had hastily written in the silence of the night were brought. Wetti recapitulated the whole story, rose from his bed, and prostrated himself on the floor, asking forgiveness and praying that his visitors intercede with God for him.

During the entire day, the following night, and the next day, he constantly worried, moaned, sighed, and commended himself to each of them. Finally, when twilight had given way to night, before the assembled brothers, he declared that the end of his present life had come, and for that reason he asked them to sing psalms. When the chants were finished, he was breathing very weakly. The monks returned to bed. As for him, he tossed and turned because of his imminent death. After receiving extreme unction, he died.

This text raises the question of the religious aspects of dream phenomena.

God, Dreams, Apparitions, and Visions

Attempts have been made to define different dream states: a dream when one is asleep, an apparition if awake, a vision when the soul leaves the body and visits the beyond. These are artificial classifications and the important thing is to know what the men of the Middle Ages believed they had seen.

Spiritual Impact

For Christians, until about the middle of the third century, there was an obvious link between dreams and the crucial moments of their lives.

Origen (185–254) saw conversion to Christianity as the consequence of a vision or a dream. "Many have come to Christianity in spite of themselves, a certain spirit having suddenly turned their hearts from hatred of the doctrine to the determination to die for it, by presenting them a vision or a dream." Tertullian (160–240) asserted that "most men owe their knowledge of God to visions." Going further, Saint Cyprian wrote that this divine presence turns out to be permanent through dreams. "This is why the divine control constantly corrects us night and day."

Martyrs earned the most prestigious dreams, those that predicted future events. They could even bring them on. The brother of the martyr Perpetua of Carthage in 203 said to her, "My lady sister, you already have such great virtues that you are worthy of asking for a vision and it will be shown to you whether it is martyrdom or release that awaits us."

But, as we have seen, the link between the dream and the body created suspicion which would last for many centuries. Over the dream hovered the threats of Satan, heresy, and sex. In addition, the future belonged only to God, and he consented to reveal it to only a few chosen ones. The circle of privileged dreamers, limited at first principally to saints, was spread to a closed world that had not yet achieved heavenly glory but aspired to it, that is, to the monasteries.

Dreams proliferated, from Cassien in Marseille in the fifth century to Bede in the British Isles in the seventh and eighth. The East, thanks to Cassien, and the Celtic and barbarian world, thanks to Bede, influenced dream narratives, as did oral culture and folklore. Monastic circles hoarded dreams, but urban growth, the Gregorian reform, and the development of the outside world would transform the situation.

At night, holy figures might manifest themselves to show forth divine glory and power. Gregory of Tours tells the story of an aged and pious woman of Bordeaux who, according to her usual custom, entered the basilica of Saint Peter one Sunday night to light the lamps. Accompanied by a little girl, she went down into the crypt. While she was carrying out her task, night fell. The priests came in, sang the verses of the psalms, and then closed the door to the crypt, not realizing that they had locked in the old woman. She began to cry out but could not be heard. Toward the middle of the night, the doors opened and the basilica was filled with an intense light. A choir singing psalms came through the church. When the singing was finished, the woman heard men complaining that Saint Stephen was late. While they were repeating their complaints, a figure wearing a white robe entered, and the multitude humbly greeted him, saying, "Bless us, holy and sacred Levite Stephen." At their request, he explained the reason for his lateness. "There was a ship at sea in danger of sinking. They called on me, I hurried there, I saved it, and here I am. And, so that you doubt not the truth of my words, see the clothing I am wearing, it is still dripping the water with which the sea drenched it." The crowd drifted away and the doors closed again. Then the woman came to the spot where the saint had been standing, gathered with a handkerchief the drops that had fallen on the floor, and showed them to the bishop of the city.

At night, holy figures might manifest themselves to indicate their duties to the faithful. In a chapter of *La Gloire des Confesseurs*, Gregory reported that the territory of Tours contained a hillock full of thorns, brambles, wild vines, and dense undergrowth. According to report, two blessed virgins were lying in that spot. Moreover, on the eve of holy days, the faithful frequently saw light there. One, bolder than the others, was not afraid to go there one night; he saw a candle of marvelous whiteness giving off an immense light. Having contemplated it, he withdrew and reported what he had seen. At the same time, the virgins appeared to an inhabitant of the region and told him that they were buried in that spot and that they could no longer endure not being sheltered by a roof to protect them from the rain. He should therefore clear out the undergrowth and put a covering over their graves. On waking, preoccupied with other thoughts, he forgot his dream. But the following night, they appeared to him again with threatening faces and predicted that if he did not obey he would die within the year. Terrified, the man took his ax, cleared away the undergrowth, and uncovered the graves. He sent cattle and a cart to gather stones, and in summer built a shrine at the spot. When the work was done, he asked Bishop Euphronius of Tours to bless it. But the aged bishop excused himself, saying, "You see, my son, that I am old, and that winter is harsher than usual; the rains are coming, the winds are blowing strongly, the rivers are rising, and the roads are becoming narrow ribbons. It is not fitting at my age to travel on such ways." The man went home quite downcast, but as soon as the bishop fell asleep, the two virgins appeared to him. The older one spoke angrily, "In what have we displeased you, blessed pontiff? Why do you despise us? Why do you neglect coming to bless the building that a faithful believer has built for us? Come immediately, we beseech you in the name of almighty God whose servants we are." The bishop awoke and called the rector of the bishopric. "I sinned by not going with the man. Now I have just seen the two virgins who reproached me for it, and I fear I will incur God's anger if I delay going to their tomb."

In the case of Ursinus, whose story comes from the same work, doubt was the first reaction. Auguste, abbot of Saint-Symphorien in Bourges, had a vision of Ursinus one night. "Dig in the earth and look for my body," the saint said to him, "for I am Ursinus, the first bishop of this city." Auguste answered, "Where will I seek your grave, since I don't know where you have been buried?" Ursinus, taking him by the hand, led him to the spot. "My body," he said, "is under those vine roots." When the abbot awoke, he told the story to his bishop, but, taking the priest's words lightly, he took no action. At that moment, Saint Germain, bishop of Paris, came to stay with the bishop. After supper, he fell asleep. Then Saint Ursinus appeared in dreams to Germain and to the abbot of Saint-Symphorien, led them to the grave, and begged them to remove him from the spot. Awaking at the same time, they went to vigils, and then with the morning offices over, they told each other of their dreams. Consequently, the following night, they went to the place indicated with a priest carrying a candle, dug in the ground, and found the grave. They uncovered it, removed the top, and saw the holy body like that of a sleeping man, untouched in any way by decay.

And at night, holy figures might manifest themselves to punish those who had committed criminal acts. A few days after the death of Saint Nizier, bishop of Lyon, his will was read in the presence of the people. A priest of the basilica, filled with gall because the saint had left nothing to the church in which he was buried, declared, "Many people always said that Nizier had little wit; you can see it clearly now, since he has left nothing to the church in which he is buried." But the following night, the saint showed himself to the priest accompanied by two other bishops of Lyon, to whom he said, "This priest has covered me with blasphemy in asserting that I have left nothing to the building where I lie, and he does not know that I have left him what is most precious to me, that is, the dust of my body." The bishops answered, "He has acted badly by denigrating a servant of God." The saint then turned toward the priest and struck him on the throat, saying, "Sinner worthy of being trampled upon, stop speaking foolishly." The priest felt a sharp pain and had to stay in bed afflicted with terrible suffering, but having invoked the name of the confessor, he returned to health.

Five centuries later, the Holy Virgin intervened in the same way. According to Guibert, abbot of Nogent, when a knight attempted to annex to his fishing area the part of a river that had belonged to the monks for a long time, to punish him, the Virgin paralyzed several of his limbs. When he attributed the event to a fortuitous cause, "the very holy Virgin presented herself to him during his sleep and struck him several times right in the face, not without force." When he awoke, the knight came to ask the abbot's forgiveness and restored what he had usurped.

In the eleventh century, there were appearances not only of saints, but also of departed laymen. We have already had occasion to note that, falling asleep after matins one Sunday night, Guibert de Nogent's mother saw, among others, her husband, the narrator's father.

The text provides invaluable details. It is preceded by an introduction which situates its spiritual import: "You know, Lord, what faithfulness, what love, she kept for her spouse, even though he was dead, what quantity of almost daily sacrifices, of prayers, tears, and generous alms she constantly devoted to redeeming the soul of the man whom she knew to be fettered with sin. Thus it happened, by virtue of a surprising divine dispensation, that she had very frequent visions, in the course of which were revealed to her, in very expressive images, the sufferings with which my father was afflicted to expiate his sins. There is no doubt that visions of this kind come from God. In fact, since a falsely luminous beauty secures only a deplorable sense of safety, and since on the other hand the vision of suffering and punishment provides a stimulus to prayer and charity, and since the dead, or rather the angels who take care of the interests of those who have died in the faith, obviously require that we secure for them the remedy of divine service, this is sufficient proof that all this comes from God; the demons never work for the salvation of anyone. Thus the soul of this blessed woman, in her solicitude, was warmed by such signs, and the prodigious vision of the inner torments of her dead husband inflamed her by making her assiduously seek intercession in his favor."

According to Guibert de Nogent, there are thus proofs of the divine origin of dreams, essentially the request for intercession by means of prayers or charity in favor of the dead. The devil cannot wish for the salvation of a soul.

The importance of this intercession is clearly brought out in the continuation of the narrative. "My mother asked her husband if prayer, charity, and the holy sacrifice provided him some relief: she was indeed aware of frequently offering all that for him. He answered that it did and went on, 'But among you there is living a certain Luitgarde.' My mother understood that he named that woman so that my mother would ask her to remember him in her prayers. The said Luitgarde was a woman who truly practiced poverty of spirit, not participating in the habits of the world, but living for God in her simplicity."

In addition to her husband, Guibert's mother saw a certain knight Renaud, assassinated soon thereafter, then one of his sons who died much later, and an old woman who was her companion when she began her conversion. Renaud, who had committed many sins on earth, was seen on a board above a well containing human ghosts. Knees bent, leaning down toward a pyre, he swelled his cheeks and blew. Guibert's brother, who had sworn terrible oaths on the body and blood of the Lord, was on the same board. The old woman, who had always publicly been busy punishing her body, had shown, it was said, a spirit of vanity. Guibert's mother saw her carried off by two very black demons.

At the time when they had lived together, they had made a mutual promise: the first one who died, if God permitted, would make known by an apparition what her condition then was, good or evil. The old woman in question, on the point of dying, herself had a vision: she saw herself stripped of her body and going toward a temple with many others like her, and it seemed to her that she was carrying a cross on her shoulders. When she reached the temple, she remained outside, for the doors were closed. After she died, she appeared to another person, in the midst of a great stench, and she thanked her heartily: thanks to the prayers of this woman, she could escape from that infection and from her pain.

In bringing these two things together, Guibert's mother understood that she had seen the places where sinners are punished in Hell.

Did the fact that she had seen two still living people indicate that the suspicion of the Church toward dream interpretation had disappeared? In the thirteenth century, after setting out the problem, Saint Thomas Aquinas concluded: "Using dreams to know the future is a legitimate thing if they are 1) dreams derived from a divine revelation; 2) dreams dependent on a natural cause, internal or external, provided that you do not go beyond the limits of that cause's influence. But if the divinatory dream has as its origin a diabolical revelation consequent on an explicit pact with the demons called upon or on a tacit pact, since the divination goes beyond the limits to which it can legitimately lay claim, this is superstition and sin. The difficulties are thereby resolved."

With the vision of Guibert's mother, we reach the subject of journeys to the beyond. Such visions practically did not exist until the seventh century because of the Church's concern with keeping its distance from a folklore that it considered linked to paganism. They grew more frequent from the seventh to the tenth centuries, particularly in monastic circles. In many respects they resemble Wetti's vision. In the course of his sleep, the hero, monk or layman, finds himself in the beyond with a saint or an angel for a guide. The emphasis was at first placed on hell, so that men, sinners, would become aware of their sins, would repent, and could be saved, like Drythelm or Charles the Fat.

Drythelm was a pious layman who fell ill and died one evening. But at dawn he returned to life. He then decided to distribute his belongings and he withdrew to a hermitage. There, he told of having been led by a figure to a very broad and deep valley. To the left were flames, to the right hail and snow, on the slopes a host of human souls. But this was not yet hell. Drythelm wandered through places that were darker and darker. Suddenly, balls of fire containing human souls came out of a well and fell to earth; at the same time there were sounds of crying and snickering, and a fetid odor spread through the air. The demons were attacking five souls, among whom Drythelm could distinguish a priest, a layman, and a woman. When the devils surrounded him and seemed about to seize him with fiery tongs, his companion, who had momentarily left him, returned and led him toward a luminous place. Drythelm soon received explanations from his guide. The valley surrounded by flames and cold is the place where souls who confess belatedly are punished. Because they repented on the point of death, they will be saved at the Last Judgment. Furthermore, the prayers of the living, charity, fasts, and especially masses will allow them to bring the hour of liberation nearer. As for the well vomiting flames, it is the mouth of Gehenna; anyone who falls into it can never get out again.

A vision written down shortly after the death of Charles the Fat in 888, to serve the cause of his nephew Louis, is presented in the form of a narrative told by the emperor. One Sunday night, after the holy office of nocturn, Charles was going to bed when a voice announced to him that his spirit would leave him for a good hour; a vision would then reveal to him the judgment of God.

His guide, who was holding a ball of glowing wool, ordered him to take hold of a thread so that he might be guided through the labyrinth of infernal sorrows. Charles was thus led through deep valleys full of wells in which were burning pitch, sulfur, lead, wax, and soot, and in which were the prelates of his father and his uncles, for they had sown discord. The same torments were inflicted on practitioners of homicide and banditry.

When demons attempted to grab him, Charles and his guide climbed very high mountains of fire. Burning rivers with various bubbling metals were flowing down the mountains. In them were a host of men and notables who served his father and his brothers, some immersed up to their hair, others to the chin, others to the navel. They told him that, in the course of their earthly life they had liked to engage in battle and to commit homicides and robberies.

At the moment when dragons came hurtling forth, jaws open and full of fire, sulfur, and pitch, to swallow Charles up, his guide wound the woolen thread around him three times and pulled him forward forcefully. They then descended into a valley that was dark but burning like an oven fire on one side, while on the other it seemed to be extraordinarily pleasant. In the burning darkness, seeing several kings from his family, Charles felt great anguish, for he feared he would suffer the same torment. He also saw his father Louis standing up to his thighs in a pool filled with boiling water. "If you quickly come to my help, you and my loyal followers, bishops, abbots, and members of the clergy, with masses, offerings, psalms, vigils, and alms, I will soon be delivered from this pool of boiling water." Then he added: "Look to the left. Those two very deep pools have been prepared for you if you do not mend your ways and do penance for your abominable crimes."

Thus the realm of hell contained several places, depending on the gravity of the crime. And the prayers of the living were capable of shortening the torment of those who had not been damned for eternity.

Paradise could also contain several parts. After going through hell, Drythelm reached a long, high wall, which he mysteriously got over. He then found himself in a vast flowering meadow where there were men dressed in white. His guide, reading his thoughts, told him that this was not the Kingdom of Heaven. Our hero crossed the meadow, and as he went forward, the aroma became ever sweeter, and the light seemed ever brighter. But he had to turn back, because his companion did not want to lead him any further. He gave him explanations when they were back among the men in white. These figures had died in the midst of good works, but their insufficient holiness had not allowed them immediately to reach the Kingdom of Heaven; they would enter it on the day of the Last Judgment. Those who had been perfect in all respects reached it immediately. If Drythelm, who had to return to his body and live among men, were to lead a life of righteousness and simplicity, he would come back to be among the blessed spirits.

From the late twelfth century on, as Jacques Le Goff has shown with *Le Purgatoire de saint Patrick*—a text written between 1180 and 1220 by a Cistercian monk of Saltrey—an intermediate space separated hell from paradise: purgatory, from which purified souls would then go to paradise.

Curing Bodies

Visions were not only spiritual in nature. Not infrequently, a saint would appear to a sleeping sick person and, as God's intermediary, bring about a cure or show him what to do to be cured. Let us imagine the basilica of Saint Martin in Tours at the time of Bishop Gregory, the celebrated historian of the Franks.

In the atrium of the church is a crowd of the sick. Some are settled along the portico to shelter themselves from the wind, others have been lucky enough to secure a cell to pass the night. The best places are near the tomb. Sometimes it was a matter of a long wait in difficult conditions, since a bed was often nothing but a pallet. The disabled transported on carts and unable to get down stayed on the vehicles near the basilica. Other pilgrims waited at the gates out of a spirit of humility. The ill were often not alone, but accompanied by relatives, friends, and, if they were great personages, by slaves who watched with them.

Night has fallen, the doors have been closed. The guardian makes his rounds, making sure that the lights are out, except for the light at the tomb which glows in the cell. Plunged into darkness, with fitful illumination from the moon projecting phantom figures, the church takes on a mysterious or even fearsome appearance. Incense and the smoke of candles has made it difficult to breathe.

The sick are awake, for watching is obligatory, stretched out or sometimes on their knees. Fatigue sometimes wins out, especially when there is more than one restless night. They pray, fall asleep, and sometimes, roughly awakened by a dream, cry out,

"Lord Martin, deliver me," awaiting the slightest sound in the hope of hearing the saint.

The saint soon appears—many of them will relate their cures to Bishop Gregory who will scrupulously record their statements—and makes the sign of the cross on their diseased limb. There is a sharp pain, and they are cured. The miracle sometimes takes place at night, sometimes a little later, at matins.

On a journey as an adolescent, Saint Gal, Gregory's paternal uncle, once stepped on a thorn. He nevertheless continued limping on his way. But on the third night, the wound was suppurating and he felt great pain. Calling on the protection of Saint Julian, he prostrated himself before his tomb. Then, with the vigil over, he returned to bed, invoking the virtue of the martyr as he lay down, and fell asleep. When he awoke, he realized that he felt no pain and looked at his wound. He could not see the thorn that had penetrated his flesh, and realized that it had been taken out. He searched for and found it in his bed, wondering how it had come out.

Because it was brought about by the saint, sleep was associated by the sick with their cure. Let us transport ourselves to Brioude. A woman named Fédamie, completely paralyzed, is carried by relatives to the basilica of Saint Julian. She spends Sunday night there, under the portico adjoining the building. Lying asleep on a little bed, she sees a man in a dream who reproaches her and asks her why, while others are keeping vigil for God, she has failed to do so. She answers that her extreme weakness makes it impossible for her to walk. She then feels as if lifted up by the man and carried to the saint's tomb, where she prays while remaining asleep; at the same instant, it seems to her that a great quantity of chains are falling from her limbs onto the floor. Awakened by the noise, she realizes that she has completely recovered her health. She immediately rises from her bed and goes into the basilica, giving thanks in a loud voice. Some report that she often portrayed the man who had spoken to her: he was tall, dressed in white, full of elegance, with a smiling face; he had blonde and white hair; his movements were graceful, his voice open and gentle, his skin whiter than lilies. From this, several concluded that it was the blessed martyr Julian who had appeared to her. This woman was cured after eighteen years of illness.

Another paralytic, who had lost the use of all his limbs, was brought on a cart to the monastery of Saint Julian. While spending the night on his cart in front of the basilica, he saw it suddenly lit up with a radiant light and had the impression that he heard a host of men's voices singing psalms. During this time, he was praying, plunged into a kind of stupor and forgetting his illness. He tried to move forward; the light he had seen disappeared. He then came to himself and realized that he had recovered his health.

Like the ill, prisoners were among the unfortunate and benefited from similar miracles. The horn that King Gontran used to assemble his dogs and hunt deer had been stolen. Irritated, he put many people in prison and confiscated the wealth of some of them. Three of them then came to the tomb of Saint Seine. When the king learned of this, he ordered them to be chained hand and foot. But at midnight, a light brighter than earthly light appeared in the church; the rods holding the leg irons were broken, the iron rings holding the hands split, and the chains fell. As soon as he learned of the event, the king granted the prisoners their freedom.

When a dream turned into a nightmare, the patient would call on the saint's help; the dumb would recover speech. Moreover, Satan tried to deceive the sick while they slept, to put their faith in danger, but the saint would put the devil to flight by making the sign of the cross.

Cure generally took place during sleep. A woman long afflicted with quartan fever could no longer eat or sleep. Moaning, she kept watch and prayed at the tomb of Saint Venantius, remaining motionless until daybreak. In the morning, she fell asleep, and when she awoke, felt no more pain and went off cured. But can we really speak of incubation, that is, of healing sleep, in the Middle Ages?

The rite of incubation existed in Antiquity. In his *Sacred Speeches* of the second century A.D., Aelius Aristidus provides vivid evidence of this. He reports his cures in the temples of Serapis and Asclepius, the dreams in which the god gave him the formulas for cure, and the very intense exercises, like running or swimming, that he carried out at the god's command. The god showed himself in dreams and brought about the healing of the sick.

There was a development in the process in the course of Antiquity. While in Epidaurus in the fifth and fourth centuries B.C., the god cured the sick during the vision, in the Tiber island sanctuary in Roman times, he merely indicated the remedies and the cure only took place thereafter.

After the victory of Christianity, some worshipers behaved in Christian edifices in the same way as Greeks and Romans had in pagan temples. Incubation was probably practiced in eastern sanctuaries.

The situation seems less clear in the West. We have seen a certain number of texts drawn from the *Livres des miracles* of Gregory of Tours. They speak of healing, but there is no allusion to the wish to sleep in order to listen to the saint. The important thing is to watch and pray. Sometimes sleep even seems to be ruled out; for example, in a miracle that took place in Candes, where Saint Martin had died. Léomère, a serf belonging to a resident of Angers, had a paralyzed hand and was unable to speak as the result of a stroke. A long time afterward, he obeyed the dictates of faith by watching in the saint's basilica, and his hand was immediately cured and he was able to speak without trouble. "Here is what God's saint has carried out this night," he declared to everyone. When he returned to his master, he reported the miracle, but the unbelieving master set him to his usual work. He was immediately overcome by paralysis. Then the master sent him back to the holy place to which he had already gone, and there, after spending the night in devout prayer, the man was restored to health at daybreak.

Many elements of the incubation of antiquity were present: illness, presence of the patients in the church at night, allowing for dozing off, the appearance of a healing saint. But if sleep did occur, it was not sought after.

In the feudal period, watching and praying in pilgrim sanctuaries persisted. Night, the desire to be cured, and the narratives of miracles carried out by the saint predisposed the sick to sleep and to imagine that the saint appeared to them.

According to Pierre-André Sigal, author of a work on men and miracles in the eleventh and twelfth centuries, in which he provides an excellent discussion of incubation, only 40 percent of cures linked to a vision took place in the course of that vision. Generally, the saint showed himself in a dream, but sometimes the patient was awake or thought he was awake. The saint sometimes had clear features, sometimes blurred, took on the form of an animal or an object, came out of the tomb or through a window from heaven. He fulfilled the patient's desires, that is, healing, but he did it in different ways depending on circumstances. He might behave like a doctor or a surgeon: Saint Benedict, with the help of a knife, cut the film that covered the eyes of a blind man. But more frequently he acted in a non-medical way: with fingers or hand, he touched the diseased place, the eyes of the blind, the ears of the deaf, the throat of the dumb. He might intercede with holy water or with oil. Sometimes he even merely gave an order to the patient, who was cured by following it. In a dream, a paralytic received the order to rise; he did and awoke in good health.

To what extent was the cure linked to the voluntary pursuit of sleep? There is nothing probative in Gregory of Tours. On the other hand, in the second half of the twelfth century, a blind man learned in a dream that he would be cured if he went to sleep in front of the altar of Saint Rictrude in a church near Lille. Once inside the sanctuary, he begged the saint to intercede on his behalf and then, the author writes, following the custom of the afflicted, he went to sleep. There then appeared to him a very beautiful woman who moved the sleeve of her dress before his eyes. When he awoke, the blind man realized that he was cured. Similarly, a woman suffering from dropsy went to the abbey of Saint-Bertin. She prayed in vain in front of the tomb of Saint Bernard the Penitent, for she did not recover her health. But at home, the saint appeared to her and told her to return to the sanctuary and to sleep in a different spot from the first time. The woman obeyed and woke up cured.

If there was incubation, it differed from the kind practiced in Antiquity, in the sense that prayer was necessary to achieve a cure; prayer was in fact mentioned more frequently than sleep. In addition, there were many other procedures without a connection to night, like drinking dust from the tomb mixed in water. It was sufferers from fever who were the greatest beneficiaries of the rite of incubation, perhaps because a few hours of rest were more able to cure fever than deafness or paralysis.

This was the case with Guibert de Nogent. When he was still a small boy, he was taken with a severe fever during Easter time. Nearby was a church dedicated to Saints Léger and Maclou, for which his mother supplied the oil for a perpetual lamp. Since Guibert could take no food, she ordered two priests to take him into the sanctuary. They set a bed before the altar where all three could rest for the night. In the middle of the night, loud noises echoed through the church. Shaken from sleep, the two priests began to worry that fear had made Guibert even more ill. As for him, reassured by their company and by a lamp, he was only slightly afraid. So the night passed, and he returned to his mother's house in perfect health, as though he had felt no discomfort.

The nocturnal presence of God was an element in the unconscious of medieval man. But there was also a conscious and voluntary presence.

CHAPTER 7

Prayers

ight was a propitious time for prayer for laymen and clergy alike, as well as for union with God.

LAYMEN

Individual Piety

Designed for a single woman, virgin or widow, a "Christian day" by Pierre de Luxembourg—cardinal at fifteen in 1384, who died three years later in Avignon in an odor of sanctity—contains a program of daily devotions which shows the importance of nocturnal prayer. "You may be satisfied with sleeping six or seven hours without harming your health. You will get up every night as close to midnight as you can and, when you are awake, you will lift your eyes on high with all your heart toward your gentle master Jesus Christ on the cross, you will make the sign of the cross on your forehead, then on your palm. . . . And when you have gotten up, you will kneel as humbly as you can, and will hail Our Lord by saying at least one Our Father with attentiveness. Then, you will hail the Virgin Mary with a Hail Mary, or more, according to your devoutness; then you will say your matins. And in all your service, by day as well as by night, banish

199

from your heart as much as you can all worldly thoughts, and attach your heart to God. When you have said your matins, you will think of the passion of Jesus Christ with all your heart, praying to him to feel the pains that he suffered for you, thanking him for the mercies he has granted you. Then, you will commend yourself devoutly to Our Lady and to the saints to whom you pray. Then, according to the length of the nights and to your ardor, you will say once or twice, by night as well as by day, the following prayer: first, you will pray for the Church and for the prelates and the people of the Church, the princes of the earth and all the people in their charge; afterward, for all the men and women to whom you owe obligations, and also for all people in tribulation, for the dead to whom we are tied, and for all those in purgatory. You will not say too large a quantity of prayers, but you will accustom yourself to think often of one or the other of the following things: first of the goodness of God and of your evil; then of the glory you wish to have and the punishment you have deserved; finally of the hour of our death and the day of judgment. And then you will lie down again for a bit and rest. . .

"When evening has come, you will say your vespers and your vigils, if you know them and are able to do it, that is, during the week, three psalms and three lessons; on Sundays and holy days, nine psalms and nine lessons. After supper, when you have given thanks, you will quickly retire to your bedroom and close the door behind you." The woman should remain alone with God, not talk until the next day, except in case of great necessity. After accusing herself of her lapses and saying various prayers, she will go to bed.

To a married woman who was the mother of a family, a Franciscan of the first half of the fifteenth century declares, "I believe, my very dear daughter, that the most profitable hour for you and for all of us is midnight after sleep, once digestion has been accomplished and the work of the world put to rest, when the neighbors will not see you, when no one will look at you, except God." And a little further on, he insists, "Even though, at every hour and at all times, we must, as it has been said, be ready continually to raise our thoughts to God, the special hour is the hour of midnight."

Thus between the thirteenth and the fifteenth century, the clergy recommended to their lay followers an existence comparable to that of people consecrated to God. However, domestic constraints required some compromises. The Franciscan just quoted advises, since his follower has a husband, a household, children, and a family, that she keep a time for meditation in the evening after supper, between seven and nine. And Saint Antonin similarly declares, "For the reason that you are married and owe submission and obedience to your husband, I cannot tell you to get up at night like nuns to recite the office, but I heartily advise you to get into the habit of rising early." When it seems impossible to pray at night, the authors of "Christian days" advise taking moments that are close to night or even are practically part of it, since one recommends after dinner between seven and nine, and the other dawn.

These recommendations applied to women who, unlike their husbands, had no concern with external matters. In general, however, the clergy recommended that they sleep enough. Except for Simone Fidati, who prohibited that his follower, a virgin, go to bed before becoming exhausted and recommended nocturnal vigils, the authors of "Christian days" advised from six to eight hours of sleep. Waking was to be early (at dawn in summer, before sunrise in winter).

And indeed many texts show laymen and women praying at night. For the Merovingian period, the works of Gregory of Tours are full of examples. Queen Clotilde, widow of Clovis, spends nights in pious vigils. The mother of Count Eulalius perishes in the following circumstances. She often reprimanded her son for behaving unreasonably, so that he developed great hatred for her. As she frequently gave herself over to prayer in the chapel of her house and very often spent nights in prayer vigils accompanied with tears, while the servants were sleeping, she was found strangled with the hair shirt with which she was praying.

The future Saint Radegonde, wife of King Clotaire, had no hesitation in leaving the conjugal bed at night for long prayers, stretched out on a hair shirt, growing so cold that, writes her biographer Fortunatus, the warmth of the bed did not manage to warm her up. Of course, this attitude caused sharp recriminations from Clotaire, who exclaimed, "I married a nun and not a queen."

To show the piety of certain laymen, less frequent than among women, Gregory of Tours customarily reports that they get up at night without disturbing others—a sign of humility—to pray. When still a layman—he later became an abbot—Brachio left his bed two or three times every night to prostrate himself and pray to God. In contrast, if Mérovée the son of Chilpéric spent three days without interruption in fasting, vigil, and prayer, this was because he had placed on Saint Martin's grave the Psalter, the book of Kings, and the Gospels, and he was trying, after praying, to learn the future, thus mixing superstition and religion.

Prayer Vigils

It was fitting to honor God, not only individually in the solitude of a bedroom, but also in the company of other worshipers. Vigils drew hosts of people during the Merovingian era.

When a saint's day was celebrated, ceremonies would begin toward the middle of the night. Residents and pilgrims went to the church to attend vigils, a long and important ceremony which continued until dawn. The congregation stood unmoving and sang psalms, prayers, and hymns. For example, the priest in charge of the basilica of Saint Julian exhorted everyone to keep vigil with him, for the next day the relics of the patron saint were to be set in that place; the night thus was spent singing sacred hymns and heavenly chants. In another passage, a young girl, who is almost blind, goes to this same basilica with her father to attend vigils. The calendar of Saint Perpétue of Tours, left to us by Gregory, contains sixteen vigils in all. They constituted a preparation for the festival which took place after dawn. Normally, eating before mass was forbidden, but this prohibition was seldom observed by the laity or by some clergy.

The vigils were long ceremonies, and obviously the crowd that attended without participating actively did not always show a respectful attitude. Priests feared excesses. Laymen would talk without concern for annoying their neighbors. They even got into quarrels or noisily left the church. To remain still for a part of the night was not easy. As for the clergy, who could hardly stay away, they sometimes fell asleep.

Sometimes, there was an outburst of joy. A miracle had just occurred. A mute had recovered speech, a paralytic had walked, a blind man had seen. People immediately jostled each other to get closer to the person miraculously cured. Praises were sung and the priest gave thanks to the saint. On other occasions, the ceremony was troubled by cries of the possessed struggling under the control of the devil. The people believed that the saints attended vigils and the possessed called on them. The arrival of the saint might be revealed by the spread of a sweet aroma through the church.

The ceremony ended at dawn. The congregation, overcome with fatigue, went to sleep until nine, and matins drew few people. Before ten o'clock mass, the church had to be cleaned. The crowd had left refuse behind it. Drunken men had vomited. Worshipers sleeping in remote corners of the building were awakened by the guard on his rounds. The sick sometimes kept vigil for many successive nights in the basilica to obtain their cure, fasting near the tomb.

In addition to nocturnal ceremonies established by tradition, impromptu events, generally misfortunes, drew crowds to the church. As the bubonic plague was devastating the population of Reims, the terrified people of the city rushed to the grave of Saint Rémi. After lighting a great number of candles and lamps, they spent the entire night singing hymns and psalms.

These prayer vigils that were so frequent in Merovingian times continued in the succeeding centuries. The congregation was made up mostly of pilgrims, and the crowd at Saint-Martin of Tours was dense because the place was celebrated for its cures.

Churches were normally open at night. But, perhaps to avoid disorders, an old custom prohibited entry into the church of Mont-Saint-Michel before the matins bell, for, it was explained, angels and saints appeared there. Whoever did not respect this prohibition risked severe punishment.

A passage in Guibert de Nogent suggests that sometimes the doors were closed at night and then reopened only at the time of vigils. Otmond, a monk in Ely, who had become a church porter, harshly ejected a poor man who was importunately asking for charity; this was during the day. When night came, he went to open the doors and to announce the hour of vigils, when the devil appeared to him in the shape of the poor man. "I specify that this monk had just opened the doors of the barrier between the clergy and the people, and he was going on from there to open the other doors through which the people came in, when suddenly, while these doors were still closed, the man leaped on him, as though to strike him from the middle of the church, through the intermediary doors."

Efforts were sometimes made to prevent worshipers from coming into the building, but without success. In the second half of the tenth century, the monks of Sainte-Foy de Conques, no longer able to stand the cries and the uproar of the congregation, tried to close the church at night; but one morning they observed that the doors were open and that many pilgrims were inside. It is probable that the impatient crowd gathered in front of the sanctuary had broken down the doors. The document indicates that the faithful, armed with candles and lamps intended to lighten the darkness, had come to the holy place to keep vigil near relics, and that they spent their time in song, sacred songs for the clergy, and secular songs for the laity. The miracles of Saint Vulfran describe a vigil in the church of Saint Laurent in Rouen in 1053. On the night between Saturday and Sunday, the crowd, too large to be entirely contained within the church, had spilled out onto the church porch. Some were sitting, others standing, but all of them, writes the author, showed an attitude full of devotion. Like the people of Reims, the Rouennais prayed to Saint Vulfran, whose relics had just been brought, to preserve them from an epidemic.

It seems that vigils took place most often between Saturday and Sunday. The terms used apparently emphasize the nocturnal vigil near the relics rather than prayer. The attitude of the faithful wishing to spend the night near the remains of the saint differed rather deeply from that of the clergy, who emphasized the liturgical aspect of the gathering. Priests and monks, troubled by the crowd, would have tried to give a more ritual form to these vigils. It has been noted that the emphasis placed on the liturgy, moreover, may have inhibited the practice of incubation. However, in the feudal period, this development had only begun, and the disturbance caused by the presence of the faithful appears at several points in the text: secular songs being mixed with sacred songs; the actions of professional musicians like a *jongleur* from the town of Saintes, who often displayed his talent by playing melodies on his instrument in the basilica of Saint Eutrope and prevented the faithful from praying.

In any event, thanks to the opening of churches even at night, vigils permitted Christians to engage in perpetual prayer for a certain number of days. The novena, frequent in modern times, is barely attested in the Middle Ages. However, a document from the late twelfth century notes that anyone suffering from fever who spends nine nights praying in the chapel dedicated to Saint Mary Magdalen and Saint Adjuteur near Vernon, and who sleeps in the saint's bed will be cured. In the late thirteenth century, the custom of the abbey of Sainte-Croix in Bordeaux granted a loaf of bread and a measure of wine every day to people carrying out a novena.

Night thus frequently involved liturgical vigils. But mass was not to be celebrated before daybreak, according to a constant doctrine of the canonists inserted into Gratian's *Decretal*, as Henri Gilles has demonstrated. The *Liber pontificalis*, compiled in the early years of the sixth century, attributes to Telesphorus (pope in 125, died a martyr in 136) the prescription for celebrating mass on Christmas Eve, followed by the prohibition of nocturnal masses "before the third hour." The text, incorporated into various canonical collections, seems to have been the rule in the West in the fifth century. On September 2, 469, having gone to the church of the Maccabees in Lyon to take part in ceremonies for the anniversary of the death of Saint Just, Sidoine Apollinaire reports that a nocturnal procession took place near the bishop's tomb. Then, after matins, the assembly dispersed, but the pilgrims remained nearby, for they had to be present at terce, when the priests would perform the divine service.

As for the preceding period, in the absence of documents dealing with the question, only hypotheses are possible. During the persecutions, Christians generally came together at night, as recorded in a celebrated letter from Pliny the Younger to Trajan. In the third century, Tertullian considered that nocturnal masses were permitted, but his text suggests that they were becoming exceptional.

However, the hour of terce required by canon law concerned only public masses, that is, those in which the faithful gathered first around the bishop in the cathedral, then around the priest in the parish church, or the monastic community under the leadership of the abbot, and not private masses, which began to spread in the ninth century. But, to assure that the faithful would attend the parish mass, a canon whose substance is repeated in the decrees of Théodulf, bishop of Orléans, in the early ninth century, prohibits monks from celebrating a private mass in public on holy days.

Legislative documents of the thirteenth century still required that mass be performed during the day. However, they allowed very busy Christians who wished to hear a daily mass to do so before daybreak, on condition that it be shortly before daybreak. The fact that this practice was exceptional can be seen in that those who wished to take advantage of it asked for a dispensation from the pope, which was very unusual. Urban IV, for example, only granted three: to Count Henri de Meissen, to Count Alphonse de Poitiers of Toulouse, and to his wife Jeanne.

Who were the people interested in these nocturnal masses? On one hand were eminent lay figures who had private chapels. In the fourteenth century, among the favors granted by the pope was the right to hear mass before daybreak. On the other were legates and nuncios to whom the sovereign pontiff had entrusted a mission.

The material context and the idea that the mass recalled the death of Christ on the cross explain the exceptional character of nocturnal masses.

THE CLERGY

The fact of a pious priest getting up at night in order to pray makes up a kind of *topos*. After the death of his wife, Grégoire, the maternal great-grandfather of the historian of the Franks Gregory of Tours, was elected by the people and ordained as bishop of Langres. Since his house in Dijon adjoined the baptistery containing the relics of many saints, he got out of bed during the night without being seen and went to pray in the baptistery, the door to which opened miraculously, and there he meditatively sang psalms. When he had finished, he returned to bed and moved with such care that no one was aware of his absence.

Of course, the clergy participated in vigils, while the laity sometimes showed little enthusiasm and did not attend. An illustration is provided by this anecdote drawn from the life of Saint Nizier, bishop of Lyon. A man speaking to a priest declared that the whole community should keep vigil to obtain from the saint a peaceful year. The priest, overjoyed, had the bell sounded for vigils. Although the priest, the clergy of his church, and all the people came, the man, who was inclined toward gourmandise, was in no hurry to come. Finally, the vigils were ended, morning arrived, and the man who had first spoken of celebrating them had not attended.

It is enough to skim the works of Gregory of Tours to note that he frequently got up at night to go to religious offices. For example in the *Gesta Francorum*, while Gregory was participating in Paris in the council charged with judging Prétextat, the bishop of Rouen, messengers came to attempt to bribe him "after the singing of nocturnal hymns." One night, a great prodigy—stars glowing in the sky—appeared to him while he was celebrating the vigil of Saint Martin. While he was staying in the basilica of the blessed Julian in Paris, he got up in the middle of the night to give thanks to the Lord.

In the course of the night before Easter and during the day itself, there were particularly important celebrations to recall the Resurrection of Christ. During the nocturnal ceremony, the archdeacon lighted the paschal candle. He went up into the pulpit and prayed with the worshipers. He recalled the goodness and mercy of the Lord, gave thanks for the death of Christ that had saved all men. The ceremony concluded with the blessing of the baptismal fonts and the celebration of a baptism. During the vigil of Pentecost, the priest blessed milk, honey, and water, and catechumens were baptized. Monastic rules provide details about nocturnal devotions. Cassien, who had probably been living in Marseille since 415, wrote the *Institutions* at the request of Castor, bishop of Apt. As each day began in the evening, following the eastern custom, he first describes and comments on the evening offices. The day must be devoted to activities of the spirit, and night, the realm of evil, to activities of the body (sleep); but since it is necessary at night especially to fight against the temptations of the devil, it is important to supplement sleep with vigils and prayers.

The nocturnal schedule seems to have gone as follows: after singing psalms, the monks rested until an unspecified time. Awakened by brothers entrusted with the task, they recited psalms. Cassien wished for nocturnal vigils not to last too long, for it was good to prolong them with private vigils and manual labor in the cells. However, apparently many monks went back to sleep. Saturday vigils, which began on Friday after vespers according to Jewish custom, were distinctly longer. Since they lasted until the fourth crowing of the cock, there were in winter two hours of sleep remaining before the time of rising. Sunday vigils were ordinary, which may indicate Jewish influence.

But it was with the Rule of Saint Benedict that the order of offices was really organized in a complete way and that prayers were meticulously established. In winter, after reciting Psalms 3 and 94, as well as six others with antiphons, the abbot gave his blessing, everyone sat down on benches, and brothers took turns reading three lessons from a book set on the lectern, interspersed with the singing of three responses. After the third lesson, the cantor recited the Gloria. Everyone then rose from his seat as a sign of respect for the Holy Trinity. During vigils, texts drawn from the Old and New Testaments were read, as well as commentaries by the Church Fathers. These were followed by six psalms and the lesson of the Apostle.

From Easter to the calends of November, the singing of psalms remained the same, but because of the shortness of the nights, in place of the three lessons, there was only one from the Old Testament. The rest was carried out as noted, that is, during noc-

turnal vigils, never less than twelve psalms were recited, not
including Psalms 3 and 94.

On Sundays, they got up earlier for vigils, which at first contained schematically the same elements as in winter. But in addition to the psalms and the four lessons, they read four other
lessons with their responses. After that, they recited four can-
ticles of the prophets and one versicle, then the abbot gave his
blessing, and they read four more lessons from the New Testament. After the fourth response, the abbot started singing the
hymn *Te Deum laudamus*. When this was finished, he read the
lesson from the Gospels in front of the monks, who stood in homage and fear. He began the hymn *Te decet laus*, and after the bene-
diction, they sang matins.

This order of vigils had to be kept on Sunday in all seasons,
summer and winter, except if the monks got up late. In that case
the lessons or responses were slightly curtailed. But Benedict recommended that great care be taken to avoid this. If it were to
occur, the monk responsible for the mischance because of his
negligence should provide a worthy satisfaction to God in the
chapel.

Benedict concluded by quoting the prophet: "In the middle of
the night, I arose to give you thanks."

The Benedictine liturgy underwent changes over the course
of centuries. It was elaborated in particular at Cluny, as Guy de
Valous has shown. The nocturnal office began at two-thirty with
the *Trina Oratio* that Benedict of Aniane had introduced in the
ninth century to celebrate the Holy Trinity. The recitation of
the thirty last psalms was divided into three equal portions, the
first recited for the sake of the dead, the second for oneself, and
the third for kings and associates.

The office of matins included the nocturn celebrated following the indications of the Rule. To it were added various prayers,
including the *Miserere*, and four psalms for the sake of associates.
During Lent, the monks prostrated themselves for the recitation
of two additional psalms.

After matins took place the daily procession from the great
church to the church of Sainte Marie with the singing of two

psalms. In Sainte Marie, they chanted the lauds from the office of all saints, then matins and the lauds for the dead, followed by four psalms, and then three psalms for the dead. The monks then returned to the chancel of the great church where they sang the hour of lauds when dawn broke. After lauds came four more psalms, which were repeated at vespers and at compline, four psalms for associates, and two recited prostrate. The monks returned to bed until they were awakened around five for prime.

In all, 215 psalms were recited daily at Cluny, but the Cluny liturgy contained not only psalms. We have seen that for Saint Benedict, the lessons in vigils had to come from the Old and New Testaments. The monks of Cluny took them rather from the writings of the Church Fathers when they contained passages appropriate to the religious significance of the day. In addition, for the octave of saints' days, the lesson was drawn from their lives. If two anniversaries were celebrated on the same day, they read eight lessons from one saint and four from the other. And if the monks found no lessons for saints' vigils, they had no hesitation in composing new ones, as the abbot Odon did for Saint Géraud and Saint Martin.

The office was inordinately long. For example, for lessons, the reading of Genesis, which began in the nocturn of Septuagesima Sunday, was concluded in the middle of the week. Beginning at Easter, the nocturn lessons were shortened. But at the calends of November, that is, November 1, the long lessons of nocturn returned with, for example, the prophecy of Ezekiel completed on Saint Martin's Day, November 11. Two nights were enough to read the Epistle to the Romans.

The recitation of the supererogatory psalms added by the monks of Cluny was an obligation. Thus, in 1294, the nuns of Laveine and the monks of Roziers were rebuked by the Visitors because they did not recite the familiar psalms.

Let us conclude with two very significant examples, one because of the person, the other because of the moment.

Dominic, founder of the Preaching Brothers, was accustomed often to spend the night in church, reported Brother Rudolph, the procurator of the convent of Saint Nicolas of Bologna, during the canonization trial. He prayed a great deal and while praying shed copious tears and uttered many groans. The witness had often seen Dominic during his prayer standing on tiptoe and hands raised in the attitude of prayer. Because of his many vigils and nights spent in prayer, he frequently fell asleep during meals.

Carol Heitz has studied how the canonesses of Essen experienced Easter night in the fourteenth century. The rites in question are in fact attested as early as the tenth century in many places in France, England, northern Italy, and Germany.

At midnight, canons and canonesses went to the abbey church, monks by the south gallery, nuns by the north gallery connected to their chancel. The twelve canons went under the tent sheltering the Sepulcher and took the pyx, the box containing communion wafers, from the tomb, while the canonesses sang in front of the Sepulcher.

Then the procession took place. It contained seven groups and marked off seven stations. There came in succession, candle bearers, monstrance bearers, the deacon with the cross, canons with reliquaries, the hebdomadal accompanied by candle bearers with the Eucharist, the sub-deacon with the *Liber pleonarius* (a sacramentary of the early eleventh century), and finally the canonesses. Saint-Riquier, in the Carolingian period, had a fully comparable Easter procession.

For the seven stations, in the western chancel, in front of the altar of Saint Peter, the first of the seven penitential psalms was recited. Then the procession left the church and went to the nuns' cemetery. There unfolded the bizarre rite of the mystical weighing of the abbess, who got up on the end of a board set up as a balance, while the other end of the board held a lamb. This ceremony in the cemetery demonstrated the link between the Resurrection of Christ and the coming resurrection of the dead. Returning to the church, the procession stopped in succession in front of the main altar, the altar of the nuns' chancel, the main altar of the crypt, the altar of Saint Stephen, and the altar of the Holy Cross. The hebdomadal replaced the pyx in the *sacrarium* from which he had taken it on Good Friday. And all made adoration of the Cross.

Matins was then sung. Before the *Te Deum laudamus*, the visit of the Sepulcher took place in dramatic form. In the nave, canonesses were seated in stalls on the north side, canons on the south. In front of them, in the western transept, were the pupils of the *schola*. As actors, canons represented the two angels guarding the tomb, Saint John, and Saint Peter; canonesses represented the three Maries. After the *Deo gratias,* the people sang a hymn in German. A final station in front of the altar of the Holy Cross concluded the Easter night ceremony.

The documents we have referred to are either legislative or narrative in character. That is, the former indicate what is fitting to do, while the latter give evidence of reality, a reality no doubt very different from the ideal. How many women, for example, were able to follow the advice contained in the "Christian days"? Going further, some mystics, through night, were joined with God.

THE MYSTICISM OF DARKNESS

At night, man no longer perceives the visible world and thus has a better grasp of the invisible. It is then, in the Judeo-Christian tradition, that he may encounter God.

"What is more favorable to wisdom than the night?" writes Cyril of Jerusalem in the fourth century. "Then we often think of the things of God. Then we carry on reading and contemplation of divine things. When is our thought more concerned with chanting and praying? Is it not at night? When is it that we most often recall our own sins? Is it not at night?"

Gregory of Nyssa (died 394) develops in a remarkable way this theme of the mysticism of darkness, which he sets out principally in the *Life of Moses* and even more in his *Homilies on the Song of Songs.* He considers the mystical experience not to be an experience of light, but of darkness, a doctrine that was developed from Denis the Pseudo-Areopagite to Saint John of the Cross in the sixteenth century.

For Clement of Alexandria and Origen, the theme of darkness means that the human spirit cannot know the divine essence. In a penetrating analysis, Jean Daniélou concludes that it was Gregory of Nyssa who conferred a mystical meaning on darkness:

feeling the impossibility of acceding to the divine essence constitutes the highest form of contemplation.

"Night designates the contemplation of invisible things, in imitation of Moses who entered into the darkness (*gnophos*) where God was, that God who had made of darkness his refuge. . . . Surrounded by the divine night, the soul seeks the one who is hidden in darkness." In achieving a close union with God, the soul attaches itself to Him in love. God, darkness for the intelligence, can only be known through faith. Thus is manifested the positive aspect of the knowledge of God in darkness.

Since God inhabits the soul thanks to faith, the mysticism of darkness contains the experience of divine nearness. "After it has gone beyond everything tangible, the soul is then surrounded by the divine night, in which the Bridegroom makes himself present but does not show himself. How indeed could what is not visible show itself in the night? But he gives to the soul a feeling of presence while escaping from clear knowledge, hidden by the invisibility of his nature."

Divine nearness leads the soul to go out of itself, brings about an ecstasy. Sleep allows this ecstasy expression. But this is a sleep superior to wakefulness. "Sleep normally follows drunkenness [a sober, ecstatic drunkenness]. . . . But this is an extraordinary sleep, foreign to customary reality. Indeed, in ordinary sleep, the sleeper is not awake and one who is awake is not sleeping, but sleeping and wakefulness contrast to and follow one another. But here we observe an unprecedented and paradoxical mixture of opposites."

The soul is so absorbed in the contemplation of God that it loses awareness of reality. "The soul enjoys mere contemplation of reality and, letting all bodily activity slumber, through the purity and nakedness of the spirit, it receives the manifestation of God in a divine vigil. May we make ourselves worthy of this, by bringing about through this sleep the wakefulness of the soul."

This experience of God through ecstasy undergoes infinite growth. God remains darkness, but the soul advances within this darkness in a tension, the *epectasis,* which results from the divine attraction working on it.

Gregory's thinking was to be adopted in various ways over the course of the succeeding centuries. The German Dominican Meister Eckhart (c. 1260–c. 1327) commented on several occasions on the verse from John, "The light shines on in the darkness"; this darkness represents for him the One in whom the Word is eternally engendered.

But although night permitted the encounter with God, it was feared. For Jean Tauler (c. 1300–c. 1361), disciple and continuator of Meister Eckhart, if there is darkness "in which the spirit is introduced into the unity of unity," there is also darkness experienced as an abandonment by God, following the example of Jesus crying out on the Cross: "My God, why have you abandoned me?" But these were temporary ordeals.

It was the Spanish monk John of the Cross (1542–1591) who most clearly expressed the mystery of darkness. For him, that night was first of all an experience of divine transcendence, but it was accompanied with torments that made of it an obscure night.

> *On a dark night*
>
> On a dark night,
> afflicted and aflame with love,
> O joyful chance!
> I went out unnoticed,
> my house lying silent at last.
>
> .   .   .   .
>
> O you my guide, the night,
> O night more welcome than dawn,
> night that drew together
> the loved one and the lover,
> each transformed into the other!
>
> .   .   .   .
>
> I stayed; I surrendered,
> resting my face on my Beloved.

Nothing mattered.
I left my cares
forgotten among the lilies.*

Night of the senses. Night of the spirit. It is not our purpose to study the mysticism of Saint John of the Cross. We will merely take note of a few passages from his writings:

"The soul which God is about to lead onward is not led by His Majesty into this night of the spirit as soon as it goes forth from the aridities and trials of the first purgation and night of sense; rather it is wont to pass a long time, even years, after leaving the state of beginners, in exercising itself in that of proficients. . . . [Nevertheless] the purgation of the soul is not complete (for the principal part thereof, which is that of the spirit, is wanting, without which, owing to the communication that exists between the one part and the other, since the subject is one only, the purgation of sense, however violent it may have been, is not yet complete and perfect). . . ."*

The supreme goal is to attain to union with God, and John of the Cross reminds us of this goal at the beginning of the commentary on his poem. "Before we enter on the exposition of these stanzas, it is well to understand here that the soul that utters them is now in the state of perfection, which is the union of love with God, having already passed through severe trials and straits, by means of spiritual exercise in the narrow way of eternal life whereof Our Saviour speaks in the Gospel, along which way the soul ordinarily passes in order to reach this high and happy union with God."*

---

* *The Poems of St. John of the Cross*, trans. Ken Krabbenhoft (New York: Harcourt, Brace, 1999), 19–21.
* Saint John of the Cross, *Dark Night of the Soul*, 3rd ed., trans. and ed. E. Allison Peers (Garden City, N.J.: Doubleday-Image, 1959), 91–92.
* Ibid., 35.

Conclusion

$\mathscr{N}$ight is the place, night is the being where he [the child]
    rests, where he withdraws, where he gathers his
    thoughts,
Where he comes back in. And he comes out of it refreshed.
    Night is my most beautiful creation.
. . . .
It is night that is continuous, where being immerses itself,
    it is night that makes a long unbroken thread,
An unbroken thread without end where days are only days.
They open only as days.
That is, like holes, in a fabric where there are days.
In a fabric, in an openwork cloth.
It is night that is my great black wall
Where days open only like windows
With a troubled and with a trembling
And perhaps with a false light.

Thus Péguy, in *Le Porche du mystère de la deuxième Vertu,*
replies to Puck the fairy of *A Midsummer Night's Dream.*

    The ambivalence of the medieval night! To the violence
linked to night is opposed the safety provided by the light of the
sun. To the long working day is opposed restful nightly sleep,

although some preferred to give their nights to play. Night was the domain of Satan and also the high point of monastic prayer.

The things of this world are never so clear cut. On the level of language, as Gérard Genette has shown, the relationship between day and night is not only one of mutual exclusion, but also of inclusion; the term "day" has two meanings, one excluding, the other including night. Day represents the essence of which night is merely an accident, an underside. One cannot speak of night without thinking of day, while any talk of day can do without reference to night. And the glorification of night by Péguy can only be done at the expense of day.

The French language made night feminine and day masculine, reinforcing the sexual characteristics inherent in the two elements. Night is the woman whom love connects to day, sometimes by opposing it:

Ah! Night, if so many times, in the arms of love,
I admitted you to the pleasures that I hid from day. . .

writes Boileau in *Le Lutrin*. And this woman is a mother, "universal mother," according to Péguy, "no longer only mother of children (that is so easy), but mother of even men and of women, which is so difficult." This mother night which gives the day will recover it in the end.

Night—woman. While medieval man experiences anguish and repulsion for the troubling darkness in the same way as he does for the mysterious feminine body that the male penetrates and where the human being is formed, contemporary man, who, thanks to technology, has conquered the darkness of night and has given to woman control over her body, can apparently adopt a different attitude.

Nevertheless, if one continues the analysis, one may be struck by a strange resemblance with the Middle Ages. Is modern night not different especially in that man has separated himself from God? By substituting man for God, he has thought to bring light and mastery everywhere—the "night *of* the Middle Ages" was followed by the Renaissance, the Enlightenment, our

BIBLIOGRAPHY

PRIMARY SOURCES

Baye, Nicolas de. *Journal de Nicolas de Baye, greffier du Parlement de Paris, 1400–1417.* Edited by A. Tuetey. 2 vols. Société de l'Histoire de France. Paris, 1885–88.

Benedict, Saint. *RB 1980: The Rule of St. Benedict in English.* Edited by Timothy Fry. Collegeville, Minn.: Liturgical Press, 1982.

Boccaccio, Giovanni. *The Decameron.* Translated by Guido Waldman. Oxford: Oxford University Press, 1993.

Boileau, Étienne. *Le Livre des métiers.* Edited by R. de Lespinasse and F. Bonnardot. Paris, 1879.

Bueil, J. de. *Le Jouvencel suivi du commentaire de Guillaume Tringant.* Edited by L. Lecestre and C. Favre. 2 vols. Paris, 1887–89.

Capitularia regum Francorum. Edited by R. Boretius. 2 vols. In *Monumenta Germaniae historica, Legum sectio.* 1881–1897.

Cent nouvelles nouvelles. Edited by R. Dubuis. Lyon, 1991.

Césaire d'Arles. *Sancti Caesarii Arelatensis Sermones.* Edited by C. Morin. 2 vols. Corpus christianorum, Series latina, 103 and 104. Turnhout, 1953.

Chastellain, Georges. *Oeuvres.* Edited by Kervyn de Lettenhove. 8 vols. Brussels, 1863–66.

Choix de pièces inédites relatives au règne de Charles VI. Edited by L. Douet d'Arcq. 2 vols. Paris, 1863–64.

Chronique du Religieux de Saint-Denis, contenant le règne de Charles VI, de 1380 à 1422. 6 vols. Documents inédits sur l'Histoire de France. Paris, 1839–52.

Deschamps, Eustache. *Oeuvres complètes.* Edited by A. Queux de Saint-Hilaire and G. Raynaud. 11 vols. Société des anciens textes français. Paris, 1878–1904.

Documents relatifs à l'histoire de l'industrie et du commerce en France.
Edited by G. Fagniez. 2 vols. Paris, 1898–1900.

Les Évangiles des Quenouilles. Edited by M. Jeay. Paris, 1985.

Farces du Moyen Age. Edited by A. Tissier. Paris, 1984.

Fauquemberghe, Clément de. *Journal de Clément de Fauquemberghe, greffier du Parlement de Paris, 1417–35.* Edited by A. Tuetey and H. Lacaille. 3 vols. Société de l'Histoire de France. Paris: 1903–15.

Flamenca. Roman occitan du XIIIe siècle. Edited and translated by J.-Ch. Huchet. Paris: 1988.

Fortunat, Venance. *Vita prima sanctae Radegundis.* Edited by B. Krusch. In *Monumenta Germaniae historica, Scriptores rerum merovingicarum,* II, 364–377. 1888 (reprint 1956).

Froissart, Jean. *Chroniques.* Edited by S. Luce, G. Raynaud, and L. and A. Mirot. 15 vols. to date. Société de l'Histoire de France. Paris, 1869–1975.

———. *Chroniques.* Edited by Kervyn de Lettenhove. 26 vols. Brussels, 1870–1876.

———. *Poésies.* Vol. II, edited by A. Scheler. Brussels, 1871.

Gervais de Tilbury. *Le Livre des Merveilles. Divertissement pour un Empereur* (part three). Translated by A. Duchesne. Paris, 1992.

Giry, A. *Les Établissements de Rouen.* 2 vols. 1883–1885.

Gregory of Tours. *The History of the Franks.* Translated by Lewis Thorpe. Harmondsworth: Penguin, 1974.

———. *Miracula et opera omnia.* Edited by B. Krusch. In *Monumenta Germaniae historica, Scriptores rerum merovingicarum.* Vol. I, 2. 1885.

———. *Les Livres des miracles et autres opuscules.* Edited and translated by H. Bordier. 4 vols. Paris, 1857–64.

Guibert de Nogent. *Autobiographie.* Edited and translated by E.-R. Labande. Les Classiques de l'Histoire de France au Moyen Age. Paris, 1981.

Guillaume de Lorris and Jean de Meun. *The Romance of the Rose.* Translated by Charles Dahlberg. Princeton, N.J.: Princeton University Press, 1995.

Hansen, J. *Quellen und Untersuchungen zur Geschichte des Hexenwahns und der Hexenverfolgung im Mittelalter.* Bonn, 1901.

Heito. *Visio Wettini.* Edited by Duemmler. In *Monumenta Germaniae historica, Poetae latini medii aevi.* Vol. II, 267–275.

Hildegard von Bingen. *Hildegardis cause et curae.* Edited by P. Kaiser. Leipzig, 1903.

Institoris, H., and J. Sprenger. *Le Marteau des sorcières*. Translated by A. Danet. Paris, 1973.

Isidore of Seville. *Isidori Hispalensis episcopi Etymologiarum sive Originum libri XX*. Edited by W. M. Lindsay. 2 vols. Oxford, 1911.

John of the Cross, Saint. *Dark Night of the Soul*. Translated and edited by E. Allison Peers. Garden City, N.Y.: Doubleday-Image, 1959.

———. *The Poems of St. John of the Cross*. Translated by Ken Krabbenhoft. New York: Harcourt Brace, 1999.

John of Salisbury. *Policraticus: Of the Frivolities of Courtiers and the Footprints of Philosophers*. Edited and translated by Cary J. Nederman. New York: Cambridge University Press, 1990.

Journal d'un bourgeois de Paris de 1405 à 1449. Edited by C. Beaune. Paris, 1990.

La Marche, Olivier de. *Mémoires*. Edited by H. Beaune and J. d'Arbaumont. 4 vols. Paris, 1883–88.

Lecouteux, Cl., and Ph. Marcq. *Les Esprits et les Morts*. Paris, 1990.

Leges nationum germanicum. 4 vols. In *Monumenta Germaniae historica*. 1920–37.

Leroux de Lincy, A., and L.-M. Tisserand. *Paris et ses historiens au XIVe et XVe siècles*. Paris, 1867.

Lespinasse, R. de. *Les Métiers et Corporations de la ville de Paris*. 3 vols. Paris, 1886–97.

Longnon, A. *Paris pendant la domination anglaise, 1420–1436*. Société de l'Histoire de Paris et de l'Ile de France. Paris: 1878.

Mansi et al. *Sacrorum conciliorum nova et amplissima collectio*. Reprint with continuations. Paris, 1901–.

Marie de France. *The Lais of Marie de France*. Translated by Robert Hanning and Joan Ferrante. New York: Dutton, 1978.

Le Ménagier de Paris. Edited by J. Pichon. 2 vols. Paris, 1846–47.

Monstrelet, Enguerrand de. *Chronique, 1400–1444*. Edited by L. Douet d'Arcq. 6 vols. Paris, 1857–62.

Ordonnances des rois de France de la troisième race. 22 vols. Paris, 1723–1849.

Prier au Moyen Age. Pratiques et Expériences (Ve–XVe siècle). Edited by N. Bériou, J. Berlioz, and J. Longère. Turnhout, 1991.

Proverbes français antérieurs au XVe siècle. Edited by J. Morawski. Paris, 1925.

Les XV Joies de Mariage. Edited by J. Rychner. 1967.

Raoul Glaber. *Les Cinq Livres de ses histoires (900–1044)*. Edited by M. Prou. Paris, 1886.

Recueil de documents concernant la commune et la ville de Poitiers. I., *de 1063 à 1327.* II., *de 1328 à 1380.* In *Archives historiques du Poitou,* vols. 44 and 45. Poitiers, 1923 and 1928.

Recueil général et complet des fabliaux des XIIIe et XIVe siècles. Edited by A. de Montaiglon and G. Raynaud. 6 vols. Paris, 1872–90.

Recueils des documents concernant le Poitou, contenus dans les registres de la Chancellerie de France. Vols. I–XI (1302–1474), edited by P. Guérin, in *Archives historiques du Poitou,* vols. 11, 13, 17, 19, 24, 26, 29, 32, 35, 38. 1881–1909. Vol. XII (1475–1483), edited by P. Guérin and L. Celier, in *Archives historiques du Poitou,* vol. 41. 1919. Vols. XIII–XIV (1483–1502), edited by L Célier, in *Archives historiques du Poitou,* vols. 50 and 56. 1938 and 1958.

Reginon de Prum. *Libri de synodalibus causis et disciplinis ecclesiasticis.* Edited by F. W. H. Wasserschleben. Leipzig, 1840.

Registre criminel du Châtelet de Paris du 6 septembre 1389 au 18 mai 1392. Edited by H. Duples-Agier. 2 vols. Paris, 1861–64.

Rufinus. *The Herbal of Rufinus.* Edited by L. Thorndike and F. S. Benjamin. Chicago, 1945.

Villon, François. *Poésies complètes.* Edited by Cl. Thiry. Paris, 1991.

Vogel, C. *Le Pécheur et la Pénitence au Moyen Age.* Paris, 1969.

SECONDARY SOURCES

[Works most utilized are indicated by an asterisk]

*Alexandre-Bidon, D., and M. Closson. *L'Enfant à l'ombre des cathédrales.* Lyon, 1985.

*Ariès, Philippe, and Georges Duby, eds. *A History of Private Life.* Vol. 2, *Revelations of the Medieval World.* Cambridge, Mass.: Harvard University Press, 1988.

Aubrun, M. "Caractères et portée religieuse et sociale des *Visiones* en Occident du VIe au XIe siècle." *Cahiers de civilisation médiévale* (April–June 1980): 109–130.

Bachelard, Gaston. *La Flamme d'une chandelle.* Paris, 1961.

Baroja, J.-C. *Les Sorcières et leur monde.* Paris, 1972.

Barroux, M. *Les Fêtes royales de Saint-Denis en mai 1389.* Paris, 1936.

*Bautier, R.-H. "Contestations de la personne du roi et de l'autorité royale (XIIe–XIVe siècle). L'exemple d'Orléans (1284)." In *Violence et contestation au Moyen Age,* 207–234. Paris, 1990.

Becker, R. de. *Les Machinations de la nuit.* Paris, 1965.

*Biarne, J. "Le temps d'après les premières règles monastiques d'Occident (IVe–VIe siècle)." In *Le Temps chrétien de la fin de l'Antiquité au Moyen Age. IIIe–XIII siècle,* 99–128.

Billot, Cl. *Chartres aux XIVe et XVe siècles: une ville et son plat pays.* Paris, 1980.

*Boureau, A. "Satan et le dormeur. Une construction de l'inconscient au Moyen Age." *Chimères* 14 (1991–92): 41–61.

Boutonnier, J. *Contribution à la psychologie et à la métaphysique de l'angoisse.* Paris, 1945.

*Braet, H. *Le Songe dans la chanson de geste au XIIe siècle.* Ghent, 1975.

Bruyne, E. de. *Études d'esthétique médiévale.* 3 vols. Bruges, 1946.

Carbonnier, J. "Nocturne." In *Mélanges Henri Lévy-Bruhl,* 345–50. Paris, 1959.

Carozzi, Cl. *Le Voyage de l'âme dans l'au-delà d'aprés la littérature latine (Ve–Xiiie siècle).* Unpublished thèse d'État. Paris, 1989.

Cartellieri, O. *La Cour des ducs de Bourgogne.* Paris, 1946.

Cassagnes-Broquet, S. *La Violence des étudiants toulousains de 1460 à 1610.* Thèse de 3e cycle, École des Hautes Études, 1982. Typescript.

*Champion, P. *François Villon. Sa vie et son temps.* 2 vols. Paris, 1913.

———. *La Vie de Paris au Moyen Age. I., L'Avènement de Paris. II., Splendeurs et misères de Paris (XIVe–XVe siècle).* 2 vols. Paris, 1933–34.

*Chevalier, B. *Les Bonnes Villes de France du XIVe au XVIe siècle.* Paris, 1982.

———. *Tours, ville royale (1356–1520). Origine et développement à la fin du Moyen Age.* Louvain and Paris, 1975.

Chiffoleau, J. *La Comptabilité de l'au-delà. Les hommes, la mort et la religion dans la région d'Avignon à la fin du Moyen Age (vers 1320–vers 1480).* L'École française de Rome 47. Rome, 1980.

Cohen, G. *Histoire de la mise en scène dans le théâtre religieux français du Moyen Age.* Paris, 1926.

———. *Le Théâtre en France au Moyen Age. I., Le Théâtre religieux. II., Le Théâtre profane.* Paris, 1928 and 1931.

*Cohn, Norman. *Europe's Inner Demons.* New York: Basic Books, 1975.

Colliot, R. "Soleil, lune, étoiles à l'horizon littéraire médiéval ou les signes de la lumière (textes du XIIIe siècle)." In *Le Soleil, la Lune et les Étoiles au Moyen Age,* 39–52.

Combarieu du Grès, M. de. "Le jour et la nuit dans le Roman de Béroul." *Tristiania* 11, no.1 (November 1976): 12–31.

———. "Scènes de nuit dans le *Roman de Renart.*" In *Mélanges Alice Planche,* 117–125.

————. "Le soleil et la lune dans le cycle du Lancelot-Graal." In *Le Soleil, la Lune et les Étoiles au Moyen Age*, 53–80.

*Contamine, Philippe. "The Use of Private Space." In *A History of Private Life*. Vol. 2, *Revelations of the Medieval World*, edited by Philippe Ariès and Georges Duby, 425–505. Cambridge, Mass.: Harvard University Press, 1988.

————. "Prodige et propagande. Vendredi 20 août 1451, de 7 heures à 8 heures du matin: le ciel de Bayonne." In *Observer, Lire, Écrire le ciel au Moyen Age*, 63–86.

————. *La Vie quotidienne pendant la guerre de Cent Ans. France et Angleterre (XIVe siècle)*. Paris, 1976.

Corrain, L. "Raffigurare la notte." In Sbriccoli, ed., *La Notte*, 141–162.

Coulet, N. *Aix-en-Provence. Espace et relations d'une capitale (milieu XIVe siècle-milieu XVe siècle)*. 2 vols. Aix-en-Provence, 1988.

Crouzet-Pavan, E. "Potere politico e spazio sociale: il controllo della notte a Venezia nei secoli XIII–XV." In Sbriccoli, ed., *La Notte*, 46–66.

*Daniélou, J. "Mystique de la ténèbre chez Grégoire de Nysse." In the article "Contemplation," in *Dictionnaire de spiritualité ascétique et mystique*. Vol. 2, col. 1872–1885.

*Delamare. *Traité de la police*. Vol. 1. Paris, 1722.

Delort, R. *Le Commerce des fourrures en Occident à la fin du Moyen Age*. 2 vols. Rome, 1978.

————. *La Vie au Moyen Age*. Paris, 1982.

Delumeau, Jean. *Sin and Fear: The Emergence of a Western Guilt Culture*. Translated by Eric Nicholson. New York: St. Martin's Press, 1989.

*————. *La Peur en Occident (XIVe–XVIIIe siècles)*. Paris: Fayard, 1978.

Deluz, Ch. "Un ciel mieux étudié que la terre, d'après quelques textes sur le monde (XIIe–XIVe siècle)." In *Le Soleil, la Lune et les Étoiles au Moyen Age*, 91–109.

*Demians d'Archimbaud, G. *Les Fouilles de Rougier (Var). Contribution à l'archéologie de l'habitat rural en pays méditerranéen*. Paris, 1980.

* *Le Diable au Moyen Age (Doctrine, Problèmes moraux, Représentations). Sénéfiance 6* (1979). Aix-en-Provence.

Dinzelbacher, P. "Körperliche und Seelische Vorbedingungen religiöser Träume und Visionen." In *I Sogni nel Medioevo*, 57–86. International Congress, Rome, 1983. Rome, 1985.

————. *Vision und Visionsliteratur im Mittelalter*. Stuttgart, 1981.

*Dubost, F. *L'Autre, l'Ailleurs et l'Autrefois. Aspects fantastiques de la littérature narrative médiévale (XIIe–XIII siècles)*. Thèse de doctorat d'État, III. Paris, 1989. Typescript.

Dupuy, M. "Nuit." In *Dictionnaire de spiritualité ascétique et mystique*. Vol. 11, col. 519–525.

Durand, Gilbert. *Les Structures anthropologiques de l'imaginaire. Introduction à l'archétypologie générale*. Paris, 1969.

Faral, E. *La Vie quotidienne au temps de Saint Louis*. Paris, 1938.

Favier, J. *Paris au XVe siècle. 1380–1500*. Paris, 1974.

Favreau, R. "Aspects de l'Université de Poitiers au XVe siècle." *Bulletin de la Société des antiquaires de l'Ouest* (1959–60): 31–71

———. "Les vues de Poitiers au Moyen Age." *Bulletin de la Société des antiquaires de l'Ouest* (1979): 223–238.

Frappier, J. "Le thème de la lumière de *La Chanson de Roland* au *Roman de la Rose*." In *Histoire, Mythes et Symboles*, 181–198.

*Gauvard, Cl. *"De grace especial."* In *Crime État et Société en France à la fin du Moyen Age*. 2 vols. Publications de la Sorbonne. Paris, 1991.

Gay, V., and H. Stein. *Glossaire archéologique du Moyen Age et de la Renaissance*. 2 vols. Paris, 1887 and 1928.

Genette, Gérard. "Le jour, La nuit." In *Figures II*, 101–122. Paris: Seuil, 1969.

Geremek, Bronislaw. *The Margins of Society in Late Medieval Paris*. Translated by Jean Birrell. New York: Cambridge University Press, 1987.

*———. *Le Salariat dans l'artisanat parisien aux XIIIe–XVe siècles*. Paris and The Hague, 1968.

———. *Truands et Misérables dans l'Europe moderne (1350–1600)*. Paris, 1980.

*Gilles, H. "L'interdiction canonique des messe nocturnes." In *La Religion populaire en Languedoc du XIIIe siècle à la moitié du XIVe siècle*, 419–428. Cahiers de Fanjeaux 11. Toulouse, 1976.

Ginzburg, Carlo. *Ecstasies: Deciphering the Witches' Sabbath*. Translated by Raymond Rosenthal. New York: Pantheon, 1991.

Gonthier, N. *Cris de haine et rites d'unité. La violence dans les villes. XIIIe–XVIe siècles*. Turnhout, 1992.

———. *Délinquance, Justice et Société en Lyonnais, fin XIIIe siècle-début XVIe siècle*. 4 vols. Thèse. Lyon, 1988. Typescript.

Gouiran, G. "*Flamenca*: du 'grand soleil d'amour chargé' aux 'princes de la nuit'." In *Le Soleil, la Lune et les Étoiles au Moyen Age*, 141–157.

Hasenohr, G. "La vie quotidienne de la femme vue par l'Église: l'enseignement des 'journées chrétiennes' de la fin du Moyen Age." In *Frau und Spätmittelalterlicher Alltag*, 19–101. Vienna, 1986.

*Heitz, C. "La nuit pascale des chanoinesses d'Essen du XIVe siècle." In *La Femme au Moyen Age*, 33–48. Maubeuge, 1990.

Huizinga, Johan. *The Autumn of the Middle Ages.* Translated by Rodney J. Payton and Ulrich Maunitzsch. Chicago: University of Chicago Press, 1996.

*Jarousseau, G. "Le guet, l'arrière-guet et la garde en Poitou pendant la guerre de Cent Ans." *Bulletin de la Société des antiquaires de l'Ouest* 8 (1965): 159–202.

Jeay, M. "Sur quelques coutumes sexuelles du Moyen Age." In *L'Érotisme au Moyen Age,* 123–141. Montreal, 1977.

Jones, Ernest. *On the Nightmare.* New York: Liveright, 1951.

Jonin, P. "L'espace et le temps de la nuit dans les romans de Chrétien de Troyes." In *Mélanges Alice Planche,* 235–246.

*Laharie, M. *La Folie au Moyen Age. XIe–XIIIe siècle.* Paris, 1991.

*Landes, David S. *Revolution in Time: Clocks and the Making of the Modern World.* Cambridge, Mass.: Harvard University Press, 1983.

*Langlois, Ch.-V. *La Vie en France au Moyen Age de la fin du XIIe au milieu du XIVe siècle.* 4 vols. Paris, 1926–28.

Lavaud, B.-M. "L'angoisse spirituelle selo Jean Tauler." *Études carmélitaines* (October 1938): 82–91.

Leclercq, H. "Incubation." In *Dictionnaire d'archéologie chrétienne et de liturgie.* Vol. VII–1 (1926), col. 511–517.

———. "Nuit." In *Dictionnaire d'archéologie chrétienne et de liturgie.* Vol. XII–2, col. 1808–1809.

Lefèvre, Y. *L'Élucidarium et les Lucidaires.* Paris, 1954.

*Le Goff, Jacques. "Au Moyen Age: temps de l'Église et temps du marchand." *Annales, ESC* (1960): 417–433.

———. "Aspects savants et populaires des voyages dans l'au-delà au Moyen Age." In *L'Imaginaire médiéval,* 103–119. Paris, 1985.

*———. *The Birth of Purgatory.* Translated by Arthur Goldhammer. Chicago: University of Chicago Press, 1984.

*———. "Le christianisme et les rêves (IIe–VIIe siècle)." In *L'Imaginaire médiéval,* 265–316. Paris, 1985.

———. "Le désert-forêt dans l'Occident médiéval." In *L'Imaginaire médiéval,* 59–75. Paris, 1985.

———. "Le temps du travail dans la 'crise' du XIVe siècle: du temps médiéval au temps moderne." *Le Moyen Age* 69 (1963): 597–613.

———. "Les rêves dans la culture et la psychologie collective de l'Occident médiéval." *Scolies* 1 (1971): 123–130.

Le Goff, Jacques, and René Rémond, eds. *Histoire de la France religieuse.* Vol. 1, *Des origines au XIVe siècle.* Paris, 1988.

Le Goff, Jacques, and J.-Cl. Schmitt, eds. *Le Charivari.* Actes de la table ronde organisée à Paris, 25–27 April 1977. Paris, The Hague, and New York, 1981.

Leguay, J.-P. *Un réseau urbain au Moyen Age: les villes du duché de Bretagne au XIVe et XVe siècles.* Paris, 1981.

———. *La Rue dans les villes françaises de la fin du Moyen Age.* Rennes, 1984.

*Le Roy Ladurie, Emmanuel. *Montaillou: The Promised Land of Error.* Translated by Barbara Bray. New York: George Braziller, 1978.

*Lorcin, M.-Th. "Le soleil, l'oeil et la vision au Moyen Age." In *Le Soleil, la Lune et les Étoiles au Moyen Age,* 215–228.

Louis de la Trinité, P. "L'obscure nuit du feu d'amour." *Études carmélitaines* (October 1938): 7–32.

Luce, S. *La France pendant la guerre de Cent Ans.* Paris, 1890.

Luchaire, A. *Les Communes françaises à l'époque des Capétiens directs.* New edition revised by L. Halphen. Geneva, 1977.

Lucien-Marie de Saint-Joseph, P. "A la recherche d'une structure essentielle de la nuit de l'esprit." *Études carmélitaines* (October 1938): 254–281.

*Maguin, J.-M. *La Nuit dans le théâtre de Shakespeare et de ses prédécessurs.* 2 vols. Lille, 1980.

Maire-Vigueur, J.-Cl. "Valenze della notte in alcune esperienze religiose medievali (Italia centrale, XIII–XIV secolo)." In Sbricolli, ed., *La Notte,* 23–29.

Mantini, S. "Notte in città, notte in campagna tra Medioevo ed Età moderna." In Sbricolli, ed., *La Notte,* 30–45.

*Marignan, A. *Études sur la civilisation française.* I., *La Société mérovingienne.* II., *Le Culte des saints sous les Mérovingiens.* Paris, 1899.

Mehl, J.-M. *Les Jeux au royaume de France du XIIIe au début du XVIe siècle.* Paris, 1990.

Muchembled, Robert. *La Sorcière au village (XVe–XVIIIe siècle).* Paris: Gallimard-Folio, 1991.

———. *La Violence au village. Sociabilité et comportements populaires en Artois du XVe au XVIIe siècle.* Turnhout: Brepols, 1989.

"La nuit." *Corps écrit* 14 (1985).

Observer, Lire et Écrire le ciel au Moyen Age. Edited by B. Ribemont. Actes du colloque d'Orléans, 22–23 April 1989. Paris, 1991.

*Pacault-Legendre, V., and Ch. Guilleminault. "Troubles du sommeil." In *Encylopédie Médicale et Chirurgicale,* Psychiatrie, 37129A10, 7. Paris, 1984.

Pastoureau, M. "Du bleu et du noir: éthiques et pratiques de la couleur à la fin du Moyen Age." *Médiévales* (1988): 9–21.

*Paul, J. "Le démoniaque et l'imaginaire dans le *De Vita sua* de Guibert de Nogent." In *Le Diable au Moyen Age*, 371–399.

*Pavant, E. "Recherches sur la nuit vénitienne à la fin du Moyen Age." *Journal of Medieval History* 7 (1981): 339–356.

*Payen, J.-Ch., and Y. Legros. "La femme et la nuit ou recherche sur le thème de l'échange amoureux dans la littérature courtoise." *Sénéfiance* 7 (1979): 515–525.

Pelle-Douël, Y. *Saint Jean de la Croix et la nuit mystique*. Paris: Seuil, 1992.

Pesez, J.-M. "L'habitation paysanne en Bourgogne médiévale." In *La Construction au Moyen Age. Histoire et archéologie*, 219–237. Actes du congrès de la Société des historiens médiévistes de l'Enseignement supérieur public, Besançon, 1972. Paris, 1973.

———. "Le foyer de la maison paysanne (XIe–XVe siècle)." *Archéologie médiévale* 16 (1986): 65–92.

Pietri, L. *La Ville de Tours du IVe au VIe siècle: naissance d'une cité chrétienne*. L'École française de Rome 13. Rome, 1983.

Quenedey, R. *L'Habitation rouennaise. Études d'histoire, de géographie et d'archéologie urbaines*. Rouen, 1926.

Ramnoux, Ch. *La Nuit et les enfants de la Nuit dans la tradition grecque*. Paris, 1959.

———. "Histoire d'un symbole. Histoire antique de 'la Nuit'." *Cahiers internationaux du symbolisme* 13 (1967): 57–68.

Reypens, L. "La 'nuit de l'esprit' chez Ruusbroec." *Études carmélitaines* (October 1938): 75–81.

Richard, J.-M. *Mahaut, comtesse d'Artois et de Bourgogne (1302–1329)*. Paris, 1887.

Riche, P. *La Vie quotidienne dans l'Empire carolingien*. Paris, 1973.

Rossiaud, J. *La Prostitution médiévale*. Paris, 1988.

Sbriccoli, M., ed. *La Notte. Ordine, sicurezza e disciplinamento in età moderna*. Città di Castello, 1991.

———. "Nox quia nocet, I giuristi, l'ordine e la normalizzazione dell' immaginario." In Sbriccoli, ed., *La Notte*, 9–19.

Schmitt, J.-Cl. "Les revenants dans la société féodale." In *Le Temps de la Réflexion*, vol. III, 285–306. Paris: 1983.

———. "Rêver au XIIe siècle." In *I Sogni nel Medioevo*, 291–316. International Congress, Rome, 1983. Rome, 1985.

———. "Le suicide au Moyen Age," *Annales ESC* (January–February 1976): 3–28.

*———. "Les 'superstitions'." In Jacques Le Goff and René Rémond, eds., *Histoire de la France religieuse*, I, 417–551.

*Sigal, P.-A. *L'Homme et le miracle dans la France médiévale (XIe–XIIe siècle)*. Paris, 1985.

* *Le Soleil, la Lune et les Étoiles au Moyen Age. Sénéfiance* 13 (1983). Marseille.

* *Le Temps chrétien de la fin de l'Antiquité au Moyen Age.* Colloques internationaux du Centre national de la recherche scientifique, Paris, 9–12 March 1981. Paris, 1984.

Théry, P. G. "Denys au Moyen Age." *Études carmélitaines* (October 1938): 68–74.

Toussaert, J. *Le Sentiment religieux, la vie et la pratique religieuse des laïcs en Flandre maritime et au 'West Hoeck' de langue flamande au XIVe, XVe et début du XVIe siècle.* Paris, 1963.

*Valous, G. de. *Le Monachisme clunisien des origines au XVe siècle. Vie intérieure et organisation de l'ordre.* Vol. 1, *L'Abbaye de Cluny. Les monastères clunisiens.* Paris, 1970.

Van Marle, R. *Iconographie de l'art profane au Moyen Age et à la Renaissance et la décoration des demeures.* Vol. 1, *La Vie quotidienne.* The Hague, 1931. Vol. 2, *Allégories et symboles.* The Hague, 1932.

*Vaultier, R. *Le Folklore en France pendant la guerre de Cent Ans, d'après les Lettres de rémission du Trésor des Chartes.* Paris, 1965.

Verdon, Jean. "Dormir au Moyen Age." *Revue belge de philologie et d'histoire* (forthcoming).

———. *Isabeau de Bavière.* Paris, 1981.

———. *Les Loisirs au Moyen Age.* Paris, 1980.

———. "Recherches sur la société religieuse et la nuit au Moyen Age." In *Mélanges Bernard Guillemain* (forthcoming).

———. "Sur l'ambivalence de la nuit au Moyen Age." Paper delivered at the Premier Congrès européen d'études médiévales, Spoleto, 27–29 May 1993.

Vicaire, M.-H. *Saint Dominique. La vie apostolique.* Paris, 1965.

*Voisin, A. "Notes sur la vie urbaine au XVe siècle. Dijon la nuit." *Annales de Bourgogne* 9 (1937): 265–279.

Weil, M. *De la circonstance de nuit en droit pénal.* Marseille, 1910.

*Zannettacci Stephanopoli, M. "La lumière naturelle dans l'habitation médiévale." In *Le Soleil, la Lune et les Étoiles au Moyen Age,* 451–465.

Zink, M. "Froissart et la nuit du chasseur." *Poétique* 41 (February 1980): 60–77.

INDEX

JEAN VERDON is professor emeritus of literature and humanities at Université de Limoges. His works include *Les Loisirs au Moyen Age* and *Isabeau de Bavière.*